Gaia's Wager

People, Passions, and Power

Social Movements, Interest Organizations, and the Political Process

Series Editor: John C. Green

Gaia's Wager

Environmental Movements and the Challenge of Sustainability

GARY C. BRYNER

ROWMAN & LITTLEFIELD PUBLISHERS, INC.
Lanham • Boulder • New York • Oxford

ROWMAN & LITTLEFIELD PUBLISHERS, INC.

Published in the United States of America
by Rowman & Littlefield Publishers, Inc.
4720 Boston Way, Lanham, Maryland 20706
www.rowmanlittlefield.com

12 Hid's Copse Road
Cumnor Hill, Oxford OX2 9JJ, England

British Library Cataloguing in Publication Information Available

Library of Congress Cataloging-in-Publication Data
Bryner, Gary C., [date]–
  Gaia's wager : environmental movements and the challenge of sustainability /
Gary C. Bryner.
     p. cm.
  Includes bibliographical references and index.
    ISBN 0-8476-9488-7 (alk. paper)—ISBN 0-8476-9489-5 (pbk. : alk. paper)
   1. Environmentalism.   2. Environmental policy.   3. Sustainable development.
I. Title.

GE195.B78   2001
363.7'05—dc21   00-059063

Printed in the United States of America

∞™ The paper used in this publication meets the minimum requirements of
American National Standard for Information Sciences—Permanence of Paper for
Printed Library Materials, ANSI/NISO Z.39.48-1992.

to Jane

Contents

Tables

Preface

Sustainability has caught on in dramatic form, perhaps more quickly and more pervasively than any other idea in environmental affairs and public policy. There are many critics and skeptics of the idea, and sustainability may prove to be a passing fad, too vague a notion to ever compel significant actions. It may be unmeasurable, undefinable, and little more than a value to which one can appeal for about anything one wishes to do. It may never serve as the basis for public policies and private behavior. The warnings and cautions of skeptics are useful, valuable checks against unreasonable expectations and unrealistic promises.

Nevertheless, I believe the idea of sustainability is of fundamental importance. It has and will even more so in the future create important expectations. It captures powerful sentiments and reflects deep commitment to ethical choices. Debates over values do not alone determine public policies and influence private behavior. Narrow economic self-interest creates powerful incentives. Vested interests fight aggressively to protect their interests. But other values matter as well, and sustainability taps into fundamental notions of fairness, responsibility, and concern for future generations. My goal is to engage students and other readers who seek to explore the contours of sustainability. This book is not a study of the policies required to achieve the goal of sustainability and how that goal should itself be defined, but rather an inquiry into the politics of the shift from environmentalism as currently practiced to sustainability. This book focuses on three questions. First, what is the nature, strength, resources, and capacity of environmentalism? Second, how well is it positioned to deal with current and emerging environmental issues? Third, how can its capacity be enhanced in order to more effectively respond to the challenges posed by the goal of ecological sustainability?

There are great uncertainties concerning the causes and consequences of global environmental threats; just as uncertain are the possibilities for fundamental political changes that would allow effective responses to these threats to develop. I hope this book contributes in some way to that debate and I invite your comments and responses.

Gary Bryner
Boulder, Colorado
gary.bryner@colorado.edu

Acknowledgments

I greatly benefited from being at the Natural Resources Law Center at the University of Colorado School of Law during the last stages of writing this book. The Center is itself dedicated to the sustainability of natural resources, focusing primarily on the American West. While this book on the politics of sustainability stretches the scope of research usually undertaken at the Center, I hope it can make a modest contribution to the fine work that others have so skillfully and thoughtfully produced there. I appreciate very much the support of the William and Flora Hewlett Foundation for this and related projects at the Center.

I also benefited from the support given by the Department of Political Science and the College of Family, Home, and Social Science to the Public Policy Program at Brigham Young University, where much of the research for the book was gathered. Research support to professional meetings and conferences also was invaluable in undertaking this project. I thank my many colleagues who offered comments and suggestions as I presented various parts of this book as papers at meetings of the International Studies Association (particularly panels sponsored by the Environmental Studies Section), and the American Political Science Association, at panels organized by its Science, Technology, and Environmental Politics study section.

Special thanks go to William Lafferty and James Meadowbrook, conveners of a group of scholars from Canada, Western Europe, and the United States that studies sustainability in high-consumption societies. I learned much from them and from others involved in the COMPSUS research team: Susan Baker, Christiane Beuermann, Katarina Eckerberg, Olulf Langhelle, Marie-Louise van Muijen, Elim Papadakis, Miranda A. Schreurs, Glen Toner, and Stephen C. Young. Funding from the U.S. Information Agency and the U.S. Embassy in Berlin also gave me the opportunity to learn more about German environmental politics.

I thank Jennifer Knerr of Rowman & Littlefield Publishers for her interest in and enthusiasm for this project and for great encouragement and support. John Green, editor of the series *People, Passions, and Power: Social Movements, Interest Organizations, and the Political Process*, was similarly supportive and provided many helpful suggestions, including the title of the book. Suggestions by anonymous reviewers also improved the book in numerous ways, as did the careful copyediting by Jackie Fearer and the efforts by Lynn Weber and others at Rowman & Littlefield.

I thank all on whom I have relied for this book and officially absolve them of all blame for faults and share with them credit for anything of value readers might find herein. The references in the endnotes and the suggested readings at the end of the book only begin to acknowledge the expansive and impressive writings of academics, activists, journalists, policy makers, and others, and I acknowledge with gratitude all I have learned from so many others.

Finally, I acknowledge the support of my family—Jane, Ben, Nick, and Jon—in this project and in all I do.

Introduction

The December 1999 Seattle trade summit, attended by the trade ministers of 135 countries, was organized to initiate a new round of negotiations under the World Trade Organization (WTO) and establish a timetable for reducing tariffs, eliminating export subsidies, and addressing the interaction of trade rules and labor standards. As the summit began, some 35,000 environmental and labor activists joined forces to protest globalization—the spread of freer markets and more open commerce—because of its impact on U.S. workers and on U.S. environmental laws. Protesters blocked delegates from entering the meetings and peppered delegates with demands to disband the talks or at least broaden the negotiations to include how to protect jobs and environmental quality in the face of the growing power of global markets. The peaceful demonstrations and protests turned into a riot as a group of anarchists, in a well-planned operation, sprang from the anti-WTO protesters and vandalized stores in Seattle. The black-clad anarchists took aim at stores owned by international companies like Nike and Starbucks to focus attention on their demand to end private property, the symbol of the broader political and economic system they detest. The demonstrations-turned-riots took on a surreal aura, as demonstrators who earlier railed against the corporate practices of multinational corporations now tried to protect their downtown Seattle storefronts from attacks by the anarchists. As the anarchists and protesters clashed and argued, many protesters began to acknowledge the anarchists' arguments about the need for radical change.[1]

The Seattle police and the National Guard eventually gained control of the streets of Seattle and arrested protestors and anarchists alike. From their King County jail cells, the labor and environmental protesters continued to work on their plans for more protests against the WTO, including a march on Washington, D.C., in the spring of 2000, to pressure Congress not to ratify the Clinton administration's bid to admit China into the global trade organization. The protests helped pressure President Clinton to defend some limits on more open trade, such as antidumping laws, which allow the federal government to sanction countries that sell goods in the United States at prices lower than production costs. The trade ministers of all 134 countries attending the Seattle Summit called for a change in U.S. antidumping policy, but the U.S. delegation refused. Clinton also urged that strong environmental and labor provisions be added to trade agreements. By the end of the week the delegates were weary, and the talks dissolved when the U.S. trade negotiator suggested they take a "timeout."[2]

As the twentieth century drew to a close, some commentators used this victory of environmental and labor groups to reflect on the power of environmental and other nongovernmental groups to shape public policy. Editorial writers for *The Economist*, for example, saw the battle of Seattle as "only the latest and most visible in a string of recent NGO victories." According to *The Economist*, the watershed for these groups was the Earth Summit in Rio de Janeiro in 1992, when the NGOs helped generate public pressure for global agreements on biodiversity and climate change. Other victories include a meeting of the World Bank in 1994 where protesters launched a "Fifty Years Is Enough" campaign to force the Bank to reconsider its goals and methods. In 1998, consumer and environmental advocates helped to sink the Multilateral Agreement on Investment (MAI), a draft treaty aimed at harmonizing rules on foreign investment that had been proposed by the Organization for Economic Cooperation and Development. Another coalition of NGOs, called Jubilee 2000, has lobbied successfully for reducing the foreign debts of the poorest countries. One of the "biggest successes of the 1990s," according to *The Economist*, was the campaign by hundreds of NGOs to outlaw landmines. NGOs have also been successful in targeting corporations like Nike for labor practices in its factories in developing countries, Nestlé for its sale of powdered baby milk to poor mothers who are often forced to mix it with polluted water, and Monsanto for marketing genetically modified food. A 1995 case, in which Greenpeace prevented Royal Dutch/Shell from dumping its Brent Spar oil rig into the North Sea caught industry by surprise. The editors asked whether these citizen groups were "the first step toward an 'international civil society' (whatever that might be)? Or do they represent a dangerous shift of power to unelected and unaccountable special-interest groups?"[3]

In contrast, a gathering of environmental leaders in Washington, D.C., also in December, 1999, painted a much more pessimistic picture of environmental political clout. A summary of the meeting reported that participants believed that, "to date, environmentalists have largely been excluded from forums where decisions affecting the world are made" and "must find a place in the center of world politics." Philip Shabecoff, a long-time reporter on environmental issues and author of a book on the history of American environmentalism, observed that the American environmental movement was nearing the limit of its effectiveness and warned that environmental groups must get "bigger, stronger, richer and more powerful."[4] Denis Hayes, a key founder of Earth Day, argued that the United States has been a poor example of environmental protection. Jane Lubchenco, head of the American Association for the Advancement of Science and the Ecological Society of America, declared, "We are in the process of changing the planet" on an unprecedented scale and rate, but environmentalists have been largely unsuccessful in countering the views that these trends are not worrisome. She warned of the "junk science" arguments made by opponents of those favoring actions to combat issues like climate change and the prevailing view that potential problems should be ignored for as long as possible and emphasized that environmental groups need to educate the public and political leaders on the need to take strong action.[5] Conservationists in other meetings also painted gloomy pictures of environmental gains that had been overtaken by population and economic growth, and saw little cause for optimism. Some rivers have been restored to health, a few species have been brought back from the brink of extinction, some lands have been protected from development, but more and more species are lost, more open lands are being appropriated for human use, and pressures on land and resources continue to grow. The title of an article about the meeting parsimoniously summarized their view: "Conservationists Win Battles but Fear War Is Lost."[6]

Is environmental politics dangerously dominating world politics (and interfering with global commerce), or is it struggling to have an impact on economic and political forces that for now seem to overwhelm environmental concerns? These two viewpoints represent only a tiny sliver of the debate that rages over the health of the global environment and its future. Diagnoses range from impending catastrophe to unbridled optimism. The purpose of this book is to join this debate by raising questions and exploring answers regarding three interrelated issues. First is the current political capacity for responding to global environmental threats: What are the political resources, infrastructure, processes, institutions, and regimes in place and how well are they working? Second, how effective is environmental politics in focusing attention, mobilizing efforts, and producing results? Third, in what ways does this political capacity need to be enhanced to effectively respond to these global environmental problems—what is needed to produce the kind of political, social, and economic changes required to significantly reduce or eliminate these problems and secure a healthy environment?

Answers to these questions are, of course, widely contested. Much of the debate turns on the way global environmental problems are characterized. If, for example, we believe that environmental conditions are generally improving and that we are largely on track in eliminating threats and maintaining ecological health, then we need only have relatively modest expectations for politics and policy making. If the analysis of the global environment points to stability and sustainability, then a continuation of politics, with the ability to adjust and respond as new problems arise, is all that is required. The debate focuses on how to generate the political support for the incremental changes needed to make policies more efficient and effective. If, in contrast, environmental conditions are not improving but are likely to decline precipitously, if current trends are not sustainable, then fundamental political changes are required, and the current political and economic structure order must be radically transformed. The way the current health of the planet is diagnosed determines the basic answers to the questions posed above.

I argue here that while there are clearly significant signs of progress, the most compelling reading of the assessments of global environmental health by ecologists and other scientists is that the threats to the planet are serious and pervasive and that we are not currently on a trajectory that allows for a continuation of life as we know it. If current trends continue, we will likely face major disruptions, changes, and catastrophes. Nor can we even assume that conditions may gradually worsen. Instead of gradual deterioration, we may see discontinuities—rapid shifts, spikes, exponential shifts, surprises, and synergistic effects that produce changes much greater than the progress of individual effects. Some scientists argue that we are facing an increased threat of rapid, unexpected change that will overwhelm any adaptive efforts.[7]

Scientific assessments alone, however, do not compel a particular set of environmental policies and private actions. Because the stakes are so high, the consequences so potentially devastating, and the developments irreversible, at least in the scale of human lifetimes, a conservative, cautionary approach is in the interest of all humankind. Because of the nature of the distribution of the burdens of global environmental problems, and the ways those who are least responsible for worldwide ecological risks are most likely to suffer the consequences and lack the resources to mitigate their effects, such a cautionary approach is morally compelling. It is prudent to assess our current political capacity for environmental policy making and prospects for a relatively peaceful, planned transition toward new ways of producing and consuming goods and services, even as research continues on the health of the biosphere, the nature of environmental threats, and the kinds of mitigating efforts that might be required. Arguments based on ecological science and public ethics call for a cautionary approach because we know very little about the consequences of our consumption and production on our health and the health of our ecosystems, and because the consequences, whatever they may be, will not be distributed fairly throughout the world. The ethical argument for precaution is rooted in a sense of our responsibility for the actions we take, especially when those who benefit from industrialization and high levels of consumption impose burdens on others who do not enjoy those same benefits. But prudence is also in our species' self-interest.

The title of this book comes from a famous wager suggested by the French philosopher Blaise Pascal, who suggested that people should believe in God out of self-interest. If God doesn't exist, they haven't really lost anything; if he does, and they believe, they are saved from damnation. Pascal aimed his wager argument at people who were not yet convinced of the truthfulness of Christianity, who were neither believers nor disbelievers but had suspended judgment on the issue. He argued that it was to their advantage for people to believe, that belief was the only reasonable, rational course of action: "If you win, you win all; if you lose, you lose nothing."[8] A person who wagered on God would give up some pleasures but would find others. Similarly, it is in our self-interest to pursue ecological sustainability, because if it turns out that environmental problems are not so serious, we have lost nothing. If environmental problems are as serious as we fear, then we will have acted to protect ourselves against them. In the pursuit of sustainability, we will give up some pleasures, but also find new ones. The shift from fossil fuels to renewable energy sources and other transitions will be painful to some interests but will open up great opportunities for others. There is no question that the transition will be difficult and disruptive, but it is a rational path to follow.[9]

Gaia is the name given by the Greeks more than two thousand years ago to Mother Earth. The idea that the Earth is a living entity has been widely held as a religious belief. Scientists have been more hesitant to make the argument. James Hutton, a founder of the modern science of geology, speaking before the Royal Society of Edinburgh in 1785, suggested that the Earth was alive. More recently, James Lovelock published a book in 1979 that proposed the Gaia hypothesis, that the "biosphere is a self-regulating entity with the capacity to keep our planet healthy by controlling the chemical and physical environment."[10] Lovelock argued that entropy, as expressed in the Second Law of Thermodynamics, means that all energy will eventually dissipate into heat and be unable to perform useful work. But life on earth continues because, as Lovelock argued, "the entire range of living matter on Earth, from whales to viruses, and from oaks to algae, could be regarded as constituting a single living entity, capable of manipulating the Earth's atmosphere to suit its overall needs and endowed with faculties and powers far beyond those of its constituent parts."[11] Gaia includes the earth's biosphere, atmosphere, oceans, and soils which combine to form a feedback or cybernetic system "which seeks an optimal physical and chemical environment for life on this planet."[12] The Gaia hypothesis suggests, among other things, that human activity may alter the balance of power between this complex human system and its most potent species. As a result, Gaia may make adjustments that are quite inhospitable for human life. Gaia may flourish, but human life may be much different, constrained, and limited.

Gaia's wager suggests the need for an environmental politics that is capable of generating fundamental changes in our personal practices and public policies. The prospects for such a transition is the subject of this book. There are, of course, many different ways of assessing environmental politics, also referred to here as environmentalism, environmental culture, and the environmental movement. I focus on two aspects of environmentalism. First is the evolution of the environmental movement and the current level of commitment to environmental protection and conservation in private behavior and public debate. Second, I examine the transition from the environmental movement to an institutionalized element of government and its expression in institutions of governance and in public policies. Like other social movements, a key to understanding environmentalism is to examine how well it strikes a balance between 1) maintaining its role as a dynamic change agent, pressuring and prodding governments, industries, and consumers to become more environmentally sensitive, and 2) having its platform institutionalized, with its leaders in positions of authority or at least with access to others in those positions. The more environmentalism becomes legalized, bureaucratized, and formalized as part of the political power structure, the more likely its agenda will be implemented as public policies. But its success as public policy threatens its vitality and power as a social movement, able to recruit new activists and to push for action as new challenge emerge.

Given the problems that plague governments or appear to be inevitable elements of early twenty-first-century governments—policy gridlock, dominance by vested interests, inflexibility, slowness in taking action, and elections funded disproportionately by narrow interests—and the transformations that are required to produce ecologically sustainable policies, environmentalism will need to maintain its energy and vitality as a social movement even as the policies it champions are enacted and implemented. Because the transformation to sustainability requires changes in consumption and production beyond those that can be mandated effectively by government, even if policies and regulations are fully implemented, environmentalism will continue to face the challenge of changing cultural beliefs and practices to promote sustainability. Most importantly, because the environmental movement itself must undergo a dramatic shift toward sustainability, its vitality as a dynamic, adaptive social movement is critical.

The strength of the environmental movement can be assessed through public-opinion polling, assessments by social observers, the activities of organized groups, and other measures. Anthropology and sociology, in addition to political science, are the relevant disciplines in looking for indicators of the strength of environmental ideas in daily discourse and behavior. The emphasis here is on the dynamic nature of environmental culture—the core elements of belief and whether commitment is increasing or decreasing. It includes the private actions of consumers and businesses that affect environmental quality; the activities of environmental activists in grass-roots, national, and international groups aimed at shaping public values and culture; and their efforts to mobilize in elections, lobbying, and media campaigns to shape the institutions of government and the policies they pursue. Public policies are themselves a measure of the strength of environmentalism, as is the extent to which they are effectively implemented and vigorously enforced.

The primary inquiry here is the extent to which the movement is sufficiently strong to produce the changes required to achieve the precautionary environmental goals that are what I call here Gaia's wager. Without attempting to build a comprehensive case for the assumption that radical change is needed, it may be useful to offer a brief explanation of why this assumption is compelling.

In an earlier study, *From Promises to Performance: Achieving Global Environmental Goals*, I examined some of the major challenges facing policy makers as they seek to achieve the goals embodied in major global environmental agreements.[13] The first set of challenges includes the problem of implementation in general—how to achieve major public policy goals with limited governmental powers, integrating environmental with other public policies, creating incentives for participation and compliance, and ensuring that policies are adjusted in light of changing conditions. The second set of challenges focused on alternatives to traditional environmental policies, particularly those that rely on market-based instruments to bring about change in practices and behavior. A third set of issues examined the capacity of international institutions for devising global accords, coordinating these efforts with other international obligations such as reducing poverty, and monitoring compliance with treaties and agreements, and how international institutions interact with regional, national, and subnational governments and nongovernmental organizations. A fourth area explored the intersection of international trade and international environmental problems, technology and democratic control of technological developments and their consequences, and economic and environmental policy. A final set of issues focused on the interaction of poverty and environmental degradation in the developing world and how difficult it has been to devise ways of facilitating ecologically sustainable development in these regions. That study concluded with a discussion of some of the concepts that might serve as the basis for a new environmental paradigm, rooted in a commitment to ecological sustainability, that would transform the ways we think about production and consumption, growth and development, and progress and wealth, into a new framework for policy making.

This study takes up where the last one ended: What is our political capacity to make the kinds of changes anticipated by a commitment to what I will call below ecological sustainability that transforms environmentalism into a more potent social movement? Others have made the point, quite convincingly, that environmental challenges require fundamental political change. Robert Heilbroner, in his provocative essay, *An Inquiry into the Human Prospect*, for example, argues that a "radically different future beckons" humankind:

> It seems beyond dispute that the present orientation of society must change. In the place of the long-established encouragement of industrial production must come its careful restriction and long-term diminution within society. In the place of prodigalities of consumption must come new frugal attitudes. In these and other ways, the "post-industrial" society of the future is apt to be as different from present-day industrial society as the latter was from its preindustrial precursor.[14]

Heilbroner argues and laments that the kinds of changes required will not likely come voluntarily but will require the use of force to compel more environmentally sustainable behaviors and practices:

> The passage through the gauntlet ahead may be possible only under governments capable of rallying obedience far more effectively than would be possible in a democratic setting. If the issue for mankind is survival, such governments may be unavoidable, even necessary. . . . Contemporary industrial man, his appetite for the present whetted by the values of a high-consumption society and his attitude toward the future influenced by the prevailing canons of self-concern, has but a limited motivation to form such bonds. There are many who would sacrifice much for their children; fewer who would do so for their grandchildren. Indeed, it is the absence of just such a bond that casts doubt on the ability of nation–states or socio-economic orders to take now the measures needed to mitigate the problems of the future.[15]

Because of our inability to transform and reconstruct "the material basis of civilization itself," we should expect "compulsive change"—change that is "forced upon us by external events rather than by conscious choice, by catastrophe rather than by calculation."[16]

William Ophuls and A. Stephan Boyan Jr., in *Ecology and the Politics of Scarcity Revisited*, argue that:

> The external reality of ecological scarcity has cut the ground out from under our own political system, making merely reformist policies of ecological management all but useless. At best, reforms can postpone the inevitable for a few decades at the probable cost of increasing the severity of the eventual day of reckoning. In brief, liberal democracy as we know it— that is, our theory or 'paradigm' of politics—is doomed by ecological scarcity; we need a completely new political philosophy and set of political institutions.[17]

Their conclusions are similar to those of Heilbroner; they believe that the "need for a world government with enough coercive power over fractious nation–states to achieve what reasonable people would regard as the planetary common interest has become overwhelming."[18] However, Ophuls and Boyan fear that ecological scarcity may intensify conflict rather than promote world cooperation and the planet will be destroyed.[19] They hope for a political revolution rooted in the idea of an "ecological covenant," "an ecological ethos," a "change of heart" that would be more "ecologically sound and more truly democratic than our current one."[20] They emphasize individual virtues and ethical and spiritual commitments as central to political change. They are hopeful that it will come voluntarily, through a reinvigoration of democracy rather than by force. Whether by authoritarian edict or radical democracy, both prescriptions call for radical reforming of individual behavior and collective action.

The Rest of the Book

The plan of the book is as follows. Chapter one briefly reviews trends in environmental conditions and the arguments by ecologists that fundamental changes are required in the ways humans interact with the environment on which they depend for life. It then develops a framework for assessing the state of environmental politics rooted in social movement theory. Social movement theory and related concepts provides a way to explore the extent to which environmental politics can be understood as a social movement and its potential to transform public policies and private behavior. Social movement theory focuses attention on the way environmental concerns arise and evolve in societies and shape the views of people, and how these concerns shape political behavior and institutions. There is no question that environmentalism is a social movement throughout the world; the question is what exactly does environmental-ism mean and to what extent does it possess the capacity to transform market behavior and public policies? Theories of ecological sustainabil-ity and sustainable development are helpful here in examining the con-tent of the environmental movement and in exploring the capacity of en-vironmentalism to bring about the kinds of changes suggested by diagnoses of the health of the planet and its ecosystems.

The chapters that follow then apply these concepts to assess environ-mental politics in several forms. Chapter two examines environmental politics in the United States. It argues that environmental groups are far too fragmented to be called a social movement. Environmental politics is still largely viewed as interest-group politics, and conservationists have not gotten very far in transforming environmental politics into a social movement. Ecological sustainability is similarly underdeveloped as a guiding principle and a blueprint for environmentalism. Chapter three looks at environmental politics from a comparative perspective; while en-vironmental politics is more ambitious and developed in some other countries, and the idea of sustainability is more broadly embraced than in the United States, environmentalism has yet to challenge the political su-premacy of economic growth. The prognosis is much more bleak in tran-sitional and developing countries. Chapter four focuses on international environmental politics and concludes that, despite some significant de-velopments, any claim to a global environmental movement is premature. Chapter five explores these issues within the context of a case study—climate change policy—to describe environmental politics in more depth. There is only modest progress to report in terms of the political response that has been generated to address the most widespread and potentially threatening environmental problem facing the planet. The final chapter examines some options for the transition to a more ambitious politics that matches the nature of the threats it may be required to address. Can envi-ronmentalism evolve into a powerful social movement that transforms practices in ways that are ecologically sustainable? The appendix lists some suggestions for research, including books and web sites.

1

Assessing Environmental Politics

The twenty-first century begins for many people in the world on a note of great optimism. A number of social and political trends are quite positive. Literacy rates have increased across the world and are expected to continue to do so. Life expectancy has increased over the past 50 years, with rather dramatic increases in the developing countries (although in Russia and some parts of Africa where AIDS is rampant, life expectancy has actually declined). Other measures of health, such as infant-mortality rates, reflect significant improvements in the quality of life in many developing regions.[1] Computers and access to information have transformed communication. Genetic engineering and the promise of conquering diseases may provide humankind with unimagined benefits. The United States and many other countries have undergone tremendous economic growth. According to one estimate, global per-capita income, expressed in 1990 dollars, has grown from $675 a year in 1820, as the Industrial Revolution was beginning, to more than $5,000 in 1995 and nearly $20,000 in the advanced industrialized democracies.[2]

Many studies are confident that conditions on earth will improve. The late Julian Simon was one of the most aggressive prognosticators of a healthier, wealthier future. Simon argued that natural resources are becoming less scarce, as evidenced by the trend in declining prices; that food is becoming more plentiful, as evidenced by reduced famine and increases in the average height in developing countries; and that environmental quality is improving, as demonstrated by increases in life expectancy. Scarcity is only a short-term problem; scarcity causes prices to rise in the short run, triggering efforts to find new ways to meet needs that result in us being better off than when the cycle started. Growth in the demand for energy is no problem, he argued, because it will simply generate pressure to develop eventually new, virtually inexhaustible sources. In the long term, Simon wrote, "there is no convincing economic reason

1

why these trends toward a better life should not continue indefinitely."
Population growth drives progress because it increases the stock of useful
knowledge.[3]

Democracy continues to spread throughout the world. At the beginning
of the twentieth century, no country on earth offered universal voting
rights to its citizens. In 1900, only six of the 43 recognized nations could
be described as democratic; in 1980, only 37 of the 121 nations. But by the
end of the century, some 119 of the 193 countries could be considered
democracies. Freedom House's end-of-the-century report found that 85
nations—44 percent of all nations— could be described as free, where citizens enjoyed "a broad range of political rights and liberties." Protection
of human rights and freedom from arbitrary arrest and torture have increased. The threat of global war has diminished.[4] However, there are still
regions, like the Middle East, where democracy and freedom are weakest,
and areas in Africa and Asia where freedom is limited. The last century,
according to one estimate, saw governments kill 170 million of their own
people in relocation and other efforts and saw another 37 million deaths
resulting from war and ethnic cleansing. Many of these conflicts continue
into the twenty-first century.[5] The last decade has been plagued by ethnic
cleansing and other conflicts, the spread of AIDS, the expansion of nuclear
weapons testing, the crash of East Asian and Latin American economies,
and the continuing fear of terrorism.

The editors of the *Wall Street Journal*, in reflecting on the approaching
millennium, mocked "self-professed 'scientists'" who warn of an "energy
crisis" or "global warming" that are "a recipe for bigger government, extreme regulation, and higher taxes." "The last crisis went away," they explained, "when Ronald Reagan was elected president, decontrolled the
price of oil and got the economy right." While they acknowledged that
"climatic change has certainly occurred over the millenniums, with powerful effects on the human experiment," there is no need to worry:
"mankind coped and will again."[6] But the reality of continuing political
unrest and conflict, growing economic inequality, the consequences of
population pressures, poverty in the developing world—especially
among women,—consumption of nonrenewable resources, and global environmental degradation makes unbridled optimism a remarkable and
naïve leap of faith.

The Nature of Global Environmental Problems

Allen Hammond has argued that between 1950 and 2000, global economic
activity has grown on average 3 percent a year; if this continues, economic
growth will be about two times population growth, and humankind as a
whole will be richer. The gross world product (GWP), the total of goods

and services produced and consumed per person, has grown much faster than population; it doubled between 1950 and 1975 and continued to grow until 1991, when it fell for the first time. About three-fourths of these goods and services are consumed in the advanced industrialized countries. But economic, like population, growth will not be even; the gap between the wealthy and the poor countries will likely widen. Even if growth in industrial regions is only moderate and growth in developing regions is very rapid, for example, the gap in per capita income, about $20,000 in 2000, will more than double, reaching perhaps $50,000.[7] While it is clear that wealthier nations have more resources to invest in cleaner technologies, economic growth is likely to result in increased pollution for a time, until sufficient resources are available to invest in ways that cause emission levels to decline. The problem is what happens while we are still on the upward side of the curve.

The developing countries have made great progress since the 1950s in reducing poverty: Child mortality and malnutrition have significantly declined; life expectancy, access to clean water and sanitation, and opportunities for education and health care have expanded.[8] But the progress of the 1960s and 1970s did not continue in many places in the 1980s and 1990s. About a hundred countries, for example, have suffered from economic stagnation during this period. Conflict in 30 countries has made economic and social progress almost impossible. The rise in health threats from communicable diseases like HIV and AIDS has been greater than expected and poses a major threat to well-being in many developing nations, particularly those in sub-Saharan Africa.[9] Only modest progress has been made in recent years in reducing poverty and malnourishment and in increasing access to clean air, water, sanitation, and health care. Incomes in Africa are 1.4 percent lower than in 1992.[10] In the Commonwealth of Independent States, life expectancy has dropped five years or more since the breakup of the Soviet empire.[11] Economic growth has often bypassed the poor and failed to increase their earnings and employment opportunities.

Recent Human Development Reports published by the United Nations Development Program (UNDP) have emphasized the increasing gap between the rich and the poor in the developing countries. In 1960, for example, the difference between the per capita income of the industrial and the developing countries was $5,700; in 1993, the difference had almost tripled to $15,400. In 1960, the bottom 20 percent of the world's population received 2.3 percent of the total global income; in 1991, they received 1.4 percent; in 1994, they received only 1.10 percent of global income. In 1991, the ratio of the income of the richest 20 percent of the world's population to the poorest 20 percent was 61:1; in 1994 it had grown to 78:1. Seventy-seven percent of the people of the world earn only 15 percent of its income. The average income in the North is 18 times greater than that in the South.[12] The globalization of markets and economic activity has benefited some interests in the developing world but has not reached the poorest of the poor, especially those in rural areas, where three-fourths of the developing world's poor reside.[13]

The UNDP measures poverty in two ways. First, *income poverty* is a function of daily income: Poverty is defined as less than $1 per day in the poorest regions of the world, less than $2 per day in Latin America and the Caribbean, less than $4 per day in the Commonwealth of Independent States (CIS) (formerly the Soviet Union), and less than $14.40 per day in the developed world. Some 1.3 billion people live below the income poverty line.[14] Second, *human poverty* is more broadly measured in terms of the percentage of people who die before age 40, are illiterate, and lack access to water and basic health care, and the percentage of children who are underweight. In 1997, the UNDP concluded that 507 million people were not expected to reach the age of 40, that 1.2 billion lacked access to safe water, and that there were 842 million illiterate adults and 158 million malnourished children under the age of five in the developing world.[15]

Women and children bear much of the brunt of poverty in the world: they suffer from maternal-related deaths, respiratory diseases (from inhaling the smoke of cooking fires), and other maladies that result from poverty. Much of the work done by women is underpaid and undervalued. Wide disparities exist between men and women, and female literacy is only about two-thirds that of males. Women are often prevented from owning property. Primary school enrollment for girls is only a little over half that of boys. Women's wages remain at two-thirds those of males.[16] Discrimination, which is manifest in land-ownership laws, employment practices, education, and development programs, contributes to the global feminization of poverty. Because of the low status of women in most societies, development projects often ignore their role in local economies, despite the fact that women comprise 50 percent of the agricultural labor force and more than 70 percent of some industries such as clothing manufacturing.[17] Development projects often ignore the plight of women because their efforts are largely outside of the formal economy.[18] The number of deaths from communicable diseases has fallen and is expected to continue to do so during the next 25 years, while maternal mortality rates have changed little: About 585,000 women die each year from complications arising during pregnancy and childbirth, and more than 99 percent of these deaths are in the developing world. For every death, an additional 30 women suffer from debilitating health problems resulting from problem pregnancies and childbirth. Most of these deaths and disabilities could be prevented with adequate prenatal and postnatal care.[19]

Since 1950, the world's population has expanded by about 2 percent a year. While there are numerous projections of what will happen during the next 50 years, a range of between 7.7 and 11.2 billion people in the world by 2050 is likely. The regional growth in population may be more critical than the total numbers; population growth will be much greater in the developing world, where, as discussed below, environmental conditions are, in some ways, much worse than in the developed world. Population will likely remain steady in North America, Japan, and Europe, and will likely decline in Eastern Europe. In contrast, it is expected to more than double in sub-Saharan Africa and in North Africa and the Middle East; increase by nearly 50 percent in India (both India and China may grow to a population of 1.5 billion by 2050), and grow by one-third in Latin America. By 2050, the most populated region of the world is projected to be sub-Saharan Africa, where environmental problems and poverty will be most acute.[20]

Population growth in the developing countries may undermine much of the progress made in those nations to protect ecosystems and natural resources. The rate of global population increase has slowed slightly: in 1996, it grew by 80 million, an increase of 1.4 percent. The rate of population growth has gradually declined since its peak of 2.2 percent in 1963. Some 98 percent of the growth occurs in the developing countries. The slowed growth rate is due to a number of factors, including declining fertility rates, a decrease in the life expectancy in the CIS, and diseases such as AIDS that have slowed growth rates in sub-Saharan Africa.[21] The number of people considered by the UN to be eligible for assistance as refugees declined slightly between 1995 and 1996, to 26.1 million, but has otherwise grown steadily since the 1970s. This number does not include refugees who are displaced within their own country, most of whom do not receive international assistance. Nor does it include the number of people displaced because of natural disasters such as floods and earthquakes, who have been estimated at 100 million to 250 million a year and compete with refugees for scarce relief assistance.[22] The aging of developed countries' populations poses major challenges for preservation of retirement pensions and the welfare state, as fewer and fewer workers must support more and more recipients of transfer payments.[23]

Population growth itself must be understood within the broader context of consumption and the consequences of technology. The environmental impact of human activity is a function of population, consumption, and technology. Global environmental problems are largely a result of high-consumption lifestyles that use disproportionate amounts of resources and produce large quantities of pollution. The levels of consumption and the environmental effects of the dominant technologies in industrial production and energy are not sustainable. There do not appear to be enough resources available nor is the planet able to absorb the wastes generated by a population of 6 billion or more people who consume at levels approaching those in the industrialized world.[24]

Trends in food production are also worrisome. The world grain harvest, measured in kilograms of grain for each person on earth, fell from a peak of 342 in 1984 to 299 in 1995, and has fluctuated between 299 and 328 during the past five years.[25] There seems to be complacency over levels of food production, but grain yields have been increasing at less than 1 percent a year in the 1990s, compared with a 2.1 percent yearly increase throughout the 1980s.[26] Per-capita soybean production peaked in 1994 and then fell slightly; one troublesome sign is that China has recently become a net importer of soybean and grain, and its transformation from exporter to importer puts increased pressure on global food supplies.[27] The global fish catch, in per capita terms, has also declined from a high in 1988 of 17.2 kilos to 15.9 in 1996; 13 of the 15 major global fisheries are in decline. "If current trends of overexploitation and habitat destruction continue," the Worldwatch report warned, "fish will no longer be 'the protein of the poor.'"[28]

Environmental trends are troubling at both the global and regional levels. Worldwide energy use is projected to grow 250 percent, and manufacturing activity, 300 percent, between 2000 and 2050, posing challenges for environmental problems like climate change that are shaped by total emissions of pollutants. Growth in emissions from energy sources, for example, are projected to increase by five or six times in sub-Saharan Africa, Southeast Asia, India, and China, and emissions of toxic pollutants from eight to ten times in these regions. Population growth in sub-Saharan Africa and China, in particular, will place great pressures on the amount of fertile land and water available to support these burgeoning populations.[29]

Some critical indicators of natural resource use and pollution production show the daunting challenges ahead. Consumption of fossil fuel, which provides 85 percent of the world's commercial energy, continues to grow, and the use of coal, oil, and natural gas set new records in 1996: Coal use grew by 1.8 percent, oil by 2.3 percent, and natural gas by 4.5 percent. Worldwide carbon emissions from the burning of fossil fuels increased by 4 percent between 1992 and 1996 and by 2.8 percent between 1995 and 1996, the highest increase since 1988. These emissions have increased by 400 percent since 1950.[30] The use of chlorofluorocarbons (CFCs) and halons peaked in 1988 but fell 76 percent by 1995. CFC use has largely ended in the developed world, which must now try to reduce methyl bromide and hydrochlorofluorocarbons (HCFCs). In contrast, in some areas of the developing world, CFC use has risen rapidly. Between 1986 and 1994, for example, CFC use rose by 95 percent in China, 109 percent in the Philippines, and 193 percent in India.[31] Between 1991 and 1995, there has been a net loss of tropical forests of about 12.6 million hectares a year, a continuation of the annual loss throughout the 1980s of 12.8 million hectares. Tropical forest cover, wetlands, and other sensitive areas declined by 3.5 percent since 1992.[32] These figures likely understate the problem, as some logging leaves a residual cover and is not counted as deforested but nevertheless disrupts ecosystems, nor does it differentiate between old-growth forests, which are much richer in biodiversity, and plantation forests planted and harvested in cycles.[33]

A 1996 World Resources Institute study concluded that while significant progress has been made in reducing urban environmental problems, they "remain significant contributors to regional and global environmental burdens;" are themselves areas of serious environmental problems such as air pollution and inadequate water and sanitation; and are "expanding into fragile ecosystems" in ways that threaten surrounding ecosystems and resources.[34] Other global trends are alarming as well. While some developing countries "are moving rapidly toward population stability...other countries are experiencing rapid population growth, usually accompanied by high levels of poverty, limited progress for women, and high levels of internal and international migration." The continued growth of global population "places enormous pressure on natural resources, urban infrastructure and services, and governments at all levels, especially in the poorest countries where growth is most rapid."[35] Demand for water is rapidly increasing and "many current patterns of water withdrawals are currently unsustainable." Some 1 billion people have no access to clean water and about 1.7 billion have inadequate sanitation. Between 13 and 20 percent of the world's population will live in water-scarce countries by the year 2050, according to one estimate. Water scarcity contributes to agricultural problems and combines with soil erosion and degradation that threaten our ability to increase global food production. Even if food production is expanded, "the inability of poor nations to pay for food imports, along with an inadequate distribution infrastructure and the inability of poor families to buy food, means that many people will continue to go hungry."[36] Projections of energy use suggest that increased consumption is inevitable, particularly in the developing world, and that will translate into increased levels of local and regional air pollution and global greenhouse gases. Other major environmental threats that will likely increase are degradation of coastal habitats and destruction of old-growth forests.[37]

Many believe that climate change is the preeminent environmental problem of the twenty-first century. Human activities such as the burning of fossil fuels have increased the concentration of carbon dioxide (CO_2) and other gases that help trap heat in the atmosphere. The accumulation of these gases threaten to magnify the planet's natural greenhouse effect and to disrupt and change current climate patterns. There is much uncertainty about the magnitude of the change that will occur, when changes might take place, the nature of the changes, and their geographic distribution. There may be some benefits in some areas: increased levels of CO_2 and warmer temperatures, for example, might stimulate plant growth in areas that are now colder and less productive. However, in some areas, climate disruption is likely to have adverse impacts such as increased flooding, more frequent and more disruptive storms, new forms of pests and other threats to agriculture, and loss of biodiversity. The areas that are most likely to suffer from these adverse impacts are often in developing countries, where residents have contributed relatively few greenhouse gases and lack the resources to mitigate the adverse effects. The magnitude and extent of the disruption that might result from climate change, and the grossly unfair distribution of the burdens of dealing with it, many argue, are compelling reasons to take precautionary actions to reduce the threat of climate change by reducing greenhouse gas emissions.

A more immediate threat for some people is the lack of access to clean water. More than a billion people in developing countries lack access to clean water and suffer disease, malnutrition, high infant mortality, and other maladies as a result. Lester Brown of the Worldwatch Institute has focused attention on the critical problem of water depletion. As a result of increasing withdrawals, many of the world's major rivers—such as the Colorado River in the United States, the Yellow River in China, the Nile in Egypt, and the Indus in India—barely reach the sea. Water tables of groundwater have fallen precipitously as withdrawals exceed recharging from rain and snow. Water shortages pose major challenges to food production: Grain markets are growing fastest in North Africa and the Middle East—areas where water tables are also declining most rapidly. Solutions include setting realistic prices for water, creating incentives for conservation, and changing worldwide dietary patterns (for example, if less water is used to raise animals for food, more can be used to raise crops for direct human consumption).[38]

Environmental conditions vary greatly across the world; in some prosperous areas, environmental quality is improving due to modernization, shifts to cleaner fuels, and conservation, all prompted by market forces and government regulation. Levels of air and water pollution have fallen, environmental assessments are required before public projects proceed, and environmental laws are enforced in most advanced industrialized nations. Environmental conditions are, on the whole, worse in the developing world, where older, less-efficient technologies predominate and where there is a less-effective regulatory governmental presence.

The nature of global environmental threats was succinctly summarized in the 1993 "World Scientists' Warning to Humanity" by some 1,670 scientists from 71 countries, including the majority of the living Nobel Prize winners. It cautioned:

Human beings and the natural world are on a collision course. Human activities inflict harsh and often irreversible damage on the environment and on critical resources. If not checked, many of our current practices put at serious risk the future that we wish for human society and the plant and animal kingdoms, and may so alter the living world that it will be unable to sustain life in the manner that we know. Fundamental changes are urgent if we are to avoid the collision our present course will bring about.

The warning focused on six critical environmental problems:

- **The Atmosphere.** Stratospheric ozone depletion threatens us with enhanced ultraviolet radiation at the earth's surface, which can be damaging or lethal to many life forms. Air pollution near ground level, and acid precipitation, are already causing widespread injury to humans, forests, and crops.
- **Water Resources.** Heedless exploitation of depletable groundwater supplies endangers food production and other essential human systems. Heavy demands on the world's surface waters have resulted in serious shortages in some 80 countries, containing 40 percent of the world's population. Pollution of rivers, lakes, and groundwater further limits the supply.
- **Oceans.** Destructive pressure on the oceans is severe, particularly in the coastal regions, which produce most of the world's food fish. The total marine catch is now at or above the estimated maximum sustainable yield. Some fisheries have already shown signs of collapse. Rivers carrying heavy burdens of eroded soil into the seas also carry industrial, municipal, agricultural, and livestock waste—some of it toxic.
- **Soil.** Loss of soil productivity, which is causing extensive land abandonment, is a widespread by-product of current practices in agriculture and animal husbandry. Since 1945, 11 percent of the earth's vegetated surface has been degraded—an area larger than India and China combined—and per capita food production in many parts of the world is decreasing.
- **Forests.** Tropical rain forests, as well as tropical and temperate dry forests, are being destroyed rapidly. At present rates, some critical forest types will be gone in a few years, and most of the tropical rain forest will be gone before the end of the next century. With them will go large numbers of plant and animal species.
- **Living Species.** The irreversible loss of species, which by 2100 may reach one-third of all species now living, is especially serious. We are losing the potential they hold for providing medicinal and other benefits, and the contribution that genetic diversity gives to the robustness of the world's biological system and to the beauty of the earth itself.

Underlying all these environmental problems is the earth's burgeoning population, consumption of resources, and inexorable demand for economic growth and material wealth: Pressures resulting from population growth and increased consumption of resources put demands on the natural world that may overwhelm any efforts to achieve a sustainable future.[39]

The Political Challenge of Global Environmental Problems

The global environmental problems, trends, and concerns outlined above can be understood primarily in one of two ways: (1) global environmental problems are manageable, and conditions are, overall, sustainable indefinitely; or (2) they are, on the whole, getting worse, will not significantly improve under current practices, and pose an increasing threat to at least future generations if not the current one. This categorization is, in reality, better viewed as a continuum, with threats that are, in terms of current laws, institutions, and political support, manageable to unmanageable. That is, although clearly oversimplifying things and masking tremendous differences, analyses of global environmental conditions suggest either that things can continue as they have in the past, or threats are so serious that trends cannot continue without resulting in calamity.

Similarly, the nature of the response required parallels the continuum. If one believes that problems are manageable, then the kinds of policies that are required are incremental, are consistent with current economic and consumptive practices, require adjustments in prices (so that full costs are reflected), and other adaptations. Political changes can likely be made through the existing structure of environmental groups, litigation, interest-group bargaining, and other political arrangements that characterize current national and global environmental politics. At the other end of the continuum, problems that are unmanageable and unsolvable under current conditions require fundamental restructuring of social and economic practices, new institutions, and, more fundamentally, new paradigms, discourses, and ways of thinking. This level of political change suggests social movements, transformational politics, and fundamental changes in the way people think, are socialized, and act individually and collectively.

The purpose here is not to resolve how to characterize environmental threats as to whether they are manageable or not under current economic and political institutions and practices. That is a complex question that requires at least a book-length exploration of its own. But it is nevertheless essential to make a choice here. If one assumes that the problems are largely manageable with current policy structures and processes, an analysis should determine how to maintain the current political strength of environmentalism and make incremental improvements as needs arise. Certainly there is much room for tinkering—for incremental adjustments in political strategies and approaches. But by defining the problems and their solutions in this way, there is no need for fundamental change. If, in contrast, the assumption is that the problems require more than incremental solutions, then a political inquiry is essential to assess whether the foundation for such transformative politics is in place and whether the prospects for radical, paradigm-shifting change are realistic.

My purpose here is to pursue this second assumption—that environmental risks are so profound that radical changes are required—and explore the political prospects for such a dramatic change in policy commitments and private behavior. While I have chosen here to explore the consequences of assuming that a transformative political change is required, these choices are not mutually exclusive. That is, one could decide that, as David Orr has argued, we should take immediate actions to stabilize the ecological health of the planet and, at the same time, begin to undertake the long-term changes that are required. Short-term remedies can complement more fundamental shifts in policies and practices that will eventually be required.[40]

In his essay "Is Humanity Destined to Self-Destruct?" Lynton Keith Caldwell answers in the affirmative: Humanity is indeed capable of self-destructing. "If humans pit themselves against the fundamental dynamics of cosmic nature, they are certain to lose," he writes. The "ingenuity of humans may impel them to their own demise," and there may be "no further future for humanity." He suggests that natural resource shortages, pollution, and population growth may combine to cause the collapse of human life and that, presumably, much if not all of human life would be extinguished, perhaps a result of a runaway greenhouse effect or a series of calamities.[41] However, these three plagues—pollution, population, and exhausted resources—need not produce collapse. They may, Caldwell acknowledges, be chronic concerns that are better understood as a "climacteric," a situation with which future generations are destined to grapple rather than an environmental crisis that may one day be "solved." Or environmental degradation may be a more a function of economic class or geography than systemic meltdown. Climate change, for example, may decimate warm areas but enrich colder ones. Wealthy humans may be able to buy sufficient mitigation from ecological collapse, while poorer ones will not be insulated from harm, a morally unacceptable outcome, without question, but not the same as wholesale collapse. Disease spread through ecological disruptions, wars prompted by conflicts over increasingly scarce resources, scarcity of critical natural resources, and the public health impacts of pollution may produce a long, gradual decline in the number of human beings able to live on the earth. Perhaps the consequence will be a decline in our standard of living. If our current practices "so alter the living world that it will be unable to sustain life in the manner that we know," as the "Warning to Humanity" cautions, we will not have the same levels of consumption, but we may still be around in large numbers.

Perhaps the optimists are correct in predicting that pollution in the Western world will end during our lifetimes, that environmental threats like runaway global warming will not occur, and that billions of people yet to arrive on this planet will take a constructive place in the natural order.[42] But ecology suggests a cautious, conservative approach given the enormity of the stakes for current and future generations. At minimum, we should explore the prospects for fundamental change because it is possible that it will be necessary. What is our collective, global, political capacity to address these problems? Is it sufficient to meet these challenges? If not, how might it be enhanced?

Assessing Political Capacity and Options for Enhancing It

Assessing the political capacity to make basic changes in public policy and private behavior can be undertaken in many different ways. Two conceptual frameworks are particularly useful: social movement theory and the theory of ecologically sustainable development. Social movement theory helps assess the breadth, depth, and power of environmental sentiment. Sustainability helps assess whether the nature of that sentiment is aimed in a direction that effectively addresses underlying ecological conditions and imperatives.

Social Movement Theory

Social movement theory provides a useful lens for looking at environmentalism. Environmentalism was one of the most successful social movements of the twentieth century and will likely continue to be so in this century. The success of social movements hinges on their ability to strike a balance between the need to have their platform and priorities institutionalized so that broad and enduring changes are made, and the need to remain flexible and dynamic enough to adjust to new realities and then generate the pressures necessary for adaptation. The movement's goals need to be embraced by the prevailing power structure, but the movement also needs to maintain its ability to prod, cajole, and even threaten governing institutions when new actions are required or more ambitious policies need to be pursued. That balancing act occurs as social movements engage in politics—from interest-group lobbying and litigation to campaigning in elections. Environmentalists are constantly confronted with choices of strategy. Should they compete as one interest battling another (big business, for example) or should they form a new political party? Should they broaden their agenda to include social justice and other progressive concerns, or should the focus be on goals that are less ambitious but may be more widely embraced and politically feasible (such as pollution reduction)? As environmentalism moves toward sustainability, those choices become clearer: Sustainability requires such wide-ranging changes in economic, political, and social life, that political parties and linkages with related social movements seem inevitable. This greatly raises the expectations of environmentalism and increases the likelihood of frustration and disappointment. And it makes even more difficult the challenge of institutionalizing policy prescriptions and maintaining a radical edge.

Jo Freeman and Victoria Johnson's analysis of social movements suggests two important characteristics of social movements in general that can be used in assessing environmentalism. First, they suggest that the term "movement" is usually used in two senses: to describe the "mobilization and organization of large numbers of people to pursue a common cause," and to describe the "community of believers that is created by that mobilization."[43] Movements, in the first sense of the word, always decline over time, but the community often continues and may survive until the next movement generates a new generation of activists. Movements typically last 20 to 30 years and always prompt a backlash.[44] One can argue that the environmental movement mobilized a great number of people in the 1970s and the community of believers remain, but the energy that characterized the movement has dissipated as many people believe that the goals of the movement have largely been secured. A parallel grassroots movement mobilized additional activists, and that movement is still energized.

Second, Freeman and Johnson view social movements as part of a broader set of social actions that can be described as a continuum, with those forms that are primarily spontaneous, unstructured responses (such as fads, trends, and crowds) at one end. At the other end are stable, institutionalized interest groups. In the middle are social movements characterized by both spontaneity and structure; the tension between these two values is the key to understanding social movements. They argue that despite the idea of a continuum, there is no natural progression from spontaneity to organization.[45] In the case of environmentalism, part of the movement, as represented by the mainstream national organizations, is at the stable, institutionalized end. The grass-roots branch of environmentalism seems much more like the classic social movement, with some organization but much better understood as an ongoing, spontaneous mobilization of people than a set of formally organized institutions.

Luther Gerlach builds on Freeman and Johnson's framework in arguing that social movements are typically characterized not as bureaucratic organizations but as *segmentary* (composed of "many diverse groups, which grow and die, divide and fuse, proliferate and contract"), *polycentric* (having "multiple, often temporary, and sometimes competing leaders or centers of influence"), and *reticulate* (forming a "loose, integrated network with multiple linkages through travelers, overlapping membership, joint activities, common reading matter, and shared ideals and opponents").[46] Gerlach's studies of environmental and other social movements attributed their successes in challenging the established order, overcoming opposition and efforts to suppress, and expanding their scope and membership to these characteristics.[47] Environmentalism is not efficiently organized in the bureaucratic sense, with clear lines of authority and division of labor. It is not monolithic or bureaucratic, but organic and evolutionary. It has been effective in accomplishing its goals because of its diversity, redundancy, and shared ideals.

The different states of environmentally related activities can be grouped as follows:

- **Fads, crowds, and trends** are labels for spontaneous, unstructured responses to public problems.
- **Social movements** are spontaneous and fluid but also have some organization and structure.
- **Institutionalized interest groups** are advocates that participate in established political and policy-making processes but are outside of formal governmental authority.
- **Advocates in office** may be elected or appointed to governmental positions or at least part of their agenda is embraced as public policies.

The idea of institutionalization can be misleading here. Once a movement becomes institutionalized in the sense of becoming part of government or part of the established political economy, then it is no longer by definition a social movement. Here, institutionalization refers to stable, established relationships between the institutions of the movement and official institutions of government. Some might argue that this level of institutionalization represents a transition from social movement to interest group (as in the United States, for example) or corporatist politics (as in Western Europe, for example). Particularly important here is the recognition that the continuum represents dynamic, interactive elements. Elements of environmentalism can be found at each entry on the continuum: some of the environmental policy agenda may be institutionalized, some environmental groups are well integrated into environmental policy- making processes, some grass-roots efforts are closest to the idea of social movement, and some environmental ideas are still at the fad or trend stage. The term "social movement" may also be used to describe the range of activities that fall short of the far right end of the continuum—public policy. The key idea explored in this book is *environmentalism as social movement*—as a set of values, attitudes, behaviors, and organizations outside of government that seek to mobilize people to change their behavior in ways that are more ecologically friendly and to support those kinds of public policies.

Social movement theory suggests that the strength of collective efforts to pursue claims, such as demands for environmental protection, is a function of how widely they are embraced and how strong are the commitments to them. Meyer and Tarrow define social movements as having three components: (1) collective challenges to existing arrangements of power and distribution (2) by people with common purposes and solidarity (3) in sustained interaction with elites, opponents, and authorities.[48] They suggest three tests for determining whether collective action has become politically institutionalized, a major element of the politics of the industrialized democracies:

- First, social protest has moved from being a sporadic, if recurring, feature of democratic politics, to become a perpetual element in modern life.
- Second, protest behavior is employed with greater frequency, by more diverse constituencies, and is used to represent a wider range of claims than ever before.
- Third, professionalization and institutionalization may be changing the major vehicle of contentious claims—the social movement—into an instrument within the realm of conventional politics.[49]

Initially social movements gain adherents and influence authority—through their power "to disrupt, to surprise, and to create uncertainty."[50] They are less likely to be disruptive and contentious as they become institutionalized. Meyer and Tarrow define the institutionalization of social protest movement as the "creation of a repeatable process that is essentially self sustaining," where the actors resort to well-established and familiar routines, "ending the uncertainty and instability" that often characterize the early stages of movements. Collective action becomes routinized, those who refuse to adhere to established routines are marginalized, and challengers are co-opted into altering their claims and tactics in ways that are not disruptive. As a result, dissidents can "continue to lodge claims" and government can "manage dissent without stifling it."[51] Ordinary interest groups may adopt the methods traditionally associated with social movements.[52]

One of the challenges facing movements is that as they become institutionalized, they may lose their edge; their ability to inspire some members may wane, and their power to pressure elites may soften. But ordinary people are likely to be more willing to support forms of collective action that are not radical or violent or difficult to predict and seem out of control. Successful groups seem to be able to adapt to different targets, opportunities, and constraints, and move back and forth between conventional and unconventional forms of activism.[53]

Meyer and Tarrow find a number of factors that have facilitated social movements, including an increase in overall education levels, increased access to the media, improved access to information through sources such as the Internet, a skilled staff that keeps the movement's effort well publicized, and a core group of activists who invigorate the mass membership. Particularly important has been the professionalization and specialization in social movement organizations. This has been important in expanding and sustaining movements but also in challenging the democratic, egalitarian nature of these movements.[54]

Social movement theory suggests that individuals first group together to pursue common goals, to challenge the established order, and to solve problems. The movement is often transformed into interest groups or parties—that is, institutions that fit within the established political order. The movement loses some of its zeal but gains access and influence to policy-making process. Those in the movement who resist the co-optation may be more radicalized and more marginalized. The threat is that in the process of gaining access, the movement may be co-opted and the drive to bring about fundamental change is lost. Several outcomes develop as movements mature. Movements that form to challenge existing power structures may eventually be co-opted by the existing power structure and become integrated with conventional interest-group and party politics. The history of third parties in the United States, for example, has been characterized by protest parties forming to draw attention to problems, and then the two established parties reaching out to absorb much of the movement. One party may be more successful than the other in absorbing members of the movement, but the formation of interest groups that then become part of the established power structure is the critical development. In the United States, for example, an important way in which social movements participate in policy making is to use the courts. Access to judicial decision making is cheaper and easier than access to legislative policy making, but a reliance on litigation runs the risk of reinforcing the idea that environmentalism, or any other movement, is just another interest vying for attention.

The evolution of a social movement to interest-group politics, with some of its agenda enacted as policy, has occurred in environmentalism and other areas. A second result of social movements may be transitory or cyclical but never of sufficient strength to generate efforts at integration. They may be perceived as so extreme or so small that their impact is limited to some policy concessions to reduce the pressure generated.[55] A third, and most difficult to achieve, outcome is the transformation of a social movement into a new framework for governance. Social movements may take the form of political parties that provide an integrated, comprehensive policy agenda or even a consensus that goes beyond partisan differences to provide an underlying set of values, assumptions, and principles. In its most successful form, then, a public issue or concern evolves into a social movement, which, in turn becomes institutionalized as a new conceptual framework for making public policy and guiding private behavior. But social movements may also take the form of interest-group politics, which may be an intermediate point that can lead to the formation of a new framework of governance or a diversion and dilution of the movement so that the underlying concerns are seen as just one more interest.

Social Movement Theory and Environmentalism

Several key characteristics of global environmental problems are illuminated by social movement theory. First and foremost is the broad sweep of the causes of these problems. Contributing factors include emissions from giant factories and power plants but also the daily actions of billions of consumers. Effective solutions will require broad political support to ensure that powerful industries and major sources comply with standards and regulations, and to ensure that the changes in everyday behavior, transportation, and consumer purchases also occur. The key question here is, how strong and pervasive is environmental awareness, concern, and commitment, and to what extent has it become institutionalized in politics, policy making, and governance?

A second issue is the interaction of democracy and technical expertise. There is a long tradition in the United States of viewing environmental and natural resource issues through the lens of professionalism and expertise. The progressive era in the United States that spawned the first generation of conservation laws for national forests, for example, was built on the ideas of centralized authority and expertise. The progressives had great faith in the ability of experts to design and implement policies in ways that would serve the public interest, and democratic participation in policymaking was unnecessary.[56] While some continue to champion such deference to expertise and professionals, the demands for democratic participation are strong, not only because of the way such participation is likely to engage citizens in implementing the policies agreed to, but because democratic participation and empowerment are themselves essential values to be nourished apart from any environmental benefit. Part of the challenge is that scientific and technological issues play a greater role here than in any other area of global politics. Natural systems are to a great extent beyond the control of human systems. Scientific arguments and analyses can be tremendously influential in shaping global politics.[57]

A third challenge is the distribution of environmental benefit and burdens. Efforts to regulate or reduce pollution-producing and resource-using activities naturally evoke responses from those who benefit from those activities or who might be liable for the costs they impose. There will likely always be claims from those responsible for problems that the risks are negligible and pose no threat, are uncertain and should be studied more, or that the benefits outweigh the costs. These claims, of course, are quite problematic. They come from those with clear economic interests in minimizing the nature of the threats. Cost–benefit analysis is of limited help here because the benefits of the activity, while they may be far-reaching, are concentrated in the owners and employees of the polluting facilities and those who buy their products. The costs of the adverse health effects, while they too may reach many, are often concentrated in those who live near facilities, or live downwind and downstream, or who are elderly or already suffer from other health problems that are made worse by pollution. Political support for change will require a strong, broad base that can counter the power that narrow economic interests typically have to externalize costs on others in ways that diffuse those costs and discourage political organizing to reduce them.

Fourth, the temporal dimension of problems poses tremendous barriers to action, as costs are immediate and burdens are in the future. Environmental problems are largely long-term challenges, making it difficult to keep them on the current agenda. It is difficult to institutionalize a consideration of future interests in political deliberations; a commitment to intergenerational equity and the well-being of future generations may be part of the effort, but more immediate pressures may dominate. Some argue that commitments such as reducing poverty in current generations should override efforts to preserve resources for future generations.[58]

A fifth challenge is the nature of risk. Some believe that the most appropriate stance to take is precaution; that is, we should do all we can to protect the current operation of ecosystems because the stakes—the ecological preconditions for human life and its flourishing—are so high. Others believe that our commitment to fairness and justice should prevail, and we should minimize problems of which the distributional consequences are unfair. For example, the threat of climate change is largely a result of consumption in the privileged world, but if the threats are realized, those who will suffer the consequences and lack the resources to mitigate the effects are those in poor countries that produce proportionately few greenhouse gases. For many environmental problems, much of the risk is to be borne by future generations, while the costs of mitigating those risks will be borne by current generations. One can argue, in contrast, that the way to understand our predicament is that the current generation is failing to pay the true cost of its activities and is foisting some of those costs off on future generations by dumping toxic chemicals and nuclear waste in ways that will contaminate lands well into the future, or by dumping greenhouse gases into the atmosphere at levels that will make the climate less hospitable in the future. But there is no express representation of future interests in current political processes, and social movement theory raises the need for extending the sense of solidarity and community that movements can engender among current participants to those yet born.

A sixth and particularly important challenge is the pervasiveness and persistence of the uncertainty that characterizes our efforts to understand the young science of ecology. We may simply not understand some ecosystem functions very well and are able to make only rough guesses about what might happen in the future. Given the uncertainty surrounding environmental problems, there is a great need for political systems that are adaptive, that can learn from experience and engage in intelligent trial and error so that progress is made—even if sometimes the hard way, through problems and setbacks.[59] However, uncertainty can also prompt a commitment to the precautionary principle, requiring that potential problems posing serious consequences be avoided. Aaron Wildavsky argues that the way to respond to highly dangerous, low probability risks is to favor resilience over anticipation: to increase the pool of resources that can be used to adapt to problems as they arise rather than invest resources in reducing possible risks. The "secret of safety lies in danger"; safety should be discovered in response to events as they unfold rather than trying to protect against adversity (except when there is strong evidence that problems will occur). Trial-and-error policy making encourages the development of new solutions to problems and reductions of new hazards. Trial-and-error decision making creates new information and spurs innovation. Markets, not regulations, are best at dealing with uncertainties. Safety measures may themselves cause harm.[60] Wildavsky's formula is provocative but raises many questions. Anticipation, he argues, is appropriate, when there is "strong evidence" of a risk;[61] but what is strong evidence? What appears to meet that test from the perspective of environmentalists may not be similarly viewed by industry groups. More difficult is the distributional consequences of risks. If risks are voluntarily embraced, and the risks and benefits limited to those voluntarily assuming the risks, there is little objection to resiliency as an approach. If, however, the risks are involuntary, or the benefits and risks are not equally distributed, then prevention may be required in order to prevent the injustice of some, perhaps a few, being harmed, so that others, perhaps the majority, will have more resources. Even if all parties involved promise to direct resources to the victims once risks are realized, compensation or other forms of resilience may be inadequate responses to disease and premature death. Environmentalism as a social movement must effectively balance prevention and adaptation.

A seventh issue is the way in which global environmental politics has become fragmented. In the past, global relations were dominated by some 150 or so sovereign states. National sovereignty was reinforced through international law, even as global accords challenged sovereignty by imposing obligations on nation–states' security. A central paradox of international law has been its dual impact on sovereignty, but sovereignty has been maintained because nation–states alone possess the authority to implement and enforce the provisions of global agreements within their boundaries. The emerging multicentric world, made up of thousands of actors—nation–states, international institutions, nongovernmental organizations, and multinational corporations make traditional notions of sovereignty obsolete—and complicate considerably the options for formulating and implementing global agreements.[62]

Finally, social movement theory can provide a broad framework for assessing the functioning of interest groups. Interest-group theory suggests that the clash of organized interests produces optimal policy outcomes. The Madisonian theory of interest-group politics is that groups make policy demands and government regulates the debate and fashions policies that it believes are in the public interest. As the Federalist argued, the regulation of factions is the primary task of government. Other pluralists are more deferential to the results of interest-group bargaining, allowing the competition of the groups themselves to determine which policy proposals are to be enacted; government here is largely a disinterested broker, facilitating and then ratifying the debate among competing policy demands. They argue that groups are central to a healthy democratic pluralism; they help fill some of the gaps in representative government, such as providing opportunities for political discussion and, between elections, adding to the information available to policy makers. They also serve as a check on governmental power. Giving groups access to policy-making processes can help generate support for implementing whatever policies are ultimately fashioned.

Interest groups play much different roles in different countries. The American political system is particularly hospitable to a wide range of groups because of its fragmented, separated power structure that provides multiple access points. In other countries, such as those with parliamentary systems, interest groups may be even more powerful as they have access to executive branch officials who have the power to make binding decisions. Interest groups in Britain, for example, play a major role in shaping legislation before it goes to parliament through negotiations with civil servants. German law requires the national government, in some cases, to consult with "interest organizations" before drafting legislation. Japanese interest groups work closely with senior-level bureaucrats and members of the diet who specialize in specific policies. The formation of the European Union has produced a rich array of some 3,000 groups that have descended on Brussels to lobby, giving groups that may have lost policy battles at home to try for Union-wide mandates to achieve their goals. In France, pressure groups are more likely to take to the streets and engage in protest politics, which are seen as a normal part of democratic politics.[63]

Interest-group politics has been targeted by a number of critics. All interests are not represented, the process has an upper-class bias that favors the politically well connected and wealthy. These groups eventually choke government's ability to adapt to changing circumstances, devise new solutions to problems, and act in ways that are consistent with the broader public interest. Jonathan Rauch describes the problem as hyperpluralism that leads to demosclerosis.[64] Economists like Mancur Olson argue that groups only represent narrow interests and that the inability of groups to counter the free-rider problem discourages the organization of a wider variety of interests.[65] Interest groups are criticized from both the Left and Right: the Right, because they put demands on government to grow and become more involved in the economy and produce too much government, and the Left because they give the rich and powerful more influence. From the perspective of social movement theory, interest-group politics is an intermediate step; environmental issues are marginalized if they are reduced to simply the agenda of special interest groups. Environmentalism as a social movement must go beyond interest-group politics to serve as an underlying, structural element of the political economy rather than a force that competes for marginal influence in shaping public policies and private behavior.

Ecologically Sustainable Development

Social movement theory is a useful tool for examining the structure of environmentalism. Sustainability provides a way of assessing its content. Environmentalism can be institutionalized and occupy a central role in a political economy, but the kinds of policies it compels may be insufficiently ambitious to remedy critical problems. The idea of sustainability has well-developed roots in environmental and natural resource policy. Sustainability has been a standard for assessing the yield of natural resources (forests, for example) and a goal of policies for decades as land managers have sought to ensure that renewable resources are used no faster than they are replenished and can be used indefinitely.[66] In the 1970s, scholars broadened the notion to examine the extent to which economic activity, resource use, and pollution were consistent with the planet's carrying capacity.[67] The World Conservation Strategy proposed the concept of sustainable development in 1980.[68] But the idea of sustainable development gained real international prominence and attention with the publication in 1987 of the World Commission on Environment and Development's *Our Common Future* report, which urged all nations to commit to the idea of sustainable development, defined as "development that meets the needs of the present without compromising the ability of future generations to meet their own needs."[69] The idea of sustainable development was an essential underpinning of the 1992 United Nations Conference on Environment and Development (UNCED). The term was included in nearly half of the 27 articles that made up the Rio Declaration, a statement of broad principles to guide economic development, and was the basis for Agenda 21, a detailed plan of action aimed at implementing the idea of sustainable development.[70]

The UNCED documents never provided a clear definition of sustainable development. According to one count, there are some 70 competing definitions of the term.[71] The idea of sustainable development has evolved from its early and rather precise formulation as sustainable yield, to its current understanding, which varies widely. For some, sustainability means that we continue with business as usual, pursuing economic growth while trying, whenever it is not too expensive or disruptive of economic goals, to minimize environmental damage and resource use. Others believe that industry needs to reinvent itself in ways that promote pollution prevention, energy efficiency, and technological innovation. In addition, sustainable development can mean that ecological and environmental goals are given roughly equivalent status, that they must be pursued in tandem and in innovative ways that promote a much wider range of values than are incorporated in market prices. Or it can mean that the preservation of the biosphere is the most important collective objective and is a prerequisite for every other human endeavor; that is, it must be given priority over any economic goal.

The contested nature of the idea of sustainable development is rooted in two primary dimensions of the concept. A weak or thin form of sustainable development and the view embraced by the Clinton administration and many other proponents of sustainability in the United States is that economic and environmental concerns can and must be balanced. In the past, economic growth as been given priority and seen as paramount; now it must be refined and balanced by environmental sensitivity. But fundamental changes are not required: Current technologies and patterns of production and consumption are acceptable as long as they are tempered by environmental and resource considerations and we can largely continue to do what we have done in the past as long as we are more "sensitive" to environmental conditions. Similarly, the overall value of the natural and economic capital for future generations must be undiminished by the current generation. The goal is to ensure the same level of resources, while permitting some substitution of natural resources for an equivalent amount of capital.

This view of sustainability is reflected in the President's Council on Sustainable Development (PCSD), created by the Clinton administration in 1993 to bring together representatives from environmental groups, industry, and government to advise the president "on matters involving sustainable development." The term was defined as "economic growth that will benefit present and future generations without detrimentally affecting the resources or biological systems of the planet."[72] The council's "vision statement" argues that a "sustainable United States will have a growing economy that provides equitable opportunities for satisfying livelihoods and a safe, healthy, high quality of life for current and future generations."[73] Sustainability means that business can continue as usual and we can continue to pursue economic goals of growth and consumption, but we need to find ways of minimizing environmental damage and resource use so that the economic activity is sustainable or can continue. The key words here are balance and restraint—economic growth can continue as long as it is smart growth, sensitive to environmental constraints, and balanced with ecological concerns. This idea of sustainable development has been attractive to so many people because they have in mind the first definition and realize that it does not require fundamental changes in lifestyles, transportation, or production.

In contrast, a strong or thick form of sustainable development, what I call here ecological sustainability, holds that environmental preservation is the paramount value. It places a major constraint on economics; only economic activity that is consistent with the fundamental criterion of sustainability is acceptable. The current distribution of critical natural capital must be maintained in some form, so that the ecosystem services it provides are maintained. It cannot simply be harvested to generate economic wealth that is to be passed down to subsequent generations. Industrial activities, energy production, transportation, and consumption must be fundamentally transformed to avoid ecological disruptions and protect regenerative processes. Ecological survival simply outweighs economic growth as the primary public priority.[74] Because ecological conditions make all life, and economic activities, possible, preserving those conditions should be given priority. Balancing is not enough— ecological values must come first, and must define and limit what kinds and levels of economic activity are acceptable. Policy goals such as free trade and economic efficiency are subordinated to the preservation of biodiversity, protection of wild lands, and reclamation of damaged areas. When the idea of sustainability is invoked, the first question should be, what kind of sustainability is involved?

An important feature of this thick notion of development is its integration of ecological protection and economic activity with social equity and political empowerment. Sustainable development here gives priority to reducing poverty and helping the poor gain some measure of self-sufficiency through a more equitable distribution of resources. Political participation is a key ingredient in ensuring that decisions affecting economic and environmental conditions be made more inclusive.[75]

These two versions of sustainability differ along key dimensions. A weak form of sustainability is that the overall value of the natural and economic capital for future generations is undiminished by the current generation. The key is to ensure the same level of resources; this would permit some substitution of natural resources for an equivalent amount of capital. In contrast, a strong form, or ecological sustainability, holds that the distribution of critical natural capital must be maintained. Where in the past, economic growth has been given priority or seen as paramount, the thin version holds that economic and environmental concerns must be balanced. The thick form holds that environmental preservation is paramount and places a major constraint on economics; only economic activity consistent with the fundamental criterion of sustainability is acceptable. The weak form is that the status quo is acceptable as long as it is tempered by environmental and resource considerations; we can pretty much continue to do what we have done in the past as long as we are sensitive to the environment; the strong form emphasizes that industrial activities, energy production, transportation, and consumption must be fundamentally transformed. Sustainable development can be a radical goal, a new way of defining problems and devising responses to them, or it can be a call for modest shifts in current practices and priorities.

Sustainability and Environmentalism

Ecological sustainability has parallels with other formulations of environmentalism. One variation of the debate over the nature of environmental problems is between radical and mainstream assessments. Radical environmentalists believe that human society, as it currently functions, is unsustainable, in a state of crisis, and destined to collapse. Their diagnosis includes not only the consequences of industrialism for natural resources, but broadens the analysis to illuminate how the domination of nature inherent in industrialism spills over to include the domination of human beings along lines of race, class, and gender. Radical ecologists call for a transformative social movement to remedy environmental threats and other social pathologies of poverty, disadvantagement, and discrimination.[76] While mainstream environmentalism is reformist, aimed at reducing pollution and inefficient use of resources, radical environmentalism is revolutionary and seeks a new way of thinking, a new metaphysics and cosmology, a new environmental ethic to shape individual and collective activity.[77]

Radical ecologists vary in their prescriptions: some advocate revolution and overthrow of the existing order; others suggest widespread education and ideological conversion; and some predict socioeconomic collapse and a rebirth along ecological lines. Deep ecologists, for example, champion biospherical egalitarianism, a commitment to preservation of biodiversity and all forms of life, not just human, and a willingness to place major constraints on human activities to preserve other forms of life.[78] Ecofeminists find that the oppression of women by men is fundamentally the same as the destruction of nature by a male-dominated society. Eliminating gender discrimination and subordination of women goes hand in hand with protecting nature.[79] The radical ecological agenda requires that capitalism be replaced with a more environmentally benign system of production as well as a more egalitarian distribution of economic and political power. Many radical proposals call for a dramatically reduced level of social and political activity, where production and consumption are decentralized, and a rejection of much of the technological infrastructure of modern societies, replaced by simpler, less consumptive ways of living. Under this view, developing countries should avoid integration in global markets and find ways to improve their quality of life within the confines of village life, appropriate technologies, and insulation from global forces. Perhaps most importantly, the idea of economic growth must be rejected as fundamentally inconsistent with the ecological limits of the planet. Radical ecologists rage against the accumulated impact of capitalism and the pursuit of wealth, war and exploitation, and the destruction of the earth's ecosystems, and propose a mutinous strategy that topples humans from their privileged position and champions the flourishing of all living things.[80]

Some critics of radical ecology correctly fear the movement as a threat to the current political economy, to capitalism and our commitment to economic growth. They argue that it is a threat to whatever hope the poorer inhabitants of the earth have to ever improve their quality of life. They fear that ecological protection will come at a too high price of the loss of individual freedoms. They believe that we are able to grow our way out of problems as we expand wealth and human ingenuity.[81] Other critics of radical environmentalism argue that, despite the intentions of its proponents, such radicalism represents an ecological catastrophe in the making. Eco-extremists, they argue, simply fuel the efforts of those opposed to environmental protection and interests that seek unbridled development of resources. Radicals are linked with mainstream advocates in ways that threaten broad-based support for environmental protection goals. More broadly, critics of radical environmentalism argue that their goals threaten to destroy technological gains and undercut research and development when as they call for dismantling large organizations and replacing them with small-scale facilities, because these facilities may lack the resources to reduce pollution or find cleaner technologies. Limiting industrialization, these critics argue, especially in the less developed countries, will actually contribute to population *growth*, as industrialization has been a primary force in reducing fertility rates. Radicals who call for an end to human management and a return to natural conditions are naïve and unrealistic, their critics charge, because pristine nature is nonexistent except for a few, isolated areas. Radicals who call for a return to nature, to a life more dependent on living close to the land, are calling for a tremendous increase in human impacts on natural resources such as timber and wildlife. The radical environmental agenda relies on a massive change in popular perceptions and lifestyles, but such a widespread conversion to ecology is unrealistic and would be insufficient without policy changes. Policy changes are required, but radicals criticize those who try to find acceptable, workable, compromises and undercut the prospects for improved policies.[82]

Some argue that a capitalist economy, with effective regulations and incentives to shape and channel behavior, is more likely to generate the wealth and technological innovations for improved environmental quality than by attacking capitalism and trying to replace it. Taking on capitalism and seeking to replace it with some other form of political economy is a massive undertaking and likely an impossible task and, in any event, would divert attention from policies that could produce direct, immediate improvements in environmental quality. This kind of "guided capitalism," proponents hope, will encourage investments in human and natural resources, create strong disincentives against pollution and other destructive behaviors, and generate the resources for technological and ecological improvements.[83]

Ecological sustainability, as formulated here, is clearly a radical prescription. Its strength and its weakness is its broad sweep. Kai Lee argues that "human societies will have to change the way they understand the relationship between economics and human life." Sustainable development "is not a goal, not a condition likely to be attained on earth as we know it. Rather, it is more like freedom or justice, a direction in which we strive, along which we search for a life good enough to warrant our comforts." Sustainability requires that we "acknowledge the pace and scale of nature's teaching." The appropriate metaphor, he argues, is the garden: "a place that is bounded and organic, designed yet open to seasons and elements, natural but cultivated, sustainable and humane."[84] The impreciseness of sustainability makes it an attractive idea around which diverse expectations can congregate. But that impreciseness makes its use as a criterion for assessing environmentalism problematic.

Ecological sustainability is also problematic for other reasons. If it requires that the stock of nonrenewable natural resources be preserved for future generations, then we have long since violated its basic premise. If, rather, it allows for harvesting nonrenewable resources, in what form must the benefits of that harvesting be made available to future generations? Sustainability also suggests a static goal of ensuring that future generations have the same level of resources and ecosystem services to rely on. From an anthropocentric perspective, is sustainability in the interest of the current generation? Or is it more morally compelling for them to improve the quality of life of existing members of that generation and reduce the enormous disparities in wealth? Or is it better to set aside resources for those to come? The value of natural resources, in part, lies in their use, but human use has varied greatly: Uses of forests have changed dramatically, for example, from sources of strategic defense materials (wood for battleships) to watershed functions of cleansing water. From an ecological perspective, does sustainability make sense in light of the dynamic nature of biological evolution? Some argue that the idea of sustainability is most useful in narrow settings, where parties may be able to agree that certain practices are not sustainable and should be changed, but cannot be used to illuminate broader issues.[85]

Two arguments developed by scholars who write about sustainability are helpful here in assessing the idea of sustainability within the environmental movement. First, the nature of the problem of sustainability is rooted in the interaction of population, affluence, and technology, as shown in the following formula:

I (environmental or resource impacts) = P (population) x A (affluence, usually per capita income) x T (impacts per unit of income as determined by technology).[86]

Population trends are relatively well understood: Global population has grown in recent years by about 1.3 percent a year, down from a peak of 2.1 percent in the 1960s. About 80 percent, or 4.8 billion people, live in developing countries; 1.2 billion live in the developed nations. The United Nations projects that population growth will reach 8.9 billion in 2050. Growth is primarily a result of death rates dropping more rapidly than birth rates. The transition from high birth and death rates to low rates for both took about two centuries in Europe; in contrast, it has taken the developing countries only about one-third that time to make the same transition. There are also rather straightforward means of reducing population growth (although, as discussed below, not everyone believes that it should be reduced): increase the availability of contraceptives to prevent unwanted pregnancies; encourage smaller families by investing more in children, particularly in the education of girls; and encourage women to postpone childbearing, by increasing educational opportunities for them.[87]

In contrast, the growth in consumption is much more difficult to address. While the earth's population more than doubled between 1950 and 2000, agricultural output nearly tripled and energy use more than quadrupled. Energy efficiency has increased, and the amount of carbon used per unit of energy has declined. However, efficiency gains have been offset by growth in consumption. Solutions to consumption include increasing efficiency; finding less environmentally damaging substitutes; fostering industrial ecology advances where industry learns from nature in redesigning production processes; and increasing our commitment to reduce, reuse, and recycle. But it is far from clear that technological solutions will be sufficient, due to the fact that technology has itself been a major factor in driving environmental impacts of consumption. Part of the solution may require that we learn to want less, that we become satisfied with imposing a smaller ecological footprint. Religious teachings that discourage materialism and the simplicity movement's encouragement of less consumptive practices may reduce pressures. But they seem to be destined to be overwhelmed by the relentless emphasis on growth that is a fundamental part of the dominant economic system. Robert Kates sums up the challenge this way:

> To reduce the level of impacts per unit of consumption, it is necessary to separate out more damaging consumption and *shift* to less harmful forms, *shrink* the amounts of environmentally damaging energy and materials per unit of consumption, and *substitute* information for energy and materials. To reduce consumption per person or household, it is necessary to *satisfy* more with what is already had, *satiate* well-met consumption needs, and *sublimate* wants for a greater good. Finally, it is possible to *slow* population growth and then to *stabilize* population numbers.[88]

Economic growth is the dominant global value: Wealth is generated by production and consumption; competitive pressures to keep up with the consumption of others helps drive growth; and the great inequalities in the distribution of resources and wealth have created tremendous demands for growth. It is difficult to imagine, under current political, economic, and cultural practices and institutions, how such a transformation could occur. Sustainability is rooted in the conclusion that the Western, industrialized, high-consumption way of living is not ecologically feasible for all the planet's residents or even for a majority of them. Despite marketing and advertising efforts to encourage this level of consumption worldwide, it is not possible to do so, at least for a long period of time. The impact of 6 billion people living an American middle-class lifestyle would overwhelm the ability of natural systems to sustain that life.

The second key idea about sustainability is that it is a process rather than a set of policies. Some policies can be assessed in terms of whether they are consistent with or contrary to the elements of sustainability and, from one view, that is the importance of the idea of sustainability. From another view, its real importance lies in its potential to reshape the terms of discourse about public policy, and production and consumption. From the perspective of social movement theory, the debate over sustainabilty seeks to produce a new paradigm to guide issues of production and consumption in the twenty-first century. Neil Harrison describes sustainability as a journey, a process, rather than a policy agenda.[89] Daniel Mazmanian and Michael Kraft describe it as a third epoch of the environmental movement, the latest stage in the evolution of environmental movement from an emphasis on reducing pollution to addressing the economic, environmental, psychological, and cultural well-being of communities.[90]

Dennis Pirages argues that much as human survival and success are a result of "evolutionary mechanisms that have adapted the human body and human behavior to changing environmental constraints," sociocultural evolution is a similar process by which "survival-relevant information is passed from one generation to the next."[91] The challenge of sociocultural evolution is to identify and inculcate values and behaviors that will allow human society to learn to function in ways that are consistent with ecological constraints. Just as natural selection shapes the survival of humans, sociocultural evolution can produce norms, values, and practices that allow human society to flourish.

This emphasis on sustainability as social learning and evolution draws attention to sustainability as a long-term process that varies over time and across geographic areas and conditions. The agenda for sustainability is different for different countries. Humanity's future will be a function of how well societies modify their sociocultural genomes in order to survive and flourish. Pirages argues that this is an enormously exciting enterprise, one that can engage our best energy and creativity in trying to increase human satisfaction and happiness without increasing material consumption. Pirages and colleagues identify a host of actions that are part of the process of sustainability: devising new measures of welfare and progress and indicators of sustainability, lengthening the time that products are used, redistributing resources to meet pressing human needs and thereby increasing satisfaction, improving efficiency, using more renewable resources, and expanding recycling. Sustainability requires a combination of changes in how material resources are used and in the values and institutions that determine behavior. Creating a more sustainable world is a "dynamic, complex, and continuous process that will require decades of concerted effort."[92] Given the great diversity in human societies and ecological conditions, there is no single plan for sustainability, but rather an effort to strengthen the evolutionary capacity of societies. Its strength comes from the way in which it represents cooperative efforts on the part of participating countries that it is in everyone's interest to protect the global environment and promote environmentally sustainable economic growth to reduce the poverty that afflicts so many of the planet's residents.

Conclusion

Despite its limitations, ecological sustainability is a useful framework for assessing environmentalism for several reasons. It is part of a global agreement, the result of international discussions and negotiations, part of a global effort to identify a problem and find solutions. It calls for a comprehensive, integrated approach that includes social justice and improving the plight of the poor, transformation in economic practices, support for participatory democracy, and empowerment of citizens. Sustainability is a critically important notion in linking environmental problems in the North and the South—the advanced, industrialized world and its developing, poorer counterpart. It links the wealthy and poor countries who all share the challenge of making their economies ecologically sustainable and reflective of the needs of the poor among them and those of future generations. It promises to find a path to reconciling the stubborn conflicts between environmental protection and economic growth, equality and efficiency, and the different agendas of the North and the South.

Environmentalism has been quite successful as a social movement. But social movements need to be flexible and adaptive, able to evolve to address emerging problems if they are to remain viable and vibrant forces for change. The environmental challenge has evolved from reducing pollution and setting aside protected areas to include the much more complex and ambitious goal of ecological sustainability. The question before us is whether environmentalism will evolve and embrace the goal of sustainability—and be able to generate the kinds of changes in private behavior, political processes, and public policies that sustainability compels.

2

Environmentalism in the United States

Assessing the strength of environmentalism in the United States, or in any country, is admittedly a subjective enterprise. Environmental commitments vary across time and throughout regions. The indicators used to measure the level and breadth of commitment are limited and imprecise. This chapter, and the two that follow, suggest that three broad indicators shed some light on the nature of the commitment to environmental protection and offer some tentative conclusions about the strength of environmentalism as a social movement and its impact on political institutions and policies and the practices of individuals and businesses. The first area examined is environmental politics. In the United States, environmentalism is largely expressed as interest-group politics, with a wide range of groups competing for access and influence in policy making. Environmentalism has not made its way into party politics as a major political force: The major parties do not give priority to environmental issues, and Green Parties occupy only a very minor role in electoral politics. I argue that interest-group politics is a limited vehicle for bringing about fundamental shifts in public values and public policies, and the transformation from interest group to party politics may be one of the steps required for a more influential environmental movement.

A second indicator, public-opinion polling, shows broad support for environmental values, but commitments are not particularly deep and are typically weaker than concern for other issues such as economic growth and jobs, education, social security, and crime. The environmental movement has had a significant impact on public values, but much more needs to be done, particularly because polling data indicates that many Americans believe environmental problems are largely being addressed and other public problems are more pressing.

31

A third indicator of the strength of environmentalism is the extent to which the idea of sustainability has been embraced—whether the movement has evolved in response to the threats that are becoming increasingly prominent. Here, the assessment focuses on whether the terms of public discourse are shifting economic growth to at least a weak or thin form of sustainability, and whether the foundation is being laid for a more long-term evolution to ecological sustainability. There are some promising breakthroughs, particularly at the community level, but little evidence that such a foundation is being built.

Following the terminology developed in chapter one, I use the word *environmentalism* to refer to the accumulation of societal values, public opinion, and political activity that relate to the environment. The term *environmental movement* is largely the same idea, as environmental ideas and commitments in the United States have clearly moved beyond the "fad" stage. Environmental politics focuses on the efforts of environmental advocates to gain support for policies and practices they favor. These are dynamic, interactive terms. The assessment here focuses on the nature of the environmental movement and environmental politics, the prospects for their evolution toward the goal of sustainability, and the capacity to produce the changes required to meet the environmental challenges described in chapter one. The evidence suggests that environmentalism has not been able to move much beyond interest-group politics. Its manifestation as a social movement is strongest at the grass-roots, community level, where it shows signs of embracing the goal of sustainability. National environmental groups have also embraced that goal, but it has yet to become a primary value in the policy-making process.

Environmental Politics

The American environmental movement is a coherent, social, cultural phenomenon—one of the most successful movements in American history. It has clearly had a profound impact on the way people think about the natural world and their impact on it. It has produced a major infrastructure of laws, regulations, conservation programs, and regulatory agencies. Within a very short period of time, it replaced a haphazard reliance on common-law protection of resources and a few, specialized laws, with a comprehensive program that affects virtually every use of land, water, and air.[1] It has contributed to major improvements in air and water quality, the protection of undeveloped lands for recreation, and the preservation of biodiversity. Its influence has permeated American life. Describing its reach is no easy task.

Participants and observers have offered a number of different descriptions. Michael McCloskey, former chair of the Sierra Club, for example, finds three groups. The mainstream or center is made up of the pragmatists, like the Sierra Club and other national groups, who work for incremental changes and see industry as having different objectives but not necessarily enemies. The conservative wing includes fishing, hunting, and land-protection groups like the Nature Conservancy, who rarely criticize industry but often do not support government regulation either, preferring private-sector solutions to problems. The radical wing is formed by groups usually opposed to both industry and government as they challenge the established powers and push for fundamental changes in economics and politics.[2] This captures the core but not all elements of the movement, as Philip Shabecoff, one of the most widely published environmental journalists and writers, has written. Other groups important to the movement are not so easily categorized such as the Union of Concerned Scientists, which calls for dramatic changes in environmental and economic policy, and the E. F. Schumacher Society, which calls for a conservative, locally oriented economic and social system.[3]

The environmental movement is a dynamic, evolving organism as some groups have faded out and new ones formed. Some groups have been quite successful in maintaining their membership and support, while others have declined in popularity. Many groups have formed to deal with specific issues such as ozone-layer depletion and rain forest destruction. The greatest growth has come in grass-roots groups aimed at working in a specific community or region. According to one estimate, national environmental organizations claim 12 to 14 million members, although many members are counted more than once because they belong to several groups, and a majority of members are likely to be relatively passive dues payers.[4]

Kinds of Environmental Groups

One set of environmental groups, the earliest ones formed, has emphasized the preservation of public lands and wildlife. The National Wildlife Federation and other groups have had a significant number of hunters and fishers and have lobbied for protection of public lands and habitat for sports. But these groups have evolved as environmental threats have changed. In 1892, John Muir and others organized the Sierra Club, for example, to protect areas like Yosemite as well as to promote outdoor recreation. The club was incorporated "to explore, enjoy, and render accessible the mountain regions of the Pacific Coast; to publish authentic information concerning them," and "to enlist the support and cooperation of the people and government in preserving the forests and other natural features of the Sierra Nevada."[5] During its first four decades, The Sierra Club focused on encouraging wilderness recreation. But the rapid development and expansion after World War II prompted some members to begin worrying about the loss of wild lands. A group of "Young Turks," led by David Brower, pushed for a change in the club's statement of purpose, from "explore, enjoy, and render accessible . . ." to "explore, enjoy, and preserve the Sierra Nevada and other scenic resources of the United States."[6] By the late 1960s, the Sierra Club had broadened its efforts to include pollution and other environmental problems. In 1971, it formed the Sierra Club Legal Defense Fund to litigate cases (now called the Earthjustice Legal Defense Fund) and introduced international programs. During the 1970s, Sierra Club members became very involved in political campaigns, endorsing candidates and publicizing their environmental views and platforms. The club continued to emphasize protection of public lands and wild areas but was also a major lobbying force for clean air and water and hazardous waste legislation in the 1980s, and for policies aimed at reducing sprawl and designating new wilderness lands in the 1990s.[7]

A related but different approach taken by other groups has been to focus on the purchase of private lands for preservation. The Nature Conservancy was created by a professional association of ecologists who sought to translate their knowledge of nature into ways of preserving it. The Nature Conservancy's mission is to "preserve plants, animals, and natural communities that represent the diversity of life on Earth by protecting the lands and waters they need to survive."[8] The Nature Conservancy purchases critical habitats and manages more than 1,500 preserves on more than 1.1 million acres in the United States and has helped protect more than 10 million acres. The Conservancy's International Program also sponsors programs in Latin America, the Caribbean and the Pacific, and works with more than 45 organizations in 22 countries to provide technical and financial assistance to protect critical habitats. Its efforts have helped protect 60 million acres of land worldwide and has pioneered the debt-for-nature swaps in Latin America, where the foreign debt of these countries has been reduced in exchange for a commitment to preserve habitat.[9]

A second kind of environmental group is characterized by Environmental Defense (formerly the Environmental Defense Fund) and the Natural Resources Defense Council, both created during the great burst of environmentalist energy in the late 1960s and early 1970s. These groups combine scientists, economists, lawyers, and lobbyists who issue technical reports, provide expertise to Green-leaning members (those favoring stronger environmental protection) of Congress, and regularly sue the Environmental Protection Agency (EPA) and states for failing to take actions required of them by environmental laws, and polluters for failing to comply with the regulations imposed on them. Environmental Defense began going to court on behalf of the environment in 1967, when it sued to stop the spraying of DDT (dichlorodiphenyltrichloroethane); its efforts produced a nationwide ban five years later. More recently, it has championed the development of market-based alternatives to traditional environmental regulation and has developed business partnerships to create pollution-reduction and conservation programs, such as working with McDonald's to reduce packaging waste.[10] NRDC also has an extensive research, public information, lobbying, and litigation infrastructure aimed at achieving its broad goal to "safeguard the Earth: its people, its plants and animals, and the natural systems on which life depends" and cases it has brought to the public's attention have played a major role in shaping environmental law.

A few environmental groups focus on electoral politics. The League of Conservation Voters works to elect a Congress "more responsive . . . to environmental concerns," and seeks to educate citizens about the environmental voting records of members by publishing an annual report of votes cast on major environmental issues.[11] For years, *Environmental Action* published a "dirty dozen" list of members of Congress who regularly voted against more protective legislation. Others focus on specific issues. The Clean Air Network, for example, is an umbrella group made up of hundreds of local and national groups that lobby for and raise awareness about clean-air legislation and issues. Clean Water Action focuses on drinking water and groundwater sources. Defenders of Wildlife champions habitat preservation for wildlife. Other groups are organized regionally, aimed at preserving specific areas or species and may include education, research, and lobbying.

Some groups describe themselves as radical environmentalists. For example, members of Earth First! describe themselves as a "movement, not an organization," and promise "no compromise in defense of Mother Earth":

> Are you tired of namby-pamby environmental groups? Are you tired of overpaid corporate environmentalists who suck up to bureaucrats and industry? Have you become disempowered by the reductionist approach of environmental professionals and scientists? Earth First! was founded in 1979 in response to a lethargic, compromising, and increasingly corporate environmental community. Earth First! takes a decidedly different tack towards environmental issues. We believe in using all the tools in the tool box, ranging from grass-roots organizing and involvement in the legal process to civil disobedience and monkeywrenching.[12]

Other groups, such as the Earth Liberation Front (ELF), have been linked with direct action, such as the 1998 burning of the Two Elks Lodge and other facilities in Vail, Colorado, perhaps the single most expensive act of environmental sabotage in U.S. history. The fire was aimed at protecting the last potential lynx habitat in Colorado—three of the four documented sightings of lynx in Colorado over the past 60 years were in the ski expansion area. ELF is a "movement of independently operating eco-saboteurs" who publicize "preannounced, internationally coordinated Earth Nights"—a "call for harm to property only, never life."[13]

A final set of U.S. environmental groups are those headquartered in other countries, with offices in the United States. The largest international environmental organization is Greenpeace International, which has offices in the United States and 39 other countries, and claimed 2.4 million financial contributors worldwide in 1998.[14] Greenpeace activists have become widely known for their aggressive efforts to protest environmentally destructive actions and their ability to focus media attention on causes such as threatened whales, the hazards of nuclear testing and wastes, toxic pollution, and ocean dumping; and protection of the Arctic.

Assessing Environmental Groups

Assessments of the power and influence wielded by environmental groups are tentative because environmentalism is still relatively young, and its effectiveness is affected by so many factors. Nevertheless, there is considerable evidence that the movement is a modest, though not a dominant, force in American life and in policy making. First, the size, resources, and influence of environmental organizations in the United States has ebbed and flowed over the past three decades. Membership grew quickly during the late 1960s as the media focused attention on environmental problems and Congress enacted a flurry of environmental legislation, then leveled off during the late 1970s. The appointment by Ronald Reagan of James Watt as Secretary of the Interior and Anne Burford as EPA Administrator, two officials who were outspoken critics of existing environmental policies, resulted in a surge in membership as environmental organizations warned of weakened laws and regulations. Another surge in support for environmental groups occurred around Earth Day 1990. But by the early 1990s, even though the environment appeared to be a core value for most Americans, membership decreased again, with many of the groups reducing staffing, closing field offices, and narrowing their program focus to just a few key issues. Despite the loss of members among the largest organizations, small, grass-roots groups appeared to be gaining strength with their concentration on local or regional issues. Contribution levels to environmental and wildlife groups increased at mid-decade, growing to $4 billion in 1995, an increase of 10 percent over 1994.[15] The membership of these groups represents only a small percentage of Americans—

and they are fragmented. Christopher Bosso has argued that there is no environmental movement in the United States, but, rather, a "vast and inchoate community of organizations dedicated to the environment in one way or another." These groups all share a "core belief in the importance of the environment, but differ in priorities, strategies, and tactics." It has become a "very typical American interest-group community, albeit one with a greater than average array of policy niches and potential forms of activism."[16] Table 2-1 shows how membership in some of the largest environmental groups has changed since 1970.

TABLE 2-1
Membership Trends Among Selected National Environmental Groups, 1970–1998

Group	Year Founded	1970	1980	1990	1998
Sierra Club	1892	113,000	181,000	630,000	555,000
National Audubon Society	1905	148,000	400,000	600,000	575,000
National Parks & Conservation Assoc.	1919	45,000	31,000	100,000	500,000
Izaak Walton League	1922	54,000	52,000	50,000	50,000
Wilderness Society	1935	54,000	45,000	350,000	350,000
National Wildlife Federation[a]	1936	540,000	818,000	997,000	4.0 million
Defenders of Wildlife	1947	13,000	50,000	80,000	243,000
Nature Conservancy	1951	22,000	NA	600,000	901,000
World Wildlife Fund	1961	NA	NA	400,000	1.2 million
Environmental Defense Fund	1967	11,000	46,000	200,000	300,000
Friends of the Earth[b]	1969	6,000	NA	9,000	12,000
Environmental Action	1970	10,000	20,000	23,000	Defunct
League of Conservative Voters	1970	NA	35,000	55,000	NA
Natural Resources Defense Fund	1970	NA	40,000	150,000	400,000
Greenpeace USA	1971	NA	NA	2.35 mil.	350,000

Note: Figures are rounded and often approximations based on conflicting data or reporting dates. NA = not available

[a] Figures through 1995 are for full members only and do not count affiliated memberships (e.g., schoolchildren) of around 4.4 million in 1995. For 1998, figure is aggregate, as the NWF no longer releases data on full versus affiliated memberships.

[b] Merged in 1990 with the 30,000-member Oceanic Society and the nonmember Environmental Policy Institute.

Source: Christopher Bosso, "Environmental Groups and the New Political Landscape," in Norman J. Vig and Michael E. Kraft, *Environmental Policy* (Washington, D.C.: CQ Press, 4th ed., 2000): 55–76, at 64.

A second indicator of modest strength is the criticism aimed at environmental groups for failing to include members of ethnic and disadvantaged groups, and for failing to address the greater environmental risks affecting minority communities. The environmental justice movement, barely a decade old in the year 2000, has focused attention on the disproportionate impact of risk on low-income communities and communities of color from decisions to locate facilities that produce dangerous emissions and the weak enforcement of environmental laws in these communities. However, environmental groups have been slow to recognize the problem and support strong actions to reduce the injustices.[17] This movement emerged from a grass-roots response to the siting of hazardous waste facilities that seeks to prevent such decisions and to ensure that decision-making processes include those who are most burdened by those decisions. The rapid rise to prominence of this movement raises questions about the limited representativeness of mainstream environmental groups and points to the potential power of community-based environmental movements. But there has been some tension between environmental and justice groups, including complaints by two small but aggressive grass-roots groups in Louisiana and New Mexico that charged the largest environmental groups with racism.[18]

Another way in which the environmental movement is fragmented is the rift between grass-roots and mainstream environmental groups. They differ in style: National organizations typically pay their executive officers relatively high salaries and run massive fund-raising operations, while most grass-roots groups are strictly volunteer based and funded on minimal membership dues. Grass-roots groups disapprove of national groups because they feel they are too closely tied to Congress, federal agencies, and trade associations, and are too quick to compromise in order to be accepted by the Washington establishment. National groups, in turn, fear that grass-roots coalitions lack the technical expertise to deal with complex issues and are often dominated by industry interests when they meet in collaborative or consensus-based settings. For example, a group of local citizens, loggers, and government officials, known as the Quincy Library Group, fashioned a five-year pilot project to govern timber cuts on 70,000 acres of national forests in California; Congress enacted into law the compromise the group fashioned.[19] In the fall of 1999, a coalition of 140 environmental groups announced their intention to try to block implementation of the plan by the U.S. Forest Service. The groups were not only opposed to the "considerable amount of environmental damage that will come from this decision," as one environmental group official put it, but also feared that such collaborative efforts will allow powerful local economic interests to pressure local environmentalists to accept environmentally destructive agreements.[20] In other cases—such as the grass-roots Clearing House of Hazardous Wastes, created in response to the poisoning of the Love Canal community by the Hooker Chemical Company—local environmentalists came to distrust the EPA, national environmental groups, and their commitment to protecting communities.[21]

Schisms have appeared within some environmental groups. The Association of Sierra Club Members for Environmental Ethics, founded by dissident members in 1991, accused the Sierra Club of compromising its principles to get legislation through Congress. The group experienced a similar split in 1996 over the issue of whether The Sierra Club should support a ban on all commercial logging in national forests, with the issue pitting the club's first executive director, Dave Brower, against former Earth First! founder Dave Foreman. The highly publicized internal controversy resulted in the organization supporting the logging ban in a two-to-one vote, but it also led to the creation of another spin-off dissident group, John Muir Sierrans, which had supported the logging ban for several years. Environmental Defense has been forced out of some environmental coalitions because its support for market-based approaches to regulation and negotiations with industries have been seen by some groups as too accommodating to polluters. While such disputes may not be enough to cause a permanent rift among groups, they are symptomatic of the fragmentation in the environmental movement that keeps it from speaking as one voice in the political arena.[22]

One of the most important indicators of the limited strength of environmentalism is the power of opposing groups. Industry interests have traditionally opposed environmental rules due to the cost of compliance and the restraint on business decision-making autonomy. Businesses were initially slow to respond to the growth of environmental legislation during the late 1960s and into the 1970s. They eventually responded by forming trade associations and nonprofit research groups or think tanks to make their case. They have launched public relations campaigns to associate themselves in the minds of the public with conservation projects aimed at preserving endangered species and other Green issues. Armies of lobbyists who have invested in campaign contributions and enjoy access to members of Congress represent industry concerns on virtually every issue considered. Companies and trade associations also employ their own scientists, economists, and policy experts to challenge the claims made by environmental groups and offer their own analyses of environmental risks. The resources industry groups bring to bear on environmental issues simply overwhelm those possessed by environmental groups, but the two sides sometimes appear to be stalemated. Environmentalists are often more successful than industry groups in capturing the attention of the media, in generating favorable coverage, and in pressuring elected officials. They have considerable strength when issues are visible, and they can label actions as environmentally good or bad. Industry groups can invest major resources in the administrative process. This phase of the policy-making process is less scrutinized by the media, and environmental groups are also out-staffed and out-funded here and are largely unable to counter industry resources by working with the media to make appeals to the public to pressure policy makers.[23] As a result, environmental laws like the Clean Air Act often contain ambitious mandates and expansive goals, but their implementation is limited and narrowed in response to industry concerns.[24]

Organized labor has traditionally supported programs that involve occupational health issues such as exposure to airborne particulates and toxic chemicals, and have joined environmental groups in coalitions for clean air and other issues. As mentioned in chapter one, an environmental–labor coalition was formed to challenge open trade and the World Trade Organization. But unions have also opposed environmental regulation when they believe it affects job security.[25]

Opposition to environmental regulation has matured and become more effective, and includes farmers and ranchers, organized labor (on some issues), industry, and three grass-roots opposition movements: wise use, property rights, and county supremacy. The two issues that have most galvanized farmers, for example, have been proposals to restrict the use of agricultural pesticides and herbicides and agricultural use of water. In the case of pesticide use, rural interests have formed a coalition with chemical companies and their associations, bringing together such disparate groups as the American Farm Bureau Federation and the National Agricultural Chemical Association, along with the National Association of State Departments of Agriculture, the Association of American Plant Food, Pesticide, and Feed Control Officers, the National Association of County Agents, and the Christmas Tree Growers Association.[26]

Other groups opposed to environmental regulation have coalesced around a set of issues, including wise use, private property, and the county supremacy movement. The grass-roots opposition to current environmental policies have long roots in the West. That movement began more as a protest against the heavy hand of federal agencies and unhappiness with government policies. The Sagebrush Rebellion began in the 1970s as an effort by wealthy ranchers and others to gain control of public lands in the West. The movement had proponents in government in the 1980s, particularly Interior Secretary James Watt. The movement was reinvigorated in the early 1990s as the wise use and county supremacy movements garnered attention. The movement spread throughout the nation in the 1990s through the efforts of networks like the Alliance for America, the Blue Ribbon Coalition, and the Center for the Defense of Free Enterprise. These groups have tried to convince the media and policy makers that there is a broad movement of Americans who are opposed to environmental laws and regulations.[27] Militant opposition groups (the Sahara Club, for example) boast of vandalizing property or disrupting environmental group activities. Sporadic violence has occurred in Nevada and other Western states, aimed at federal agency facilities and employees.

From a political standpoint, the grass-roots opposition has had some successes at the state and local levels. Between 1991 and 1995, 59 western counties passed ordinances that claimed authority to supersede federal environmental and land-use laws and regulations, and 34 counties in Nevada, California, Idaho, New Mexico, and Oregon passed ordinances challenging federal control of local lands.[28] The Justice Department challenged the ordinances as illegal and sought an injunction to ban their enforcement, and courts have struck down ordinances that would have given counties the right to determine how public lands within their boundaries would be used. But the wise use movement's adherents are highly motivated and well organized through a network of web pages, e-mail, and grass-roots chapters, and they continue to press their concerns forcefully.[29]

The wise use movement has challenged the environmental movement in important ways. The private property movement and other grass-roots elements combine to pose a potent challenge to environmentalists and environmental law and policy. The wise use movement, to oversimplify, has not produced solutions to the problems of pollution. They apparently seek only to block any effort to limit what they can do on their property and seem to have little interest in workers who are exposed to toxic substances in chemical factories, or private property owners or farm workers who are exposed to dangerous pesticides on farms owned by others, or the communities exposed to hazardous wastes that come from privately owned industries. The money that funds their campaigns come from industries that can be more profitable if they are allowed to externalize some of their costs and avoid paying the real costs of the activities in which they engage. They seem uninterested in ensuring that victims of pollution can gain compensation for the taking of their life, health, and property. They unfairly and inaccurately demonize environmentalists as "liberals" and "elites" who are opposed to modern civilization.[30]

However, some wise use, private property activists raise important challenges to environmentalism. Some of them are free-market environmentalists who offer useful criticisms of environmental policy and suggest ways environmental goals could be achieved more efficiently and effectively. Others point out cases where environmental regulation has been unfairly applied in ways that neither further environmental goals nor represent basic fairness. Perhaps most importantly, they serve as a reminder that the power of environmentalism as a social movement is its universal appeal—the claim that it represents the common good, the public interest. Environmentalism cannot represent all interests: Those who want to impose costs on others in the pursuit of profits that don't reflect the true cost of production will find little representation there. But there is room for stewardship and responsibility, for the fear that some kinds of government regulation may not foster those values, for a commitment to fairness and protection of personal freedoms that don't infringe on the rights of others, and for solutions that reflect a commitment to traditional ways of making a living on public lands. These values need not be pursued themselves by environmentalists who recognize that sustainability requires changes in past practices, but they ought to be part of the debate about how to make the transition.

Jacqueline Vaughn Switzer's work on opponents of environmentalism is another reminder of the modest strength of ecological values. Switzer argues that the opposition movement is much more diverse and divided than is commonly recognized, and that their influence has varied according to the ebb and flow of public commitment to the environment. These forces have been adept at taking actions during "policy windows," openings in the cycles of political attention that provide opportunities for these groups to voice their views to sympathetic policy makers. The idea of policy windows, according to theorists like John Kingdon, suggests that opportunities arise unpredictably, infrequently, and for a short period of time before closing. Policy entrepreneurs who are in the right place at the right time and have the resources necessary to garner political attention and get on the policy-making agenda, can take advantage of those opportunities. Policy influence, then, is a function of happenstance and the ability of charismatic personalities, or those with wealth and other resources, to capitalize on opportunities. This explanation may be quite reflective of the way in which policy making takes place, but it does not offer much help in assessing the long-term strength of environmentalism. It seems to suggest that environmental concerns are primarily like other interests; the political system treats them as just one of many interests whose demands are to be balanced with others. Environmental advocates may achieve occasional breakthroughs, but their opponents may as well.[31]

Mark Dowie argues that the American environmental movement has been able to win some victories in preserving resources and has helped raise broad sensibility to environmental quality, but has "been unable to produce a significant improvement in the country's environmental health."[32] The broad, ambitious goals in environmental laws, such as the Clean Air and Water Act's promise to restore air and water to healthy and even pure conditions, compared with the modest progress in achieving those goals, are clear evidence of the failures of the environmental movement. For Dowie, assessments of environmental quality by the Council on Environmental Quality, the EPA, and others demonstrate that we have fallen far short of the goals Congress embraced in environmental laws: "American land and water are certainly in better shape than they would have been had the movement never existed, but they would be in far better condition had environmental leaders been bolder; more diverse in class, race, and gender; less compromising in battle; and less gentlemanly in their day-to-day dealings with adversaries."[33]

Critics like Dowie argue that the environmental movement grew tremendously after the 1970 Earth Day, and, by the 1990 celebration, was a "vast, incredibly wealthy complex of organizations."[34] The problem was that the movement came to be dominated by a dozen major groups, centered in Washington, D.C., who shaped and directed the movement along a strategy of working closely with and depending heavily on the federal government. That was the fatal flaw of the movement: assuming that it could work with the federal government to improve environmental quality: "civil authority and good faith regarding the environment have proven to be chimeras in Washington; they are real only in the imagination of environmental leaders."[35] This fundamental flaw, coupled with the way in which national groups undermined and alienated their grass-roots support and underestimated the power of their antagonists, have combined to render the movement to the point where it is "dangerously courting irrelevance."[36] Dowie concludes that the future of the environmental movement lies in the grass roots, in communities, in the transformation of the movement to include people of color and environmental justice issues—this will lead to a real social movement. For Dowie, environmentalism fails as a movement because it has not been transformative; its national organizations have become cautious and conservative and have failed to challenge the basic causes of environmental problems.[37]

In contrast to these moderate and pessimistic assessments of the success and impacts of environmentalism, some scholars have argued that it has already engendered a Green transformation. Americans, they believe, have come to reject unbridled growth and consumption and have become committed to environmental protection goals and some restraints on personal actions. Americans' views on the environmental issues evolved significantly during the post–World War II period—as has occurred in other industrialized democracies—as Americans have come to embrace a postindustrial, postmaterialist ethic.[38] Scholars and activists alike have discovered an environmental ethic, a "new environmental paradigm," that rejects unbridled growth and consumption, rooted in "postmaterialist" values. Some have characterized it as a new ideology. Robert Paehlke, for example, argues that such an environmental ethic includes three major elements: (1) the protection of biodiversity, ecological systems, and wilderness; (2) the minimization of negative impacts on human health; and (3) the establishment of sustainable patterns of resource use.[39] How strong and deep are such values among Americans? To what extent have Americans embraced such an environmental ethic?

First, what do people typically mean by the preservation of biodiversity, ecological systems, and wilderness? A thick notion of preservation, such as deep ecology or biocentrism, rejects the idea that claims to the use of natural resources by humans are superior to those of other species. From this view, all forms of life are to be equally valued and the biosphere in general, or any particular ecosystem, should not be managed for the primary benefit of humans, but for the interests of all living things. Alternatively, a thin notion of the protection of biodiversity and related concerns might be characterized as recognition that nature is not just a source of raw materials for human use. Not only does the preservation of biodiversity make human life possible and provide recreation and aesthetic benefits beyond resource consumption, but other species have some independent claim for survival and flourishing that humans should respect. While that is not a particularly precise formulation, it clearly differs from the view that natural resources should be viewed only in terms of their contribution to economic wealth.

While deep ecology likely finds relatively few adherents, there is considerable evidence that this thin notion of preservation is widespread. The Endangered Species Act (ESA) is one of the most powerful environmental laws; it has the potential to stop any public or private project that threatens the habitat of endangered or threatened species and to prohibit the taking of any protected species.[40] There is strong support for the act, and efforts to amend and weaken it during the past three sessions of Congress have ended in failure and adverse publicity for proponents of the amendments. Congressional Republicans were temporarily successful in using the appropriations process to place a moratorium on listing threatened and endangered species and designating critical habitat,[41] but that moratorium was lifted in an April 1996 budget bill.[42] Republicans proposed a number of riders to Interior Department appropriations bills during the 104th Congress in response to their failure to reauthorize the ESA, but the only one that passed was a rider in 1996 that exempted construction of fences and roads along the United States–Mexico border from ESA requirements.

Second, minimization of adverse impacts on human health is also an imprecise but useful indicator of an environmental ethic. Again, a thick notion or commitment to health would make it a primary value, and economic activities would be permitted only if they do not significantly impair or threaten human health. Some environmental laws, like the Clean Air Act, give primacy to human health. National Ambient Air Quality Standards, for example, are required to be set at levels that protect public health "with an ample margin of safety," and the EPA is prohibited from considering costs in setting those standards.[43] A thin view of minimizing human health impacts would require a balancing test: Adverse health impacts would be minimized, and economic growth, personal freedom, and other values would be maximized. Human health might be one of many factors to be included in a cost–benefit analysis.

The actions of Congress between 1995 and 2000 indicate that there is little agreement over this issue. Congress tried to rewrite virtually every major environmental law, including the Clean Air Act, but those efforts were largely discredited, and relatively little legislation was enacted. The Clean Air Act's commitment to a strong notion of human-health protection seems to be widely supported. But in other laws Congress has modified zero-risk provisions. In 1996, Congress amended the Delaney Clause, a provision in the Federal Food, Drug, and Cosmetic Act, that had prohibited the use of any food additive that had been shown to cause cancer in animals or humans. The 1996 law required the EPA to set standards to ensure that food was "safe."[44] In the 1996 Safe Drinking Water Amendments, the only other major environmental law enacted by Congress since the Republicans gained control of both chambers in 1995, Congress gave the EPA considerable discretion in deciding whether to regulate a contaminant and required the agency to perform a cost–benefit analysis for all future drinking-water standards.[45]

However, Congress has been repeatedly deadlocked in efforts to impose cost–benefit analysis on regulatory agencies. The Republicans' 1994 "Contract with America" promised to "roll back government regulations and create jobs."[46] One of its central pieces was the Job Creation and Wage Enhancement Act, aimed at changing administrative law and the rule-making process to ensure more scientific and economic analyses are performed; increase opportunities for regulated industries to help shape the provisions; ensure that only relatively serious risks are regulated; and require agencies to show that the benefits resulting from regulations exceed the costs of compliance. In March 1995, the House passed a major regulatory reform bill that required regulatory agencies like the EPA to demonstrate that the costs of compliance are justified by the expected benefits. The bill died in the Senate after several days of debate, passage of several amendments, and three failed votes aimed at ending debate. The House regulatory reform bill was subsequently attached to a debt-limit extension bill passed by Congress but vetoed by President Clinton in November 1995, ultimately killing the initiative for that and subsequent sessions of Congress.

Jeffrey Berry argues that environmental groups (and other liberal citizen groups) have been remarkably successful in lobbying Congress to enact legislation. The effectiveness of environmental groups in pushing for new laws is, according to Berry, a result of several factors. While there has been a decline in liberal legislation on material issues, like poverty, since the 1960s, there has been a tremendous increase in interest in postmaterialist, quality-of-life issues, like environmental quality. For many people, participation in and support of these groups has replaced involvement with political parties, as identification with these causes has become more important than partisan affiliations. Environmental groups have grown so much that they have been able to afford to develop specializations and niches such as endangered species and wilderness. Environmental groups have had great success in gaining the trust of the media, who regularly turn to them for expert opinion. Despite the power of industry and trade associations, and the perception of the privileged position of business in policy making, liberal citizen groups have growing power and have been able to influence the passage of a series of environmental laws that have been enacted over the past 35 years.[47]

The 104th Congress, 1995–1996, provides an interesting set of data for examining the power of environmental groups. Berry argues that the traditional liberal, materialist-oriented citizen groups did not do well under the new Republican Congress, suffering a "catastrophic defeat" with passage of the 1996 welfare reform act. In contrast, he argues, environmental groups were overwhelmingly successful in blocking the 12 major bills considered during that session. Timber companies won a timber-salvage provision in a 1995 budget bill, and the new Safe Drinking Water Act passed in 1995 seemed to be a compromise that environmental groups, state and local governments, and industries could accept. But for the other issues—regulatory reform, endangered species, clean water, superfund, and cattle grazing on public lands—environmental groups were able to block bills that the Republican leadership introduced to reduce the regulatory reach of environmental laws. And several bills that were enacted, dealing with pesticides, management of fisheries, and parks and public lands, were championed by environmental groups.[48] Berry argues that the success of these liberal citizen groups, in pursuing quality-of-life issues, regardless of who controls the Congress and the White House, is evidence of their maturity and power: "These are social movements all grown up. Citizen groups participate in the governmental process, not because government has been eager for these organizations to be involved, but because they mobilize millions of Americans whose values lean in a postmaterialist direction."[49]

The 105th Congress (1997–1998) also ended with little progress in reauthorizing environmental laws and addressing new problems. The 106th Congress (1999–2000) will likely end that way as well. These sessions can hardly be classified as environmental success stories or evidence of the emergence of a vibrant Green politics in the United States. They do demonstrate the ability of environmentalists to block legislation that retreats from environmental protection, but they do not have the clout to get new legislation passed. Part of the explanation may lie in mistakes made by the Republican leadership in 1995 and 1996, when they appeared to grossly overplay their hand and were unreasonably deferential to business demands.[50] House Republicans generated public skepticism and cynicism through their unabashed pro-business initiatives; reports on the new congressional leaders regularly emphasized their close ties to business. The Republican-controlled Congress's hostility to existing environmental laws and regulations does not appear to be a reflection of broader American society. Media articles highlighted then-House Speaker Newt Gingrich's communications with the executive branch during his years in Congress and concluded that he had "used his position, in a series of noteworthy intercessions, to help his own friends with special connections." [51] Many of these cases were investigated by the House Ethics Committee and contributed to the reprimand of the Speaker by the full House in early 1997. The access given in return to lobbyists during the 104th Congress was remarkable even by Washington standards. Lobbyists were invited to write bills and sit with committee members in hearings. Journalists described lobbyists ensconced in rooms next to the House Chamber, writing talking points for Republican members to use in floor debates. Senators were lambasted for having lobbyists draft bills and then having to ask the lobbyists to explain the bills they were sponsoring.[52]

Ultimately, the downfall of the Republican regulatory relief effort was its failure to take into account widespread public support for environmental, health, and safety regulations. This strong underlying support caused a split between Republicans and gave the Clinton administration the incentive to resist congressional relief efforts. Environmental law enjoyed strong bipartisan support in the 1970s, but in the 1980s it became more of a divisive issue as Republicans began responding to complaints of regulatory burdens by business interests and using the cost of regulations as an issue to strengthen their ties with business. The Reagan administration launched a major assault on environmental laws and regulations; the Democrat-dominated Congress resisted proposals to rewrite laws, but members were largely unable to block administrative changes that reduced enforcement of regulatory programs and cut spending for research on environmental problems and other agency activities. These proposals in Congress were aimed primarily at reducing the size and scope of the regulatory state, cutting the costs of compliance, and slowing down the regulatory process. Although Congress was far from monolithic on these issues—different members had different views about what ails the regulatory system, about which industry group demands needed to be accommodated, and what kinds of changes might raise the ire of voters—the predominant view among Republicans was that the cost, scope, and reach of regulation must be reduced. While environmentalists are able to mobilize grass-roots members to lobby members of Congress and participate in some interest-group bargaining, their real power may lie in their ability to shape the terms of discourse and control the symbolic language used to undermine the legitimacy of the Republican initiatives.[53] But that power is far from the power to institutionalize environmental values in policy making; environmentalists can block actions they oppose but they are, in turn, blocked by opponents in pursuing their agenda, often leading to deadlock or gridlock.[54]

While environmental politics is largely interest-group politics, there are other measures of its strength. One indicator of the limited power of environmental groups is the use of ballot initiatives to provide for increased environmental protection. From the early 1970s to 1986, for example, citizens passed eighteen environmental ballot measures. During the 1988 elections, some seventeen environment-related propositions passed. One of the most politically visible initiatives was Proposition 128, known as "Big Green," in California in 1990, which would have banned pesticides, prohibited new offshore drilling, stopped the cutting of virgin redwood forests, and mandated major reductions in carbon dioxide emissions from utility plants. Oil and chemical firms spent more than $6 million to oppose the measure, and it was soundly defeated at election time: The voters defeated the ballot initiative nearly two to one.[55] The timber and chemical industries responded with their own ballot measures, The Global Warming and Clear-Cutting Reduction, Wildlife Protection and Reforestation Act of 1990, and the Consumer Pesticide Enforcement Act, labeled by environmentalists as "Big Stump" and "Big Brown." Other measures dealing with recycling and nuclear power in other states were also voted down. Despite such defeats, the citizen initiative process is still a key strategy used by environmental groups in some states. In 1996, initiatives to protect the Everglades and Maine old-growth forests were defeated due to well-financed and well-organized industry opposition.[56]

Finally, there is a small Green Party movement in the United States: Twenty-four states belong to the Association of State Green Parties (which partners with the European Federation of Green Parties). The parties are autonomous but come together in the association to cooperate on environmental and other issues such as campaign finance and social justice issues. They have agreed to support ten "key values": ecological wisdom, social justice, grass-roots democracy, nonviolence, decentralization, community-based economics, feminism, respect for diversity, personal and global responsibility, and future focus and sustainability. About 120 Greens ran for offices in 1998 elections; some 59 Greens held elective offices in 12 states, primarily nonpartisan offices, in 1999.[57]

The Green Party of Colorado, for example, describes itself as "a political alternative for those committed to building a sustainable and just society. What makes Green politics different is a holistic, ecological outlook that recognizes the interconnection of all life and social processes, and that neither social nor environmental problems can be solved in isolation from each other. We pursue a broad conception of politics that embraces electoral efforts, the development of alternative institutions, education for empowerment, nonviolent direct action, and ecological lifestyles." In addition to a platform that includes planks on employment, energy, environment, health, indigenous peoples, nonviolence and peace, social justice, technology, and transportation, the party also holds that "fundamental reform of government and the electoral system to empower citizens and restore and protect democracy is an important part of Green activism" and calls for "resisting free trade treaties like [the North American Free Trade Agreement] and [the Multilateral Agreement on Investment] and addressing wealth inequalities in our society" in "protecting our democratic rights." The party ran candidates for governor and lieutenant governor in 1984, capturing 1.6 percent of the vote; in 1998, Green candidates for the University of Colorado Regent received 3.6 percent of the vote and for Larimer County Commissioner, 15 percent, the highest percentage of the vote any third party received.[58]

Prospects for a national Green Party are quite modest, but Ralph Nader's efforts to build one demonstrate the movement's political limitations. Nader was the presidential candidate for the Green Party in 1996 and 2000. In 1996, Nader ran but refused to campaign, spent less than $5,000, and received less than 1 percent of the vote. In the spring of 2000, he promised a much more active campaign as he took on issues such as campaign finance reform, free trade, poverty, health care, corporate welfare, and global corporations: "Big business is on a collision course with American democracy, and American democracy has been losing," he argued. Apparently, his long-term goal is to generate the 3 percent of the vote necessary to qualify for matching funds and use that to build the Green Party as a progressive alternative to the Democratic Party, which Nader believes is indistinguishable from the Republican version on most key issues, particularly those affected by corporate power. But currently the Green Party is weak, disorganized, and divided. Some members oppose involvement in campaigns while others favor other candidates besides Nader.[59]

The weakness of Green Parties in the United States is a reflection of the challenges that remain in institutionalizing environmentalism. Interest-group politics do not provide a holistic, integrated policy agenda, as do political parties, at least in theory. But that kind of integrated policy effort is exactly what environmentalism prescribes.

Environmentalism and Public Opinion

Public-opinion polls and other measures of public sentiment show strong support for environmental regulation, and most studies show that Americans favor even more protection than current efforts provide. For many years, more than 70 percent of respondents have replied in national polls that "protecting the environment is so important that requirements and standards cannot be too high, and continuing environmental improvements must be made *regardless* of cost" (emphasis in original).[60] Environmental regulation has been a major issue in many congressional, state, and local races, and has been a significant issue in presidential campaigns.

Public-opinion polling gives only limited information about the nature of public support for environmental policy. Everett Carll Ladd and Karlyn H. Bowman have described the problem this way: "Americans have been asked repeatedly in a wide variety of formulations to affirm a core value, in this case the importance of the environment. Each time, not surprisingly, they responded that a clean and healthful environmental was important to them. These questions tell us little about what a society with many demands on it is willing to do to advance the value, what trade-offs the public is willing to make for it, or what happens when one important value clashes with another."[61]

The study nevertheless found some important indicators of public sentiment in polling data from the 1980s and 1990s:

• There is strong support for the idea that economic growth and a clean environment are simultaneously attainable.
• Americans have a significant amount of confidence in government's ability to protect the environment.
• Americans believe that efforts in their country are greater than those typically found in other nations and that industry has made progress in reducing emissions.[62]

Several surveys have asked people how well they identify with the environmental movement, and, in particular, whether they describe themselves as environmentalists. In 1987, 24 percent said the term perfectly or nearly perfectly fit them; in 1994, that number was 27 percent. The percent of respondents who said the term was "totally wrong" in describing them was 4 percent in 1987 and 9 percent in 1994. Another study asked people to place themselves on a seven-point scale, where 1 indicated they did not identify, and 7 indicated they strongly identified with the term environmentalist. In 1989, 21 percent placed themselves at either 6 or 7 and the same percentage placed themselves at 1 or 2. In 1994, pollsters found the same results. Table 2-2 shows the results of a third poll, taken in 1994.

TABLE 2-2
Percent of Respondents Identifying with Environmentalism

Respondents Described Themselves As:	1992	1994
Active environmentalists	29%	23%
Sympathetic but not active	52	56
Neutral	15	16
Unsympathetic	2	2

A fourth study asked people to picture a thermometer that measured how favorably disposed they were to different groups: 0–50 meant unfavorable feelings, and 51–100 meant favorable; the mean temperature for people "seeking to protect the environment" was 71 in 1980, 77 in 1989, and 65 in 1992.[63]

It also is important to understand the value respondents place on environmental issues, how politically salient they are, and how deep their views are about these issues. Environmental issues rank very low when polls ask respondents questions such as, "What is the most important problem facing the nation?" People do not mention environmental issues nearly as often as crime, education, health, taxes, unemployment, efficient government, and the economy; these problems and concerns are seen as far more urgent than preventing pollution and protecting natural resources.[64] Yet most respondents also believe that we are spending too little on environmental quality. They were asked, "Are we spending too much, too little, or about the right amount on improving the environment?" Table 2-3 shows that respondents clearly favored spending at least as much as we are now, or more:[65]

TABLE 2-3
Views on the Appropriateness of Spending Levels for Environmental Protection

Response	1974	1978	1982	1986	1990	1994
Spending too little on the environment	59%	52%	50%	58%	75%	59%
Spending about right	27	33	32	30	21	30
Spending too much	8	10	12	6	4	8

Ladd and Bowman conclude their review by arguing that, "the vast majority of our citizens are environmentalists. But we are now more inclined to think that for most Americans the urgency has been removed, and the battle to protect the environment is being waged satisfactorily."[66]

Other analyses confirm Ladd and Bowman's. Gregg Easterbrook, in a 1995 book, *A Moment on the Earth: The Coming Age of Environmental Optimism*, argued that great progress has been made, that Americans have broadly embraced the environmental agenda, and that it is a stunning public policy and political success story.[67] Even the Heritage Foundation, source of many of the analyses on which regulatory relief initiatives were based, also recognized that public opinion strongly supports regulation:

> While a plurality feel that American businesses are burdened by too many regulations, Americans nevertheless support most environmental regulations, even when told that relaxing certain regulations could help business. Conversely, Americans do not want to add to or expand existing regulations. The status quo, it seems, is acceptable to most Americans.[68]

Michael Kraft and Norman Vig distinguish between short-term political and economic forces that affect the salience of environmental issues and long-term trends. They find in American society strong, underlying public support for environmental protection, but that support is occasionally punctured by recessions, energy shortages, and other threats to their well-being. Americans' commitment to environmental policy softens from time to time, when there are countervailing economic pressures.[69]

Finally, it is useful to compare environmentalism with other social movements. Riley Dunlap, coordinator of the Gallup Poll's environmental surveys, argues that support for environmental issues grew from 1970 to their peak in 1990, when a number of problems such as the Exxon Valdez oil spill, contamination of beaches by medical waste, and global warming were major stories. Support for environmental issues has fallen since the 1990 peak.[70] An April 2000 Gallup Poll aimed at measuring public sentiment toward environmental issues for Earth Day, found that the movement falls only behind the civil rights and women's movement, and is in a virtual tie with the abortion rights and gun control movements. Respondents were asked to rate eight important social movements in terms of their impact on the nation's policies. Table 2-4 shows their answers.[71]

TABLE 2-4
Public Assessments of the Impacts of Social Movements

Movement	A Great Deal/ A Moderate (Combined)	A Great Deal	A Moderate Amount
	%	%	%
1. Civil Rights	85	50	35
2. Women's Rights	82	42	40
3. Gun Control	74	38	36
4. Abortion Rights	75	36	39
5. Environmental	76	30	46
6. Consumers' Rights	67	21	46
7. Gay and Lesbian Rights	59	24	35
8. Animal Rights	50	15	35

Respondents were then asked to indicate to what degree they agreed with the goals of the eight movements. Again, the environmental movement trails the civil rights and women's movements but nevertheless enjoys strong support: 83 percent of Americans agree with the environmental movement's goals, as shown in Table 2-5.

While there is strong support for environmentalism and for the civil rights and women's movements, none of these issues is considered a top priority among respondents. While the most important issues on the minds of American vary from year to year, they are more typically issues such as the economy, education, health, or crime, than environmental quality or race and sex discrimination.

TABLE 2-5
Public Agreement with the Goals of Social Movements

Movement	Strongly Agree/ Somewhat Agree (Combined)	Strongly Agree	Strongly Disagree/ Somewhat Disagree (Combined)
	%	%	%
1. Civil Rights	86	49	12
2. Women's Rights	85	45	13
3. Gun Control	69	43	29
4. Abortion Rights	61	30	36
5. Environmental	83	43	15
6. Consumers' Rights	82	30	13
7. Gay and Lesbian Rights	49	15	47
8. Animal Rights	72	29	25

TABLE 2-6
Percent of Americans Actively Participating in the Environmental Movement

	% Active In the Movement	% Sympathetic Toward the Movement
1978–83 (4 polls)	7–13%	47–55%
2000	16%	55%

In contrast to strong support for the goals of environmentalism, few Americans have been active participants in the movement itself, although the percentage participating has increased according to Table 2-6.

Five percent of Americans say they are members of national or international environmental groups, while 9 percent are members of local, regional, or state groups. Respondents reported participating in a variety of environmental protection-related activities, but Table 2-7 shows that the numbers drop dramatically for activities associated with environmental activism.

In 1992 and 2000, respondents were asked by Gallup if they felt the environmental movement has done more good than harm or more harm than good. The surveys generated nearly identical responses: 33 percent say the movement has *definitely* done more good than harm, and 42 percent say it *probably* has done more good than harm. However, 21 percent say the movement has done more harm than good, compared with 14 percent who responded that way in 1992, indicating that there may be growing dissatisfaction with the movement's tactics or impacts. Nevertheless, most Americans trust environmental groups more than any other institution to protect the environment, as shown in Table 2-8.

TABLE 2-7
Participation in Environmental Protection–Related Activities

Kind of Environment-Related Activism	% Participating
Recycling	90%
Reducing energy use	83
Avoided purchasing environmentally harmful products	83
Purchased environmentally beneficial products	73
Contributed money to an environmental cause	40
Signed a petition for an environmental cause	31
Voted or worked for candidate because of environmental position	28
Attended a meeting about an environmental issue	20
Contacted a public official about an environmental issue	18
Active in an environmental group or organization	15
Complained about a product because it harms the environment	13
Bought or sold stocks based on the company's environmental record	9

TABLE 2-8
Level of Trust in Organizations to Protect the Environment

	A Great Deal	A Moderate Amount	Great Deal/ Moderate Amount (Combined)
	%	%	%
1. National Environmental Organizations	34	44	78
2. Local Environmental Organizations	28	46	74
3. Federal Environmental Agencies (e.g., EPA)	27	45	72
4. State Environmental Agencies	21	51	72
5. Local Government Agencies	12	47	59
6. The Democratic Party	15	41	56
7. Small Businesses	13	35	48
8. The U. S. Congress	10	38	48
9. The Republican Party	10	33	43
10. Large Corporations	9	28	37

Environmentalism has permeated American culture: It has some strong, dedicated adherents, and it is a solid part of public opinion. But the environmental values reflected are not transformative; they are not demands for new ways of producing and consuming, but assume a continuation of current practices. And environmentalism can rather quickly fade in the face of other, more pressing concerns. A discussion of environmentalism as sustainability, in the next section, confirms this assessment.

Environmentalism and Sustainability

One of the most important indicators of the strength of the environmental movement is the level of commitment to the idea of sustainable development. The Clinton administration created the President's Council on Sustainable Development (PCSD) in 1993. Its purpose was to bring together representatives from environmental groups, industry, and government to advise the president "on matters involving sustainable development," defined as "economic growth that will benefit present and future generations without detrimentally affecting the resources or biological systems of the planet."[72] The Council's "vision statement" argues that a "sustainable United States will have a growing economy that provides equitable opportunities for satisfying livelihoods and a safe, healthy, high quality of life for current and future generations."[73] The structure of the council reflects one of its primary themes: "Our most important finding is the potential power of and growing desire for decision processes that promote direct and meaningful interaction involving people in decisions that affect them."[74] The role of government is to "convene and facilitate, shifting gradually from prescribing behavior to supporting responsibility by setting goals, creating incentives, monitoring performance, and providing information."[75] The council is co-chaired by the president of the World Resources Institute, a Washington, D.C., environmental research center, and by a vice president of Dow Chemical Company. Members include the executives of several national environmental organizations, four U.S. government cabinet members, chairs of the board and CEOs of several corporations, and representatives from state governments, labor unions, and civil rights groups.[76]

The council proposed ten goals to guide public and private efforts in pursuit of the idea of sustainable development that address environmental quality and natural resource preservation, equity, economic growth, community and civic engagement, education, and international responsibility. It has outlined in some detail changes needed in six areas: (1) making environmental regulation more effective and efficient, (2) increasing the amount of, and access to, information concerning sustainable development, (3) encouraging community planning, reducing sprawl, and creating jobs and economic opportunities, (4) developing an ethic of stewardship to guide human interaction with natural systems, (5) expanding access to family planning and reproductive health services, increasing equity for women, and reducing illegal immigration, and (6) fostering U.S. leadership in international efforts to promote democracy, scientific research, and sustainable development.

Other federal agencies have embraced sustainability to some extent. The EPA has launched numerous initiatives that are aimed at "reinventing" government—making regulation more efficient and effective, engaging regulated interests in regulatory policy making, and integrating diverse regulatory programs—and that are consistent with many of the ideas underlying sustainable development. The U.S. Agency for International Development (USAID) has embraced sustainable development as one of the guiding principles for foreign aid. USAID, for example, regularly uses the term sustainable development in its reports on activities and projects. Its primary objectives are "achieving both sustainable development and advancing U.S. foreign policy objectives" through six programs: economic growth and agricultural development; population, health, and nutrition; environment; democracy and governance; education and training; and humanitarian assistance.[77]

More impressive than these modest federal-level efforts in sustainability are the actions taken by some local governments. Communities in the Pacific Northwest, for example, are leaders in sustainable development. The region has undergone dramatic economic growth over the past few decades and its economic base has been transformed. Metropolitan areas have aggressively developed policies to control urban sprawl and develop mass transit. Timber and ranching businesses in the region have emphasized stewardship and responsibility for sustainable use of resources. State officials in Oregon have devised indicators of sustainable development to help guide policy makers.[78] Other communities have also aggressively pursued sustainable development initiatives. The East–West/Gateway Coordinating Council in St. Louis, for example, has developed a 20-year transportation plan that integrates transportation decisions with economic, environmental, and community goals such as supporting mobility for low-income residents and ensuring that development along rail lines is based on sustainability principles. Some communities have formed sustainable development forums to bring community members together to discuss issues and formulate plans. Nonprofit organizations throughout the nation formed the Sustainable Communities Network to share information on demonstration projects and conduct outreach programs.[79]

Many U.S. cities have joined the International Council for Local Environmental Initiatives' (ICLEI) for climate change, community planning, implementation of Agenda 21 (a 40-chapter blueprint for sustainable practices produced for the 1992 Earth Summit), and other programs related to sustainability. Many cities have embraced the goal of a 20 percent reduction in carbon dioxide emissions, and several major cities have reduced emissions by as much as 15 percent since 1995. Most of the progress is being made in retrofitting municipal buildings, community energy efficiency programs, and waste management initiatives.[80] Communities throughout the United States have devised innovative, collaborative means of reducing the use of agricultural pesticides, protecting watersheds, and conserving energy, which have created a great deal of experience and interest in how communities can become more sustainable.[81] A number of innovative programs, often described as community-based environmental protection bring community members together to identify local problems and fashion broad, comprehensive solutions that include public health, environmental quality, and economic development.[82]

Proponents of environmental planning, urban ecology, management of growth, bioregionalism, appropriate technology, and a number of other efforts are all contributing to the wellsprings of a vibrant, dynamic commitment to sustainability that is having a major impact in some communities and is likely to expand in the future. There is a growing literature that describes with optimism and enthusiasm the growing interest in sustainable communities, metropolitanism, regionalism, and other collaborative planning efforts that are aimed toward the goal of sustainability.[83] Innovative industries are finding ways to contribute to the idea of sustainability, through changes in production and marketing that help conserve resources and reduce waste and pollution and also save money.[84] Solutions to urban sprawl, including preserving undeveloped lands, creating parks, promoting "smart growth," cleaning up abandoned factory sites so that agricultural lands are not used for new construction, setting urban growth boundaries, and other programs aimed at enhancing quality of life have become key elements of the idea of sustainability in communities throughout the United States.

Nevertheless, despite the wide range of activities, sustainability has yet to become a defining part of American political, economic, or social life. The Council on Sustainable Development's agenda is a strong statement of the interrelatedness of economic, social, educational, and environmental issues, but it lacks a sense of strategic purpose; of identifying opportunities, key players, and timing; and of specifying policies to pursue. There is little evidence that voluntarism is sufficient to produce the changes needed to ensure sustainable development. Specific policies that could have a major impact on environmental quality and on technological innovation, and are also relatively simple and administratively manageable, such as ending subsidies on harvesting natural resources, or taxing energy, are not proposed. It is hard to imagine a policy that would be simpler and more likely to move the United States toward sustainability than is a major energy tax increase such as a fifty-cents per-gallon tax hike, but there is little discussion of such an initiative, given the Clinton administration's ill-fated proposal in 1993 to raise energy taxes, which collapsed in controversy. Collaborative and consensus-building efforts can take a great deal of time and may never produce agreements; pollution taxes, in contrast, are simple schemes that create clear incentives to make technological progress.[85] Other studies have identified specific subsidies and tax expenditures that are environmentally damaging and should be eliminated, but it has been very difficult to challenge the political power of those who benefit from these policies.[86]

There is little discussion of the moral obligation the United States has, as the major consumer of resources and producer of pollution, to reduce its contributions to global risks that threaten others who are much less responsible for them. The tremendous mismatch between the U.S. contribution to greenhouse-gas emissions and the impact climate change is likely to have on developing countries who lack the resources to protect themselves against the consequences is a profound moral problem facing the United States. Nor is there much discussion of American isolationism, its failure to adopt the Convention on Biodiversity, the role of the United States in producing a relatively weak and non-binding climate change accord in 1992 (and the unlikelihood that the U.S. Senate would ratify the 1997 Kyoto climate change agreement), and other actions that have placed the United States behind other industrialized nations.[87]

The Council on Sustainable Development has focused primarily on the intersection of economic and environmental issues, and has not taken on some of the broader social-equity issues raised in Agenda 21. The Council's agenda fails to include a commitment to address the interaction of poverty and environmental degradation, and ignores much of Agenda 21's focus on increasing participation by women in all decision-making forums at all levels; improving health and education for children, particularly girls; empowering indigenous peoples to participate in decisions affecting them; increasing the interaction between nongovernmental organizations (NGOs), governments, and international organizations; strengthening the role of public participation in development decisions; giving increased voice to workers and unions; and a host of other issues.[88] The council recognizes that ecological, economic, and social goals are interrelated. But it does not take on the hard questions of the impact of free trade on developing countries' social and environmental problems or the overwhelming power of multinational corporations in determining resource use or the great disparity between the consumption of resources and production of pollution in the developed and the developing worlds.

Perhaps most problematic is the failure of the council and other efforts to focus attention on improved environmental policy making to engage Congress in their deliberations and encourage legislation to implement sustainable development, pollution prevention, and other goals. While it is important to encourage industries to voluntarily improve their environmental stewardship, clear incentives backed by governmental power are essential. Until Congress joins the discussion on sustainable development, we are not likely to make progress in national policy making. One policy area, energy production and use, illustrates the failure of the national government, particularly Congress, to begin taking steps toward a more sustainable future. Early in his presidency, Bill Clinton proposed a broad tax on all forms of energy in order to raise federal revenue to reduce the budget deficit. The proposed tax, called a Btu tax because it was based on the heating ability of different fuels, as measured by British thermal units, would have raised the prices of gasoline, electricity, and other energy sources. Environmentalists supported the measure as a way to promote conservation and to begin to move away from fossil-fuel consumption. The tax would have raised about $22 billion a year, only a tiny fraction of the $6 trillion U.S. economy, but opposition from Democratic and Republican senators representing energy-producing states killed the idea.[89] The administration was successful in raising gasoline taxes by 4.3 cents a gallon in 1993 as part of Clinton's deficit-reduction plan. During the 1996 campaign, when gas prices jumped 17 percent during the summer, Republican candidate Bob Dole called for a repeal of the gas tax; President Clinton called for an investigation of the oil companies and ordered the release of 12 million barrels of oil from the nation's Strategic Oil Reserve to soften the price increase.[90] Increasing energy taxes sufficient to achieve significant conservation or revenue purposes requires more political skill than recent presidents and their congressional allies have been able to muster. Congress has refused to pass recent bills to increase the Corporate Average Fuel Economy standards or other proposals to increase energy conservation. The failure of this policy debate is all the more significant considering that the price of crude oil in the late 1990s, not including taxes and adjusted for inflation, was less than one-half what it was in 1981.[91]

Sustainable development, like any other major policy commitment, ultimately requires the support of Congress and strong, effective legislation—and the greatest failure to engage in the idea of sustainable development has been here. The Republicans leaders in Congress have virtually ignored the idea of sustainable development and the United States' commitments made at the Rio Earth Summit. For them, sustainable development is a problem for other countries to worry about. The hostility many congressional leaders have toward international commitments, along with their opposition to environmental regulation, combine to create a major barrier to pursuing the idea of sustainable development in the United States. The political conflict in Congress over environmental law and regulation during the mid-to-late 1990s, as briefly described above, has been so divisive and time consuming that it has precluded the nation from moving toward the next generation of environmental laws that would incorporate the idea of sustainable development. There is little question that the system of environmental regulation could be improved. Rather than asking more fundamental questions about how to balance and integrate economic growth and ecological sustainability, however, Congress has largely been unwilling to move beyond attacking the regulatory system that has been in place since the 1970s.

Political leaders in and out of Congress have also been unwilling to take on the broader questions of American values of economic growth, sustainable consumption, technology, land use, transportation, and individual freedom. Most Americans seem determined to view economic growth as limitless, constrained only by unwise policy or business choices. They strongly resist the idea that limits should be placed on material consumption, and exhibit tremendous faith in technological solutions to whatever problems confront them. Their strong commitment to private property rights places major limits on political decisions to limit private property use for environmental purposes. Their insistence on single-occupancy vehicles and dislike for mass transit is intertwined with their fundamental commitment to individual freedom and ability to travel wherever and whenever they please. Jimmy Carter, the last major political leader to talk about limits and constraints, was widely derided for violating the American creed of limitless growth and opportunity.

Another barrier to sustainability has been the priorities of the EPA and the statutes it is responsible for implementing, which have primarily focused on public health rather than broader environmental quality. In 1987, the EPA completed a study that compared the risks of 31 major categories of environmental and health problems, ranging from global warming to oil spills, and also examined risks from four perspectives that represent the major responsibilities of the EPA: cancer risks, non-cancer health risks, ecological risks, and welfare effects. There were significant differences between the study's estimation of the seriousness of risks and the EPA's operating priorities: "EPA has been more concerned about pollution that affects public health, as opposed to protection of natural habitats and ecosystems, in all programs except surface water."[92] In some areas of high risk, such as for indoor air pollution, carbon dioxide and global warming, and nonpoint sources of water pollution, neither the EPA nor any other federal agency has any significant statutory authority. Other studies have built on the EPA assessments and criticized Congress and the EPA for failing to compare and rank risks so that the most serious are given priority.[93] Congress has not yet responded to the challenge of overhauling environmental laws in ways that ensure that the most serious problems are addressed and regulations are more efficient and effective.

Congress, the White House, the EPA, and other policy makers have failed to create effective incentives to push industries and consumers toward pollution prevention and toward sustainability. In 1989, the EPA commissioned a review of its comparative risk assessment by the agency's Science Advisory Board, which concluded in a 1990 report that the agency has largely been a "reactive" agency, insufficiently oriented toward "opportunities for the greatest risk reduction." Not all risks can be reduced, but not all problems are equally serious, and the EPA has failed to set priorities for reducing the most important problems. The agency has usually imposed "end-of-pipe controls that often cause environmental problems of their own" rather than "[p]reventing pollution at the source—through the redesign of production processes, the substitution of less toxic production materials," and so on. Pollution-prevention approaches avoid transferring "pollutants from one environmental medium to another" and "often bring substantial economic benefit to the sources that use them.[94]

Conclusion

The American environmental movement does not appear to be ready to address the challenges of the twenty-first century effectively, for a number of reasons. First, the easiest, cheapest problems have been solved— the low-hanging fruit has already been picked. The problems that remain are bigger and more complex. The opposition is better organized and financed. The public seems to believe that environmental problems are being addressed, things are under control, and they can worry about other issues.[95]

Second, the American educational system has failed to educate people as to how to live in harmony with the ecological system on which they depend. As David Orr, an environmental studies professor, puts it, "We have taught a generation to industrialize a planet without understanding the biosphere and ecosphere in which they are doing these things."[96] Orr writes that schooling is aimed at mastering basic functions, whereas learning "has to do with matters of judgment and with living responsibly and artfully" and continues throughout life. Unfortunately, even tragically, educational institutions are built on the idea that nature is to be subdued and managed, and quite independent of what we need to know to "live humanely, peacefully, and responsibly on the earth."[97]

Third, environmentalism has been unable to challenge the dominance of consumption, marketing, and the pursuit of wealth that dominate popular culture. From the late 1990s and into the beginning of this new century, the U.S. economy has enjoyed unprecedented growth, high rates of employment, and low inflation. Environmental changes have not been politically palatable because no one has wanted to do anything that might threaten prosperity. But when economic times are lean, growth is down, and unemployment is high, the argument is that we cannot afford to take preservationist actions but must do all we can to stimulate prosperity. As Ophuls and Boyan argue in *Ecology and the Politics of Scarcity Revisited: The Unraveling of the American Dream*, we appear to be hopelessly destined to ignore ecological constraints until they come crashing down on us.[98] Environmentalism has failed to take on the faith in growth and the idea that it is limitless. A host of policies, such as rechartering corporations to ensure that their actions are consistent with ecological limits and constraints, requiring environmental audits to increase accountability of industry, reducing or eliminating subsidies that create incentives to engage in environmentally harmful and unsustainable practices, and reforming tax policy to encourage conservation, renewable energy, and other environmentally friendly practices, would have profound ecological benefits but have not been successfully placed on the political agenda.

Fourth, environmental protection efforts often are overwhelmed by political forces beyond their control. Campaign finance and lobbying laws allow those with economic resources to gain disproportionate access to policy makers and make their case for reduced regulatory standards, scrutiny, and enforcement. The environmental movement, argues Shabecoff, "has been a minor, rather ineffectual player in the electoral process. Its engagement has been tentative and diffident—it plays at politics rather than going to war."[99] Some argue that environmentalists disdain politics, others that they are too well behaved, or that they have not raised the funds to allow them to be major players in financing the elections of candidates that agree with them.[100] Because environmentalists are unlikely to raise the level of money that corporations can, support for campaign finance limits and reforms like public financing of campaigns is critical.

Fifth, environmentalists have not been able to challenge the allure of technological progress and faith in science. Technological advances appear to be inevitable, beyond collective control, even when they pose great threats to the common good. Scientific and technological advances are widely viewed as being neutral despite their ecological consequences. Democratic control of scientific research and technological decision making is critical in remedying existing problems and preventing future ones, but there are few options and opportunities to increase social control of science and direct it in ways that are ecologically sustainable. Science is increasingly brought to bear on policy questions in terms of adversarial debates between dueling scientists, a forum that does not deal well with scientific uncertainty and scientific research.

Sixth, environmentalism has largely not been able to counter the tremendous pressure toward economic globalism and the dominance of market forces shaped by multinational corporations throughout the world, although there are signs that a challenge is developing. U.S. foreign policy is driven more by the goal of maintaining and even increasing American power and influence rather than ensuring that the planet's residents avoid environmental destruction.[101] Environmental issues fall well below security, economics, and politics in foreign policy making.[102] Global lending institutions like the World Bank continue to finance ecologically unsustainable projects, such as fossil-fuel development, rather than investing in renewable energy sources.[103] The global scope of environmental problems, the cross-boundary flows of pollutants, and the broad sources of threats to global commons require a more powerful international authority to develop and enforce environmental standards, but there is little support for stronger global governance. U.S. environmental groups have not been very effective in generating political support for global action or working with NGOs in other countries to develop strong global coalitions.[104]

Most importantly, the movement is divided and unclear about its goals and how to approach the issues it decides to take on. The challenges facing the movement are daunting. It is split between pragmatists and purists, those who are willing to work with industry groups to find low-cost ways of reducing pollution, and those who believe that compromise is unnecessary, counterproductive, and even immoral. The strength of environmentalism lies in its ability to label things as good or evil. Collaborative groups, market-based regulatory approaches such as tradeable emission rights, and other innovations are seen by some as the key to the future of the movement, the core of the next generation of environmental policy, and by others as a profound threat and a major retreat. Another division is between those who argue that environmentalism should focus on a relatively narrow set of issues in order to appeal as broadly as possible to the public, to avoid being pigeonholed as a liberal interest, and to be widely viewed as "the safest movement in town."[105] Others argue that environmentalists must join forces with other progressives to address a host of ecological, social, economic, and political problems that are rooted in inequality and exploitation. Broadening the movement to include social justice and other issues at the same time makes the movement more radical and less attractive to others. A related division is between the grass-roots environmental movement that is growing in power, numbers, and energy, and the mainline national movement. Grass-roots environmentalism is often built on the idea of the connectedness of economic, political, and social problems and concerns. People's connection to place and land, their commitment to a land ethic that Aldo Leopold and others have argued is so powerful in engendering care for the environment, are necessarily local, community-based. They link environmentalism with efforts to solve other pressing problems Americans are struggling with. They are as skeptical of federal agencies as they are of multinational corporations as they seek autonomy and control over their communities. And they lend ammunition to those who argue that mainstream environmentalists are too far removed from the struggles and injustices that many people face.[106] Some see the future of environmentalism in Green capitalism, in working with industry to change the way they operate; others believe that heightened criticism of corporations is the proper course of action.[107]

The most important question facing the environmental movement is whether it can transform itself to be more powerful, more capable of addressing the environmental problems, and countering the tremendous economic, social, cultural, and political forces that champion a continuation of industrial production and consumption.[108] One of the paradoxes in which the United States finds itself in the beginning of the twenty-first century is that sustainable development requires a comprehensive policy response, but that the primary focal point for sustainability is at the state and local level. The national government, fragmented and disjointed, seems incapable of coherent policy efforts in the absence of a national crisis. The prospects for the transition to sustainability as a major governing principle are explored in the final chapter.

3

Environmentalism:
A Comparative Perspective

As is true in the United States, there is great interest throughout the world in preserving environmental quality. But political systems differ considerably, making comparisons of the strength of green interest groups, parties, and public opinion uncertain. Public-opinion questions can be asked in many nations, but answers are a function of history, culture, differences in environmental problems, and other factors, which make comparisons tentative. Sustainability provides a useful benchmark because of the global commitment to sustainable development in the 1992 Rio Earth Summit, but, as discussed in chapter one, the breadth of support for sustainable development is in part a function of its vagueness.

The environmental movement has evolved considerably during the past century, and its very dynamism makes it difficult to assess. Environmentalism varies widely across the developed nations—even more so in the less developed world. The primary issue here is the ability of the movement to generate the public policies and personal behaviors required to reduce environmental risks and preserve essential ecosystems. How can that capacity be enhanced to ensure that emerging and future problems are effectively addressed? The discussion here is not a comprehensive examination of environmental politics in other countries, but an inquiry into some of the major characteristics of environmentalism as a social movement. One gross oversimplification, but nevertheless of some value, is to look at broad trends in the industrialized and developing worlds. Public opinion demonstrates strong support for environmental values, and those values are stronger in Western Europe than elsewhere. Green political parties are much more prominent in Europe than in the United States, a function of electoral systems as well as environmental concerns and demands. In the developing world, there are a great number of grass-roots environmental groups;

the movement is quite robust in some areas and has been successful in a few cases in protecting local environments. But the lack of democracy in some areas and the weaknesses of national governments in other areas have resulted in only limited success in these countries in elevating environmental policy to a national priority. In few places throughout the world has environmentalism evolved into a strong social movement and made the transition to a fundamental commitment to ecological sustainability that gives it priority over economic growth and consumption.

Green Politics

There are a number of ways one might characterize the evolution of environmental politics globally. Environmental politics differ in important ways across nations. A thorough description and assessment of these differences is well beyond the scope of this book and this chapter in particular. My purpose here is to look very broadly at overall trends rather than seeking to provide a comprehensive or systematic survey that is beyond the scope of one book. In many countries, environmental politics have roughly followed this evolutionary pattern. First, the earliest environmental movement was conservationist, aimed at protecting wild lands, scenic areas, unique ecological areas, and threatened species. The goal was to preserve areas from economic development and ecological damage. That movement was successful in preserving some magnificent landscapes and clearly could have been more ambitious and protected more lands. As scientific understanding has developed, we are now able to make some judgments about how much land should be protected in an undeveloped state based on goals of protecting biodiversity and the integrity of ecosystems that provide important ecological services. This knowledge provides some basis for setting priorities for preservation: What areas should be protected in order to preserve a representative sample of ecosystems and species? What areas should be conserved by virtue of their important ecosystems?

The second environmental movement was built on the first; it continued to emphasize preservation but added pollution to the mix of concerns and sought to reduce environmental harms that threatened public health. Again, the movement has clearly been successful in generating support for a host of new laws, regulations, and agencies to enforce them but can be just as clearly criticized for failing to achieve faster results, be more protective, and save more lives. As we learn more about the extent of environmental harms, it becomes more and more evident that the environmental movement has fallen particularly short in identifying areas where economic benefits and environmental burdens are not fairly distributed.

One can argue that people should be able to choose whether to be exposed to greater levels of pollution in exchange for access to jobs and other financial rewards, but one is hard pressed to defend policies and practices that allow some to benefit and others to pay the costs. The growing environmental justice movement is a belated attempt to remedy what should be gross violations of our collective sense of justice and fairness.

A third environmental movement is emerging that builds on the first two, incorporates their goals, embraces their policy prescriptions, and seeks to push well beyond them toward the idea of sustainability. Sustainability is, of course, frequently invoked, and a host of definitions have been offered for it, but it is clearly a more ambitious goal than environmentalism has heretofore pursued. It requires broad, comprehensive, collective efforts, and expansive public policies—a revolution in the way people think and act. It calls for transformative politics whose contours and elements are not well understood. My argument here is that the nature of the environmental challenge to which the movement is aimed is the primary basis for making judgments about the movement's capacity. While environmentalism has accomplished impressive feats, it is addressing this third level of concern with uncertainty. Most of what is described as environmental politics is still in the second phase, and while there are indicators of aggressive and ambitious grass-roots groups taking on sustainability, environmental politics throughout the world suffers many of the shortcomings reflected in American environmentalism.

Interest-Group Politics and Environmental Policy

Central to environmental politics is the role of environmental groups. Nongovernmental organizations (NGOs) play an increasingly important role in environmental policy making in developing and developed nations, but their influence and resources vary widely. They range from grass-roots organizations that depend on volunteers to groups with hundreds of professional staff members and millions of members. In some countries, they play a major role in generating pressure within their countries for their governments to comply with and implement the global agreements they have signed. In other countries, they struggle to gain access to policy-making forums. Their existence, while important in focusing public attention on environmental issues, is nevertheless evidence that environmentalism is widely viewed as one interest among many competing for influence in the policy-making process.

The increasing role of NGOs in environmental politics has not been universally applauded. Defenders argue that they play a critical role in generating support for environmentally protective actions by consumers and producers, and for more ambitious public policies. They are defended as both effective and necessary ancillaries to policy making and, as governments have moved toward privatization, have become increasingly important actors in filling the vacuum. Critics charge that NGOs weaken democratic politics by introducing fragmented, single-issue groups that are neither accountable to nor representative of the broader public. Some critics argue that NGOs infringe on business prerogatives and threaten market processes, while others lament their impact on traditional democratic institutions such as political parties, public bureaucracies, and legislatures.

Part of the question here is, what role do NGOs play in environmental politics, and what role should they play? The descriptive question is difficult because it depends on the issues, the geographic location, the strength of the organizations, the effectiveness of government agencies, and other factors. The normative question is just as difficult. From the perspective of representative democracy, responsible parties, policy-shaping elections, and similar arguments, NGOs should be discouraged because of the fragmentation they produce and the challenges they pose for coordinated and comprehensive public policy making. But champions of participatory democracy believe that the interplay of groups contributes greatly to democratic values. NGOs are an important response to the increasing perception that politicians are not willing to take on difficult issues and that multinational corporations increasingly affect people's lives.

NGOs have grown from a handful of conservation organizations formed in the 1890s—for example, the International Union of Forestry Research and the International Friends of Nature—to more than 100,000 NGOs that work on environmental issues a century later. Most of those groups started in the 1970s and 1980s. Environmental grass-roots groups are part of a much bigger movement. There were more than 20,000 international NGOs—organizations with offices in more than one country— according to a 1996 count. The United States has some two million NGOs, and India has at least one million NGOs that work on development projects alone.

NGOs play a key role in helping to set the agenda by generating public pressure for action through boycotts, protests, and lobbying; providing scientific expertise; helping to confirm legitimacy by withholding or giving support; implementing solutions; and providing services. NGOs work in concert with governments as well as independently of them. Perhaps their greatest power comes from the granting or withholding of legitimacy—being able to shape the terms of public debate by labeling proposals as good or bad. When environmental groups labeled Monsanto's genetically modified seed that would not regerminate "the terminator," it generated a strong backlash against the development.[1] NGOs become an especially potent force when they form a global network to address particular issues.

There is some concern that in Africa, foreign NGOs overtake national governments in some policy areas. Some fear that this is not politically sustainable. There is also a concern that NGO activity lacks coordination, that they are unable to produce coherent public policies that governments, at least in theory, are expected to produce. NGOs have brought about big changes, but NGOs include both preservationist and polluting interests. They can be bad or good for environmental quality.[2]

Cultural differences are the major factor behind the variations in how environmental interests are structured or how they operate. In democratic nations, the pluralist system legitimizes interest-group membership. Most comparative studies of environmental politics have highlighted the adversarial nature of environmental politics in the United States, in contrast to the more corporatist structure of policy making in Western Europe. U.S. environmental politics are typically described as much more adversarial than what happens elsewhere, dominated by litigation and conflict between environmental and industry groups. David Vogel's comparative study of environmental policy in the United States and Great Britain, for example, emphasized the close relationship between industry and government officials, unlike the tension that characterized government–industry relations in America. Vogel argued that the differences are rooted in the greater acceptance of governmental authority in Britain by business and by the general public, and greater public trust in business and confidence that its actions will be in the public interest. He concluded that the American approach of adversarial relations and strict enforcement of regulations "has been no more effective in changing corporate behavior than Britain's emphasis on voluntary compliance." The U.S. approach, emphasizing as it does the enforcement of violations and imposition of penalties creates little incentive for corporations to make voluntary changes, and consumes considerable resources in enforcement efforts. The opportunities for public participation in U.S. regulatory proceedings, while they give environmentalists the chance to challenge agency decisions, give that right to industry groups as well who may see it in their interest to delay or block the implementation of regulations.[3]

In France, government officials at all levels are expected to base their regulatory decisions on informal negotiations with industry; conduct that would be roundly criticized in the United States is expected in France as the means of formulating mutually acceptable results. Japanese environmental regulation is similarly characterized by "considerable informal interaction between government and industry." In Germany, scientific research in regulatory policy making is aimed at fostering balanced, consensual decisions, in contrast to the U.S. approach that sees scientific research as essential in defending the various positions taken in the inevitable litigation.[4] In Canada, environmental politics have focused on the concept of compatibility between economic growth and environmental protection rather than conflict, and on the need for economically painful policy changes in order to protect ecological values. Politicians have been particularly quick to embrace the idea—preferring to find "win–win" opportunities rather than condemning environmentally damaging activities—and favor voluntary over coercive measures.[5] Critics have argued that this approach ignores the need to make difficult choices in order to ensure a more ecologically sustainable economy.[6]

The European approach to environmental regulation is attractive to many industry leaders and politicians who give priority to fostering business growth because it encourages voluntary compliance, de-emphasizes aggressive enforcement, and excludes "outside" interests like environmentalists who do not understand technical processes and competitive business pressures. The advisory committees, government–industry working groups, and quasi-private committees of technical experts that dominate German and other European and Japanese policy-making processes seem superior to contentious lawsuits and intractable public debates. Differences in political culture make the transfer of institutions, processes, and expectations difficult, but there is growing interest in the United States in making regulatory proceedings less adversarial through regulatory negotiations and other business–industry–environmental working groups. But the emphasis on consensus clashes with the traditional American commitment to judicial review and the ways in which courts promote accountability to the rule of law and open decision-making processes.[7]

These studies emphasize that the differences in regulatory styles have important political implications as they encourage distrust of government and conflict (the U.S. case) and promote trust and acceptance (as in the British example). But Vogel concludes that the different styles of regulation "have led to roughly similar environmental outcomes."[8] Alan Peacock and others who studied regulation in Britain and West Germany described the style there as "negotiated compliance," in which industry and government officials acquire information through a process of bargaining that is aimed at ensuring compliance with whatever standard is agreed to. These authors concluded that "much regulation represents a codification of established practice," but does not force regulated industries to develop new technologies and devise new processes to reduce or eliminate pollution.[9] Susan Rose-Ackerman's comparative of U.S. and German environmental policy making characterized the German approach as "inadequate," and in need of reform because it fails to provide "sufficient public accountability" and opportunities for public debate. The German parliament delegates a great deal of policy authority to the bureaucracy, which has independent authority to implement laws. Ministerial processes are not open and accountable to nongovernmental groups because Germans believe that would obstruct the democratic will that results from an elected parliament delegating authority to bureaucracies. The German system emphasizes the protection of individual rights, but does not allow for participation by organized groups and fails to provide a forum for balancing the demands and interests of different groups.[10]

There are some important indicators that Western European nations are ahead of the United States in developing and implementing environmental laws. The United States produces more greenhouse gases, both in terms of total and per capita emissions, than these nations; while some of the difference is due to geography and economy, U.S. patterns of consumption account for part of the disparity. Other countries are ahead of the United States in developing a new generation of policies that emphasize integrated approaches to pollution regulation and prevention, rather than treating pollutants in each environmental medium separately. Europeans are also ahead in developing green taxes, recycling, and energy conservation.[11] Nevertheless, neither regulatory style moves policy making beyond traditional concerns or represents the prospects for a transformation to a more sustainable political economy. In Europe, the hope for such a transformation has rested not with reforms of regulatory policy making but with a shift to green politics and environmental parties.

NGOs are growing in both number and influence most rapidly in developing nations, where their roles are even broader as they sometimes fill a vacuum left by ineffective or nonexistent government programs, or where they challenge existing governments that are unresponsive to environmental and related problems. Although these trends indicate that NGOs are growing in both numbers and importance, their influence on global environmental protection is still limited by a lack of stable funding sources and political sophistication.[12] In South Korea, for example, environmental groups contributed to democratic movements in the 1990s as they protested industrial pollution problems that helped erode the legitimacy of the old government. There are now more than 260 environmental groups in the country. Similarly, environmental NGOs in Indonesia helped bring about the downfall of the Soeharto regime by disclosing information about corrupt business–government practices that resulted in environmental damage.[13]

One of the most promising trends is the growth in environmental-law NGOs in the south. Hunter, Salzman, and Zaelke, for example, argue that "South America boasts a number of the most sophisticated environmental law organizations anywhere in the world." These groups include the Sociedad Peruana Derercho Ambiental in Peru, the Fundacion Ambiente y Recourses Naturales in Argentina, the Centro Mexicano del Derecho Ambiential in Mexico, and similar groups in Costa Rica, Guatemala, and Columbia. They find that "perhaps the most innovative environmental litigation in the world now emanates from Asia."[14] The key to the growing influence of NGOs, they argue, is communications technology that provides rapid dissemination of information at very low costs and fosters the mobilizing of activists for lobbying on domestic and international issues. Technology has dramatically increased the power of NGOs. But that influence is still on the perimeter of political power, and despite impressive growth, southern NGOs' concerns have not been widely institutionalized.[15]

Just as in the industrialized democracies, cultural context is critical. In Mexico, for example, few groups are demanding better air quality despite the capital city's major pollution problems. One study of Mexican political beliefs and values concluded that Mexicans generally do not relate easily to abstract or impersonal organizations but only to the individual who leads the movement. Mexicans' *personalismo* makes it difficult to start and sustain groups that lack such high-profile figures. In nondemocratic countries such as the People's Republic of China, the government crackdown on Western influences has made it difficult even for international NGOs like the World Wildlife Fund to have much of an impact, leaving little room for environmental groups, domestic or foreign. International pressure and the government's expanded involvement in international trade and politics have led to substantial advances in China's environmental policies, but they have not come about as a result of organized citizen activism.[16]

Environmental NGOs have developed ties with other groups working on related problems such as human rights.[17] Southern NGOs are seeking greater autonomy from those in the north and forming international networks and coalitions to focus attention on issues of common concern. They have long been dependent for financial support on NGOs in the developed nations, and increasingly seek the resources and technical expertise that will permit them to set their agendas rather than follow the priorities of others. A few international nongovernmental organizations (INGOs), such as Friends of the Earth International and Greenpeace, have affiliates throughout the world and are discussed in more detail in the next chapter. INGOs are especially important in regions where environmental concern has only recently begun to emerge, as evidenced by the founding of a Russian affiliate of Greenpeace. Without the support of an international organization and its resources, environmental activists in the republics of the former Soviet Union, for example, would have little voice for their efforts to draw international attention to decades of environmental degradation.[18]

The interaction of democracy and environmental protection is critical. The progress that has been made in enacting and implementing environmental protection policies have largely come as a result of mobilization by citizens. Some of this has occurred in authoritarian regimes, but democratization has made environmental politics much more effective. The role of citizens groups in generating pressure for environmental regulation has been evident throughout the world, and suggests that democratic reforms and strengthening of grass-roots political movements are critical to the future of environmentalism. A study of environmental policy and politics in Northeast Asia concluded that public participation in the development of environmental policies has stimulated political change. In Japan, for example, the environmental impacts of the tremendous economic growth in the 1960s were not addressed until several citizens' movements organized to protest against pollution and ecologically damaging projects. Japanese environmental laws and programs for air and water pollution, put in place beginning in the mid-1960s, were prompted by fierce citizen protests against petrochemical facilities, and by an effort to garnish the nation's international credentials as it prepared to host the 1964 Olympic games. Policy efforts peaked in the 1970s and subsequently slowed as political pressure dissipated. In Korea, despite an authoritarian government, NGOs proliferated and have carried out a number of local and national campaigns. Protests against the construction of dams have been successful and demands for clean up of pollution prompted national legislation. The hosting of the 1988 Olympic games in Seoul, and concerns about air pollution, also prompted new regulatory efforts. The democratization of Korea, beginning in the 1980s, has been accompanied by governmental efforts to encourage citizen participation, and campaigns for environmental preservation have become increasingly prominent.[19]

Environmentalists in China face tremendous obstacles. The government has been increasingly concerned about polluted rivers, dirty air, and denuded mountains, but restricts private citizens from taking action, insisting instead that it will solve the problems. Successes occasionally occur, such as the creation of a "living water park" to purify a polluted river by pumping water from the river and then allowing it to trickle down through pollution-absorbing plants before returning it to the river much cleaner. Spearheaded by an American artist living in China, the idea has spread to other communities with the support of the government.[20] But success stories are rare. The Chinese government claims that "the state protects the environment and natural resources" and prevents pollution.[21] Environmental protection has gradually been given more attention by the government, but economic growth continues to be the dominant public policy. Mark Hertsgaard and others have documented China's environmental crisis of unhealthy urban air, acid rain, water pollution, urban sprawl and loss of farmland, deforestation, and water scarcity as among the most serious threats facing the planet. Many Chinese see pollution as an inevitable consequence of modernization and development and an acceptable cost. The belief that economic growth requires environmental damage is widely accepted. Public sentiment, combined with government insistence on managing environmental problems itself with little public scrutiny, produces a painfully pessimistic of China as a major source of global pollution in the future as well as a an increasingly inhospitable home for its residents.[22] As discussed chapter 5, China is the second largest emitter of greenhouse gases, and its participation in global climate change accords is critical, but resisted by many Chinese leaders who believe that economic growth is a more critical public goal.

The experience of these and other nations also demonstrates the importance of international pressures. Hosting Olympic games has been accompanied by significant pressures to clean up air and water pollution. Even China, whose leaders are often fiercely independent and reject many Western demands, has become increasingly sensitive to environmental protection prerequisites for receiving funding and technological transfers. But these political pressures can be negated by economic ones, as the Asian economic crisis in the late 1990s demonstrated. The economic downturn actually reduced pollution levels and produced some temporary environmental benefits. But those were likely outweighed by budget cuts to environmental programs and deepening poverty in countries like Thailand that will have longer lasting negative impacts on environmental quality.[23]

Green Parties

Unlike the environmental movement in the United States, which has mustered only small Green Parties at the state level and a national Green Party that has never come close to generating significant support for its candidates, Green Parties have formed in dozens of countries. They vary considerably in strength and impact on their respective political systems, in membership, and in the percentage of the electorate they represent. Green Parties often are difficult to track as they frequently change their name or form new alliances with other groups. The term "Green Party" is sometimes used generically: Greens are sometimes described as a group of activists working on a specific issue, and sometimes as a broader social movement. In Hungary, for example, the Greens were labeled "Blues" because of their formation of the Blue Danube Circle, a group opposed to the building of the Nagymaros Dam. In Poland, the largest environmental organization was not a party per se, but the Polish Ecology Club.[24]

The first Green Party apparently was the United Tasmania Group, formed in a local election in the Tasmanian region of Australia in 1972. The party was quite successful in getting environmental issues on the agenda but was disbanded in 1976. But the real center of Green Party activity has been in Europe, primarily because the structure of European political systems allows small parties a role in governance. During the 1970s, one of the first efforts to form a Green Party was in Germany, where a loose coalition of groups, the Bund Burgerinitiativen Umweltschutz (BBU), organized massive demonstrations opposing nuclear energy but exercised little political power.[25] The most cohesive and powerful environmental movements are found in western Europe, where public opinion polls have shown that support for the environment is especially strong and continues to grow. Coalition building is a common strategy, with umbrella groups like the European Environmental Bureau monitoring proposed legislation and lobbying on behalf of more than a hundred organizations within the European Union. Group activism has frequently focused on the issues of nuclear power and nuclear weapons, leading to massive public protests in 1995 when the French government resumed weapons testing in the South Pacific. But the environmental movement is Europe is best characterized as diverse, with each group developing its own structure, strategy, and style.[26]

There were high expectations for Green Parties in the late 1980s and early 1990s. Some industry groups sought alliances with Greens in order to generate goodwill with consumers. Green Parties in Sweden, Germany, Belgium, and France seemed most promising and grew quickly in the 1980s. Many Green Parties are rooted in social democratic movements and have natural ties with groups oriented toward other social issues, and alliances seemed promising. Mainstream parties began at least paying lip service to environmental goals. From the beginning, Green Parties have been plagued by fundamental debates over structure, strategy, principles, and priorities: Some activists opposed the professionalization of politics and feared the movement's integration into the political mainstream. Some believed that compromise was essential. Others resisted any tolerance for softening demands. And there was little agreement over the need for and benefits of collaborating with other interests. The problems plaguing Green Parties in their early years continue.[27] Table 3-1 lists the major Green Parties.

TABLE 3-1
Major Green Political Parties

Nation	Green Party	Year Founded
Australia	United Tasmanian Group	1972
	Nuclear Disarmament Party	1984
	Rainbow Alliance	1988
Austria	Die Grune Alternative	1982
Belgium	Agalev	1982
	Ecolo	1980
Canada	Green Party of Canada	1984
Denmark	DeGronne	1983
Finland	Vihrea Liitto	1987
France	Les Verts	1982
	Generation Ecologie	1990
Germany	Die Grunen	1980
Ireland	Comhauntas Glas	1981
Italy	Federazione delle Liste Verdi	1986
Luxembourg	Die Greng Alternativ	1983
Mexico	Partido Ecologistica de Mexico	1984
Netherlands	De Groenen	1983
New Zealand	Vlaues, Green Party of Aotearoa	1972
Sweden	Miljopartiet de Grona	1981
United Kingdom	People/Green Party	1973
United States	Green Party USA	1984

Source: Jacqueline Vaughn Switzer with Gary Bryner, *Environmental Politics: Domestic and Global Dimensions* (New York: St. Martin's Press, 1998): 40.

In exploring the strengths and weaknesses of party politics and environmentalism, the evolution of the German Green Party is particularly interesting. The challenge for the German Green Party, as for any Green Party, is how to become part of the government and assume responsibility for the broad range of policies it must pursue, while at the same time maintaining constant pressure on society, business, and government to do more to protect environmental quality. The party has faced numerous challenges as it has assumed a governing role. The German experience in green governance is too recent to assess: is the Green Party more effective in achieving its environmental protection goals as part of the governing coalition, or would it be better off remaining outside of the government, where political compromise is less obligatory? But the initial experience is instructive as it represents many of the difficulties awaiting greens in other nations as they make the transition from social movement to organized interest to governance.

Over the past two decades, the German Greens have teamed with others to form perhaps the best-known Green Party in the world.[28] But its success in reshaping German politics and policy has been limited. The Green Party in Germany started at the local level in the mid-1970s when party members began to run for positions on municipal councils. This movement brought environmental activists together with advocates of grass-roots democracy, who believed that more political decisions should be made through direct, democratic decision making at the local level. The Green movement began as a protest against the problems of urban life—a growing sense of powerlessness among urban dwellers, the loss of power by local governments resulting from political centralization, and a growing number of defectors from the established parties. Greens formed coalitions with feminists and other activists to demand changes in local government policies. Successes by Greens in local issues such as nuclear power led to the formation of the national party in 1980, led by small group of activists committed to pacifism as well as environmentalism.[29]

The German Greens have had modest and inconsistent success in winning elected offices. Their peak years of electoral success have been 1994 and 1998, where they received nearly 7 percent of the national vote. By 1998, they held scores of seats in 12 of the 16 state parliaments and hundreds of seats on local councils.[30] In 1999, three members served as ministers, including Joschka Fisher, the foreign minister and vice-chancellor, and one of the nation's most popular politicians. But the party's share of the vote fell dramatically in several state and municipal elections, and polls measuring support reported a drop from 10 percent in 1997 to 5 percent in 1999; that figure is critical, as parties with less than 5 percent get no seats in state or national parliaments.

From the beginning, the local basis of the Green movement in Germany has been problematic. Some argue that local politics do not provide an adequate platform for addressing the Green movement's goals. Local governments generally deal with the administration and implementation of decisions made at the state (lander) or federal level, and there is in place a "very tight network of legal, financial, and political restrictions," and local politics "tends to become an area of non-politics or merely symbolic politics." Once in place, Green members of councils found it difficult to remain the "voice" of grass-roots activism and still function effectively in institutional politics. They also found it difficult to resist pressures toward professionalization, as more radical Greens opposed that trend. At the same time, more established local parties began to adopt the messages and platforms of Green and other grass-roots groups.[31] But their influence is not limited to electoral politics. Some Greens have also assumed important positions in corporations and continue to pursue their agenda by shaping corporate behavior through innovations such as organic clothing and beer. But older generations fear that the wealth of Germany produced in the factories and mills will be frittered away by the Green agenda.[32]

Roland Roth argues that the Greens are not a "mass-based party," but an "intermediary project created out of the environment of the new social movements." He and others have argued that the numerous experiments with red–green local governments in some areas of Germany have been rather ineffective and their coalitions unstable. And when combined with the limited funds and power of local governments, Green officials have been able to bring about only modest changes. Greens have been unsuccessful in their efforts to strengthen local governments.[33] But Greens are not without influence. They have been able to gain the public's attention and force the established parties to address the issues they have raised: "Green topics, modified and selectively reinterpreted for different purposes, have long been introduced into the programmes of all parties in city hall. Greens have been successful in getting many of their issues on the agenda, but not in getting their programs established and implemented."[34]

Part of the challenge of strengthening the party comes from its anti-authoritarian structure. To keep any one person from accumulating power, elected officials are prohibited from also serving as party leaders, and every leadership position must be shared by two people. But all this has made it difficult for the party to function effectively. They pride themselves on being the party of issues and programs, not personalities, despite their leading figure, Joshka Fischer, Germany's foreign minister who is perhaps the best known Green to have made the transition to governing. Fischer has been increasingly criticized by his Green allies for embracing establishment values and for supporting the NATO bombing of Kosovo in 1999. His willingness to compromise has been central to efforts to keep the red–green government in power.[35] Some argue that the party's leadership was in disarray; some wanted to pull out of the Social Democrats' ruling coalition because of its declining popularity, and others lamented that too many compromises had already been made in order to be part of the coalition. The shift from protest politics to compromise and accommodation has not been easy. Greens are split between those who want to keep their agenda unsullied by the need to compromise over issues such as pacifism and the bombing of Kosovo, immigration and human rights, and genetically modified crops. In many cases, the younger party members are more pragmatic: "We, the over-40s," said one Dutch Green leader, "who were raised on opposition to the system, on the peace movement and reading Karl Marx, have the greatest difficulty in making the transition from protest politics." Or, as another Green put it, "We have never worn ties in our lives, and we are not going to do it just because we have ministers."[36]

Another challenge for the German Greens has been to develop policy positions in concert with their coalition party. German Greens have traditionally focused on three issues: the environment, the status of women, and peace. It is not a comprehensive platform, but has given the party some direction as it has begun to govern with the Social Democrats. Social Democrat Prime Minister Gerhard Schroeder, is very much a proponent of the "middle way," along the lines of Bill Clinton and Tony Blair, who all seek to balance commitments to markets and social justice, and moderate policies that keep their progressive allies on board but don't threaten business groups. The German Green Party has had to rethink its traditional opposition to motor vehicles and demands for major increases in fuel taxes. A discussion paper drafted by some party members in the spring of 2000, for example, argued that the party must accept the fact that motor vehicles are the primary mode of transportation for Germans and they guarantee independent mobility, security for women, and social status. If the party is to expand beyond its current support and attract young voters in particular, the authors of the paper argued, it needs to find ways to reconcile the party platform with social realities.[37] Similarly, the agreement between the German government and the nuclear power industry to phase out nuclear power falls fall short of the party's platform on nukes. The agreement allows power companies to generate a fixed amount of power from nuclear plants but with no deadline on when the plants are to be shut down. The Greens were forced to make considerable compromises in order to strike a deal with the Social Democratic Party and the industry.[38]

The achievements of the German Greens have not been matched elsewhere, however. In some countries, Green Parties' successes have been limited to getting their members elected at the local and regional level. In countries like Sweden, where legislative seats are allotted based on a threshold level of representation, Green Parties have struggled to attract the necessary numbers of voters or have been shut out of the process entirely. Even in those countries with proportional representation, most Green Parties have had little support, in large part due to the fact that they modeled their strategy on the atypical German model. In France, political control of the government changed five times between 1981 and 1997. In 1997, the several Green Parties agreed with the communists to field only one candidate in each constituency, and the largest Green Party, the Verts, won 4 percent of the vote and seven seats.[39] However, in 1999, Green Party members formed the political base for France's prime minister.[40]

Green Party fortunes seem to be improving since the new century began. In addition to forming the base for Germany's chancellor and France's prime minister, Greens also held offices in the governments of Italy, Finland, and Belgium, and played an influential role in Sweden's government. They doubled the number of seats they held in the parliaments of France, Great Britain, and the Netherlands; increased seats in

Belgium, Finland, Austria, and Ireland; and offered a national list of candidates in Spain for the first time.[41] The first Green to serve as a commissioner of the European Commission also took office in 1999. In 1999, Greens captured 6.4 percent of the vote for elections to the European Parliament, and seated 47 members, up from 27 in the last session. In 1999, some 200 members of the European Parliament were members of Green Parties, and Greens were represented in 12 national governments.[42] In some countries, such as Norway and Switzerland, Green Parties are not strong but the mainstream parties have embraced a Green agenda.[43]

In Eastern Europe, there have been occasional signs of progress. In October 1999, for example, the governments of Poland, Germany, and the Czech Republic announced that eight years of collaborative efforts had succeeded in turning what was the most polluted region of Europe into a green area. The three countries began the "black triangle" project in 1991, aimed at the coal-fired power plants—which produced 30 percent of Europe's sulfur-related pollutants—in the area where the three nations intersect. Modernization of the plants reduce emissions of dust by 80 percent, nitrogen oxides by 60 percent, and carbon dioxide by 40 percent from 1989 levels.[44] But, overall, the state of the environment and environmental politics in Eastern Europe is shocking. Murray Feshback and Alfred Friendly Jr. documented the widespread environmental damage wrought by Russia's communist leadership's drive for economic growth and modernization. Pesticides are ubiquitous, air-pollution levels are well above international standards, nuclear waste and fallout contaminate many regions, rivers and lakes are poisoned, topsoil is depleted, and fish resources have collapsed. These problems are reflected in the declining health of Russians, whose life expectancy has fallen, and infant mortality. The ecological problems in Russia and in the other former members of the Soviet Union are disastrous and require a transformation in economic activity and industrial production.[45] Barbara Jancar-Webster and her colleagues identified similar problems in other Eastern European countries, where environmental deterioration was a result of state socialism's emphasis on economic development and virtual disregard for the environment, and political systems in which information was limited, public involvement in environmental concerns not permitted, and political and social order imposed at the expense of environmental quality.[46]

There is little promise, at least in the short term, for the Russian political system to respond to these problems. Politically, Russia is one of the 18 countries reported by Freedom House to have suffered a deterioration in the state of political rights and civil liberties.[47] The 1999 parliamentary elections, while democratic in the sense of some level of competition, were plagued by threats, bribes, and "thuggish incompetents."[48] The Kremlin controls television, allowing it to promote allies and defame op-

TABLE 3-2
How Russians Describe Domestic Politics Today

Rise of anarchy	63 percent
Democracy building	9 percent
Old system, new names	8 percent
Approach of dictatorship	6 percent

ponents; favored candidates are given access to the media. Local governors who support opponents may find their local oil company forced out of the national pipeline network; if they switch sides, they are rewarded by having their opponent jailed. Power is turned off in public meetings where opponents of the government plan to speak. Bribes of up to $800,000 were reportedly paid to opposing candidates to resign from races. The campaign debate ignored Russia's massive health, poverty, and lawlessness problems. The Russian economy was, as the twenty-first century began, smaller than that of the Netherlands, but few candidates seemed interested in such mundane issues. Businesses in Russia have begun to sponsor candidates, overwhelming party resources and tying candidates close to them. The Communist Party reemerged in the election as the largest single party, with about 25 percent of the vote, but a coalition of parties that support the Kremlin and two other centrist coalitions control more than 40 percent of the seats. But the election, according to many observers, had turned the focus in Russia away from social stability to the search for a strong state and a strong leader.[49] Public-opinion polls record the political upheaval. Table 3-2 shows respondents' answers to the question, "How would you describe politics in Russia today?"

When asked to name the economic system they preferred, 48 percent said state planning and distribution and 35 percent responded private property and markets. Fifty-eight percent of respondents responded yes to the statement: "It would have been better if the country had stayed as it was before 1985"; 27 percent said no.[50]

Russia remains one of the great unknowns in the political equation of global environmental politics. President Vladimir V. Putin's efforts, soon after his election in 2000, to strengthen central control over the country's regions that Boris Yeltsin had given to governors in exchange for their support, and to curb the power of the Russian business "oligarchs" whose economic empires appear to be beyond governmental control, are promising.[51] While these actions do not bear directly on environmental policies, they will help determine the nation's stability and governing capacity. There are few signs that environmental quality is a pressing national commitment. But if Putin and others are successful in building the foundation for economic growth, Russia's environmental impacts on the biosphere will become increasingly important, as will be its government's ability to pursue ecologically sustainable development. Unfortunately, Russia has seen NGOs as sufficiently threatening to the government that it closed down 3,000 of them throughout the country in 2000.[52]

Russia's fledgling democracy is faring far worse than some of its neighbors, such as Poland and Estonia, and about as well as others; some commentators have admiringly noted that turnout in the December 1999 election ranged from 60 to 80 percent and that the political debate is more heartfelt than in the West. Russian instability is an enormous concern as President Yeltsin reminded the world in a testy exchange with President Clinton during the war in Chechnya. The Clinton administration had been quite critical of the attack on Grozny, the Chechnyan capital, as the Russians sought to destroy rebels in the region who favored autonomy from Moscow and who had been blamed for unrest in Chechnya and bombings in Moscow. Yeltsin warned Clinton that he should back off, that Russia still had nuclear weapons, and that it lived in a multi-polar world—not dominated by the United States.[53]

There is robust debate among scholars over how to characterize and assess the influence of Green Parties in Europe and elsewhere. According to Erich Frankland, Green Parties in Eastern Europe "helped pave the way for the downfall of each regime through their opposition and function as 'laboratories' of democracy, but they have been unable to coalesce into a political force in the transition period."[54] This is a significant indicator of the relative strength of environmentalism. The transition to democracy called out for new ways of thinking and new forms of politics, and environmentalism, if it had developed into a strong social movement, could well fill the vacuum. Its role in bringing down the old order indicated that the movement possessed some resources. The failure of Eastern European Greens to sustain their influence is a result of a number of factors. First, Green Parties were plagued by internal conflicts over strategy and personality clashes, causing many members to abandon the parties. Second, the parties' focus on environmental problems and vagueness on other issues permitted other parties to co-opt the Green issues. A third issue was the number of Green Party members who had been communists, weakening the parties' reformist credentials. Other dynamics were beyond the control of the Greens: Environmental issues became less important as the revolutions proceeded and as societies faced uncertain economic and social futures. Once the initial revolutions ended, many members of the revolutionary groups returned to traditional parties. Greens have not been able to successfully push for Green policies but serve as "ecological watchdogs on the governments' and the public's rising expectations and fear of economic crisis, which encourage irresponsible development."[55] The conclusion is pretty bleak. While some argue that the Greens offer transitional nations a "third way"—besides capitalism and socialism—their impact seems to be much more modest: serving as their nations' "conscience" but unable to prevent environmental protection becoming overwhelmed by economic and political problems.[56]

Anna Bramwell's *The Fading of the Greens* highlights the weakness of Green Parties in Europe and elsewhere:

> People are reluctant to vote for Green Parties. Protest votes sometimes produce a blip on a chart, but the experience of Eastern Europe, where environmental issues virtually brought down the old regime but where no political environmental movement has developed, encapsulates in rapid time frame two decades of party political ecology in the West, with support for the issues not being matched by support at the polls.[57]

Bramwell argues that the ecological movement was, in a sense, a victim of rising public concern over the environment: As environmental ideas became acceptable and even popular, mainstream politicians and parties embraced the changes that were politically feasible and moderate, and Green Parties moved to the background. The importance of environmentalism "forced the main political parties to take account of it, and the adoption of environmentalist goals by international and supra-national bodies that seems to have rendered national political Green Parties superfluous." The changes Greens demanded that went beyond incremental policies to reach deeply embedded values and practices remain unaddressed. Environmentalism will likely be marginalized, and the "Western political system will once again have shown its flexibility, its capacity to neutralize and then absorb its opponents." [58]

The rise of Green Parties and their limited but significant electoral successes have caught the attention of Americans who see greener pastures across the Atlantic. Europeans are further along than Americans in institutionalizing environmentalism in government, but environmentalism is still far from a transformative movement there. The Green Party approach to institutionalizing environmentalism, like the interest-group method, is fraught with difficulties. If one accepts the idea that environmental problems are manageable within the existing political economy, then the mainstreaming of the Green movement is largely a positive development and will lead to government policies that are more sensitive to environmental concerns and constraints. However, if one is convinced that transformations are required, there is a real fear that Greens are being co-opted and weakened. Their position is quite precipitous: If they maintain a hard, radical edge, they may alienate potential allies and allow opponents to caricaturize them; if they abandon the extreme positions, then there is no voice for radical change. The Green Parties' problems may not necessarily indicate the public's lack of interest in environmentalism or its saliency as a political issue, but may be a reflection of the extent to which other parties have embraced Green issues. In some northern European countries such as Norway, for example, environmental policy has become firmly integrated into the agenda of the mainstream parties. Many environmental activists, believing that political barriers to party influence in governments are too great, have shifted their energies toward affecting legislation and policy by working through NGOs.[59]

Green Public Opinion

There is considerable evidence that some level of environmental values has been firmly embraced by most of the earth's residents, at least those in the industrialized world, but that support seems to make only modest demands and has produced only modest policy and behavioral changes. The extent and causes of public inattention, incoherent views, and lack of knowledge has been widely debated. Some studies conclude that the public pays little attention to public-policy debates and has little knowledge about public issues. Others conclude that people are not ignorant of public affairs, but are not really well informed either. Still others suggest that different segments of the public are more informed about and attentive to certain issues and not others. Some people clearly feel more strongly and are more informed about some issues than the public as a whole, but how many people actually fit that description is not known, and scholars continue to disagree over how to characterize public opinion.[60] Several theories have been constructed to offer explanations of public opinion and the environment.

Mary Douglas and Aaron Wildavsky argue that strong cultural values are at the heart of public opinion. People can be divided into two broad categories: (1) individualists, who favor minimal government regulation and development over preservation, and (2) egalitarians, who use environmental regulation as a way to address inequities that are at the heart of capitalism.[61] Related explanations of how people form environmental issues focus on ideological and political party views. Many public-opinion studies have identified major differences surrounding economic and social issues. For economic issues, opinion is divided between liberals who favor working-class and low-income issues and want government to intervene to ensure more egalitarian wages, and conservatives, who favor business interests, the concerns of wealthier people, and the maintenance of incentives for economic activity that result in inequities. Liberals favor more government intervention, and conservatives want less. For social issues, liberals favor expansion of rights and government intervention to protect alternative lifestyle values and diversity. Conservatives seek to conserve traditional values and favor government intervention to maintain those values. Government is favored by both sides to encourage or protect the values they embrace. Environmentalism fits in fairly well as an economic issue in that liberals and environmentalists favor government intervention in the marketplace, and conservatives and nonenvironmentalists champion free markets and minimal regulation. Democratic politicians are much more likely than Republicans to favor environmental protection policies. In contrast, Robert Paehlke argues that environmentalism is neither a liberal nor a conservative issue, as all people depend on environmental quality and it is independent of the other issues that drive public opinion.[62]

Demographics is one variable: Young and well-educated persons are more likely to have strong environmental views than others, but age and educational levels seem to be better predictors of views on other issues than for environmental ones. Income, race, and ethnicity, variables that are highly correlated with views on other policy issues, do not seem to have much relevance for environmental views. Ronald Ingelhart suggests that public opinion is formed during a person's early years and that people from different generations develop different values. Generations that grew up during World War II, the Great Depression, and other eras in which resources were scarce or rationed are more materialist, concerned about development and production of resources, while those raised during times of plenty are more likely to be postmaterialists, who favor freedom, self-expression, and other quality-of-life issues, such as environmental protection, over economic issues and concerns.[63]

Inglehart's review of public support for environmental protection in 43 societies, for example, found that "Mass support for environmental protection tends to be greatest in countries that have relatively severe objective problems (as indicated by air- and water-pollution levels). Citizens of countries with relatively severe pollution do tend to be relatively willing to make financial sacrifices to protect the environment." A second conclusion is that "public support for environmental protection is also shaped by subjective cultural factors. People with 'postmaterialist' values—emphasizing self-expression and the quality of life—are much more apt to give high priority to protecting the environment...than those with 'materialist' values—emphasizing economic and physical security above all." These postmaterialist cultural values are critical; public support (as with the Nordics, for example) for environmental protection is highest in some of the countries that have relatively low levels of pollution. Overall, Inglehart concludes that objective and subjective factors "are about equally important."[64]

Environmental quality has improved significantly in most advanced industrialized democracies. In less developed countries, access to clean water and sanitation services are the major environmental problems; air pollution is a pressing problem as well. And these conditions are worsening. The World Values survey in 43 countries asked, "Do you approve of the ecology movement?" Sixty-two percent of the respondents answered "strongly approve," while 34 percent answered "approve."

There is great variety among respondents from different countries: 83 percent of respondents in Moscow, 82 percent in Brazil, and 81 percent in Poland said they strongly approved, while only 37 percent in Iceland, 30 percent in Denmark, and 28 percent in Finland agreed with this assessment.[65]

The vast majority of residents in these 43 areas approve of environmentalism; the more critical question is how deeply this sentiment is felt, and what happens when choices must be made between environmental protection and preservation, and jobs, highways, fossil-fuel use, and other development. When asked if they would be willing to pay higher taxes to prevent environmental pollution, 65 percent said yes. Again, the percentages varied greatly, from 78 percent in China, 77 percent in Sweden, and 76 percent in South Korea, to 41 percent in Belgium, 35 percent in Hungary, and 49 percent in West Germany. When given a contrary statement concerning willingness to sacrifice for environmental protection—"The government has to reduce environmental pollution, but it should not cost me any money"—45 percent agreed. But again, the variation across nations makes it difficult to draw any conclusions. In Portugal, 92 percent agreed with the statement, 76 percent in Spain, and 75 percent in Italy, while only 17 percent in the Netherlands, 28 percent in Iceland, and 29 percent in Denmark agreed.[66]

Perhaps the most useful results of the World Values survey ranked respondents as "high" on an environmental protection index if they agreed or strongly agreed to the following propositions: (1) "I would be willing to give part of my income if I were sure that the money would be used to prevent environmental pollution," and (2) "I would agree to an increase in taxes if the extra money is used to prevent environmental pollution," and if they disagreed or strongly disagreed with the following statements: (1) "The government should reduce environmental pollution, but it should not cost me any money"; and (2) "Protecting the environment and fighting pollution is less urgent than often suggested." The results of the survey are shown in Table 3-3.

Inglehart argues that in some cases—Russia, China, South Korea, and Mexico, for example—high levels of public support for environmental protection are a result of high levels of pollution. For other countries, such as Scandinavia, high levels of support are signs of postmodern values that emphasize quality of life more than economic growth and consumption. These changes in values are most prominent in the wealthiest nations, but are becoming increasingly common in industrializing countries. Inglehart found evidence of an intergenerational shift

TABLE 3-3
Support for Environmental Protection Policies

Country	% Scoring High on the Environmental Protection Index
Sweden	69
Denmark	65
Netherlands	64
Norway	59
South Korea	58
Iceland	54
Russia	53
Turkey	53
Czechoslovakia	52
China	52
Mexico	50
Finland	48
Brazil	48
Japan	47
East Germany	47
Moscow	46
Chile	46
Slovenia	46
India	45
Bulgaria	44
Latvia	44
Lithuania	43
Britain	42
Canada	42
West Germany	41
United States	40
Belarus	40
Austria	39
Estonia	38
Northern Ireland	36
Portugal	36
Belgium	33
Italy	31
Spain	30
France	30
Argentina	30
Nigeria	27
Hungary	24

Source: Inglehart, "Public Support for Environmental Protection," 60.

from materialist to postmaterialist values and priorities over the past three decades. Values surrounding freedom of speech, giving people more voice in what happens in their community, and a less impersonal and more humane society are strongly associated with support for environmental protection. He concluded that postmaterialist values "are an even stronger predictor of pro-environmentalist attitudes than is education."[67] Postmaterialists are much likelier to take action on behalf of environmental causes, such as joining environmental groups and contributing money. There is clear evidence, Inglehart concludes, that "pervasive changes *are* taking place in the basic values of the publics of industrialized societies throughout the world." These changes are "gradual but have a good deal of inherent long-term momentum" and "seem to have a direct bearing on public support for policies designed to deal with global change."[68] The public's willingness to pay for measures is interesting but it is not clear how helpful it is. Many respondents, for example, may believe strongly that corporate profits should be reduced in order to pay for pollution reduction, and support laws and regulations to that end.

The postmaterialist embrace of environmentalism seems to account well for the rise of concern about ecology in the developed world. But the obverse does not obtain: residents of poor countries are not necessarily uninterested in environmental quality. There is much evidence that they are very concerned about environmental quality, that they recognize that the degradation of the environment threatens their survival. They are more likely to engage in subsistence agriculture than their Northern counterparts and suffer when environmental conditions decline. They lack the resources to mitigate the effects of environmental problems such as climate change.[69] The future of the developing world is intimately intertwined with the protection of local ecosystems and the biosphere, and poverty continues to be a major barrier to ecological sustainability. One of the most frustrating characteristics of global politics is the lack of progress made in reducing poverty, particularly in Africa and Latin America. World Bank President James D. Wolfensohn warned in a February 2000 speech that "we are no better off than we were in the 1970s" in reducing poverty in Latin America, where 63 million people live in poverty. Others point to disasters across the developing world, where poverty is more intense now than in earlier decades.[70] The decline in foreign aid spending in the United States of 20 percent over the past two decades, and its last-place position in the ranking of aid given by nations as a percentage of gross domestic product are only two of a number of indicators that there is little political will for reducing poverty in the developing countries.[71]

While wealthier countries have more resources to invest in cleaner technologies, this does not necessarily mean that a developing country's residents are too poor to care about environmental quality. Many leaders from developing countries have argued, perhaps to attract foreign aid, that environmental protection will not occur without external assistance and that developing countries will not be able to comply with global environmental accords unless they are paid to do so. That is the idea behind the Global Environment Facility (GEF), established to help developing countries implement the Framework Conventions on Climate Change and Biodiversity, the Montreal Protocol on the stratospheric ozone layer, and other global accords. Projects that otherwise would not receive funding can be supported through the GEF. This creates a clear incentive for developing country leaders to minimize domestic support for environmental protection to make the best case for external assistance. That incentive dovetails nicely with the view that increased pollution is widely viewed as an acceptable tradeoff with economic growth, and that once countries reach a minimum level of well being they can begin to afford to worry about environmental quality. [72]

But there is considerable evidence that many people in developing countries are very supportive of environmental protection goals. Polling data show that there is little statistically significant correlation between level of environmental concern and per capita income. There seems to be about as much concern for environmental quality in low- and middle-income nations as there is in wealthy ones. Riley Dunlap and others have concluded, based on their assessment of the Gallup international data, that there is no evidence that residents of poor nations care less about the environment than residents in the wealthy world.[73] People in developing countries appear to be at least as willing as those in wealthy countries to pay higher taxes or prices to protect environmental values.[74]

Perhaps some level of personal wealth is a prerequisite for effective environmental activism. As is true in developed nations, a strong environmental movement need only involve a fraction of the total population, and even in poor countries there may be sufficient numbers of people who have the resources to participate effectively in environmental politics. But the sheer number of environmental groups in developing countries is evidence of a great deal of interest in environmental values.[75] And concern for environmental quality is intertwined with survival in poor countries, where people are intimately involved with nature as they seek to find adequate soil and water to grow crops for survival. Residents of poor nations, through their commitments to indigenous and other religions, traditional art, and other core elements of their cultures, value nature. While financial assistance to developing countries is essential, it should not be understood as buying environmental sensitivity. Leaders of developing countries who downplay environmental support within their nations in order to strengthen their bargaining hand in global talks may discourage NGOs from helping local groups. Given the importance of NGOs in encouraging environmentally protective policies and in fostering environmental awareness and involvement among citizens, international governmental and non-governmental institutions have an interest in understanding the factors that contribute to the strength of environmental movements in developing nations.

Other polls show wide variety in the level of environmental commitment worldwide, as Inglehart found. A recent poll by the Gallup International Institute found that people in both wealthy and poor nations express strong support for environmental protection: "Majorities in most of the 24 nations surveyed by Gallup international affiliates give environmental protection higher priority than economic growth."[76] Among the poll's conclusions:

- Environmental problems are rated as one of the three most serious problems in nearly half of the nations surveyed.
- While respondents in the less developed countries (LDCs) identify local problems such as air and water quality and lack of sewage treatment facilities as much more serious than residents of the more developed world, both groups rate similarly the seriousness of global problems such as ozone-layer depletion, climate change, and loss of biodiversity.
- When asked whether the industrialized or the developing countries are more responsible for today's environmental problems, the most frequent response from both worlds is that both are "equally responsible."
- Respondents in the LDCs believe that the most important actions that the developed world could take would be to provide educational opportunities, technological assistance, and family-planning services. Support for debt reduction is greater in the LDCs.
- There is strong support throughout the world for the creation of an international environmental agency.
- The majority of respondents in 21 of 24 nations indicated that "protecting the environment should be given priority, even at the risk of slowing down economic growth."

While these results are significant, specific policy actions supported by public opinion are less clear. Political leadership will play a fundamental role in focusing debate on the choices we face and generating support for the decisions to be made.

A 1993 study by the Gallup International Institute found a wide range of distribution of public opinion on the environment in developing and industrialized nations. Respondents in 24 countries were asked, "How concerned are you personally about environmental problems?"[77] The responses are given in Table 3-4.

TABLE 3-4
Level of Concern about Environmental Problems

Industrialized Nations	*Percent Indicating Great Concern*
Portugal	46%
United States	38
Canada	37
Great Britain	28
Japan	23
Ireland	22
Norway	18
Netherlands	16
Finland	16
Denmark	12
Switzerland	12

Developing Nations	*Percent Indicating Great Concern*
Nigeria	71
Philippines	55
Brazil	53
Mexico	50
Russia	41
Uruguay	38
India	34
Hungary	32
Chile	30
South Korea	22
Turkey	12
Poland	4

Source: Kates, "Sustaining Life on the Earth," 120.

These data are difficult to compare. Many of the countries whose citizens indicate great concern with environmental problems are those that face considerable problems. Conversely, some of the lowest levels of concern are found in industrialized countries that have already made considerable efforts to protect environmental quality; in developing or transitional nations, such as Turkey and Poland, there is low support despite the existence of considerable environmental problems.

These aggregate figures provide only a limited description of environmental sentiment. Public support for environmental regulation may vary across regions in large countries. In Canada, for example, British Columbia (BC) is a leading province for environmental activism and awareness. Of the 2,250 groups that were part of the Canadian Environment Network in 1994, 529 were located in BC, twice the province's share of the nation's population. These groups are more militant than elsewhere in Canada

TABLE 3-5
Green Consumerism in British Columbia, Canada

Activity	Percentage of Respondents Who Answered Affirmatively (All or Most of the Time)
Turn off lights when leaving room	83.8
Turn down thermostat at night	82.7
Recycle newspapers	81.2
Recycle tin cans	69.8
Compost fruit and vegetable waste	43.4
Use own bags when shopping	26.7
Buy organic fruit and vegetables	19.7
Use public transportation	14.2

Source: Blake, Guppy, and Urmetzer, "Canadian Public Opinion and Environmental Action,"
   454–55.

and have been involved in well-publicized protests over logging, such as the Clayquot Sound protest in 1993, one of the largest acts of civil disobedience in Canadian history. The province is also the birthplace of Greenpeace International.[78] Opinion polls in BC show strong support for the environment. The environment was ranked as the second "most important problem facing British Columbians today." Some 60 percent of provincial residents chose "protecting the environment" when asked to choose between jobs and the environment. Nearly half of respondents, when asked who—among industry, different levels of government, or individuals—has "primary responsibility for protecting the environment," responded that individuals do.[79] Blake, Guppy, and Urmetzer focused on three measures of the strength of environmental commitments among British Columbians: Green consumerism, Green activism, and willingness to pay for a greener environment. The tables below report the results of their survey and the activities that reflect the different kinds of environmental commitments. Table 3-5 shows British Columbian respondents' frequency of activities in support of Green consumerism.

There is strong support for a few activities around the house that have environmental benefits; as is true in the United States, there is little support for the use of public transportation, the activity that would likely yield the greatest environmental benefit. Similarly, the number of people actually engaged in environmental activism is rather small, as shown in Table 3-6.

Blake, Guppy, and Urmetzer's final measure is "willingness to pay for a better environment." They constructed a willingness-to-pay scale based on the extent to which respondents agreed or disagreed with a given position. They then asked respondents whether they agreed or disagreed with a series of statements that addressed various issues con-

TABLE 3-6
Green Activism in British Columbia, Canada

Activity	Percentage of Respondents Answered Affirmatively (Activities in the Last Year)
Donated money to support an environmental cause	46.6
Signed a petition supporting a pro-environmental issue	44.4
Boycotted a product because of environmental concern	43.4
Worked to elect someone because of their views on the environment	24.3
Displayed a bumper sticker or pin supporting pro-environmental issue	19.1
Written a public official about environmental matters	16.6
Joined an environmental group	12.7
Joined a protest or demonstration concerned with the environment	9.8
Phoned TV/radio talk show about environmental issues	7.7
Written a letter about environmental issues to newspapers	7.2

Source: Blake, Guppy, and Urmetzer, "Canadian Public Opinion and Environmental Action,"
457–58.

cerning the idea that individuals, businesses, and society as a whole should pay for the cost of preserving the environment. The percentage of respondents who strongly agree and are willing to pay is shown in Table 3-7.[80]

Shutting down businesses that fail to comply with environmental standards is the most popular action, and increasing gasoline taxes the least. Blake, Guppy, and Urmetzer found no statistical association between support for these measures and levels of income or education, except that those who have higher incomes are more willing to pay more for a better environment. Women are significantly more concerned about environmental issues than men.[81] In the case of British Columbia, there is strong support for some environmental positions, but support is softest for the issues that are most central to sustainability and the solution of major problems like air pollution and climate change that require major changes in production and consumption. Like their neighbors to the south, Canadians apparently oppose conservation-related lifestyle choices as a diminution of their quality of life.

TABLE 3-7
Support for Environmental Protection in British Columbia, Canada

Proposition	Percentage Strongly Agree
The size of BC's population must be limited even if it means less economic development.	15.0
There should be tougher anti-pollution laws, even if such laws decrease our standard of living.	29.4
We should do more to protect the environment even if it means losing jobs.	16.0
[Government should] place higher environmental taxes on gasoline.	12.2
Do you support or oppose sharply limiting resource companies' access to BC's wilderness lands, even though it would mean a loss of jobs in some areas? (% who support)	20.1
Do you support or oppose closing down businesses that do not meet environmental regulations after they've received a warning, regardless of job loss? (% who support)	31.1
Do you support or oppose requiring electric and gas utilities to spend a larger share of their budgets on ways to increase energy efficiency, even if it means higher rates for consumers? (% who support)	19.3

Source: Blake, Guppy, and Urmetzer, "Canadian Public Opinion and Environmental Action," 461–62.

Public opinion changes over time. Cultural theory suggests that changes in values occur over long periods of time. Postmaterialist theory suggests that changes occur across generational lines. But opinion shifts can also occur more quickly, in response to major events and crises, media messages, and political leadership. An interesting example of the power of natural disasters in reshaping public opinion is illustrated by the impact of hurricane Lothar which struck France in December 1999. Some 80 people were killed but far more powerful was the impact of the loss of millions of trees. "France is devastated," said one appeal for "national solidarity" in raising money to plant new trees. The storm appeared to profoundly shake French confidence in the idea of progress and humankind's ability to manage nature, and may lead to significant rethinking of environmentalism.[82]

The more the information is in line with cultural predispositions, ideological commitments, and life experience, the stronger the impact of the information on opinion. Conversely, the more the information challenges these views, the less likely the information will affect attitudes. All three will be critical if public opinion is to mature and become more responsive to the complex issues underlying environmental threats. But the interaction is hard to chart. As older generations die, postmaterial, quality-of-life values will become more dominant. The more egalitarian values are strengthened by awareness that ecological conditions bind us together, the more environmentalism will be strengthened. But individualism remains a strong, pervasive value. The more government intervention and regulation seems to be successful in accomplishing its goals, the greater the support there may be for more regulation. But that growth will also prompt opponents to argue that there is too much interference with individual behavior. Crises will likely continue to shape attitudes. What is needed is a more mature understanding of the complexities, interactions, and tradeoffs associated with environmental protection, and political leadership and education will be critical for that to occur.

Ecological Sustainability

The discussion above has occasionally broached assessments of sustainability. This section examines the level of commitment to sustainability among the advanced industrialized democracies. There are a number of ways this commitment might be assessed. One important measure of political support for environmentalism, for example, is a country's embrace of Green taxes and reform of environmentally harmful subsidies. Some Green taxes are quite modest in terms of the revenues raised, and may not appear to represent environmental commitment, but they can be an indicator of a willingness to take a first step toward strong environment-protection policies. The Scandinavian countries and the Netherlands, for example, have introduced carbon taxes that would vary according to the carbon content of the fuel. Sweden was able to produce a shift from high- to low-sulfur diesel fuel by reducing taxes on low-sulfur fuels. In Britain and Germany, proposals to raise taxes on fossil fuels have raised protests from taxpayer and industry groups.[83]

William M. Lafferty and James Meadowcroft, in a research project they organized entitled "Implementing Sustainable Development in High Consumption Societies," suggested that one way of assessing the level of commitment to sustainability is to assess the extent to which it has become an organizing principle, institutionalized, in national policy making. They argue that indicators of commitment include the express use of the term "sustainable development," and an important measure of the level of global commitment to sustainability is the extent to which it has been implemented in the high-consumption societies.[84] As one would expect, efforts to shift to sustainability have been quite modest. Most of these countries have devised strategic plans for ecologically sustainable development, including conservation of biodiversity, programs to reduce the threat of climate change, environmental-impact assessment, plans for forests and other key resources, and more general plans for greening government. Most countries have made only modest progress in moving toward sustainable production and consumption; the Scandinavian countries and the Netherlands lead the way here. Industries are much more integrated into planning and implementation efforts than are environmental interests.

Expectations for the transition to sustainability have been highest for the northern European nations, particularly the Scandinavian countries. Norway, for example, has been one of the leading proponents of sustainable development. Gro Harlem Brundtland, who served as prime minister in the late 1980s and early to mid-1990s, also chaired the World Commission on Environment and Development. Norway appears to be as strong a candidate for sustainability as any nation in the world. It is one of the least densely populated countries in Europe. It is apparently the only country in the world that bases its entire mainland electricity production on hydropower, although it is the second-largest oil exporter in the world. Norway is regularly described as an international leader in environmental issues. It is regularly ranked first or close to first in the world in terms of social and economic development and quality-of-life measures. The Norwegian political system is highly participatory. NGOs participate in official delegations to international environmental talks, and the government regularly consults with them, includes them in official consultative bodies, and helps fund their participation. Nevertheless, the government published a white paper two years after the issuance of *Our Common Future* by the World Commission on Environment and Development, which concluded that Norway would need to make fundamental changes in the use of energy and other resources for the nation to move to a path of sustainability. The paper outlined an ambitious plan that required "profound changes in the ways energy and other resources are used before development in Norway is brought within the bounds of nature's carrying capacity." Then-current trends were viewed as risking "unacceptable" and possibly "irreversible" damage to the environment.[85]

Norway's commitment to sustainability has faltered considerably, particularly after the 1992 Earth Summit. There has been a gradual softening of its ambitious goals for policies such as investing in research and development for renewable energy sources and raising the tax on electricity. Renewable energy sources produced a smaller percentage of total energy consumption by the end of the 1990s than they did in the late 1980s. There has been no broad, national discussion on sustainable development. Government ministries have been reluctant to assume responsibility for achieving goals and targets. In 1997 a new white paper called for an acceleration of implementation of sustainability in various sectors of the economy and the development of indicators for charting progress. The country has never embraced a strong commitment to significantly reduce greenhouse gas emissions, even in its 1989 white paper. There is little success to report in changing production and consumption patterns. The lack of interest in sustainability is not limited to the national government: Only one of Norway's 435 municipalities has prepared a "local Agenda 21" document as chapter 28 of Agenda 21 suggests. A Friends of the Earth Norway report chastised the nation for having betrayed the Brundtland Commission. However, Norway remains a leader in assisting developing countries and established a small fund to finance projects in developing countries to reduce carbon dioxide emissions. [86]

Sweden also has been a global leader in environmental policy. The Swedish Environmental Protection Agency was established in 1967, Stockholm hosted the first Earth Summit in 1972, and there was great support in Sweden for the 1992 UNCED meeting. Sweden has emphasized ecologically sustainable development. It has introduced the concept of producer responsibility, where producers rather than consumers and municipalities are responsible for recycling and disposing products once their use has ended. Virtually all local governments have initiated a process of implementing Agenda 21; about 50 municipalities have begun programs that have been characterized as early forms of actions that represent a shift to fundamental changes in infrastructure, resource use, and consumer choice. The government regularly consults with NGOs and helps fund their participation in decision making, and includes them in official consultative bodies and delegations to conferences such as UNCED. The political rhetoric has been ambitious, promising to rebuild the nation into a sustainable Sweden.[87]

Nevertheless, it is difficult to find evidence of a fundamental transformation. Economic growth continues to be a priority. Many of the local projects carried out under the banner of Agenda 21 are really traditional environmental policies and don't represent any kind of a breakthrough, or are the relatively cheap and easy programs—the low-hanging fruit—that have not touched more difficult and contentious problems. Sweden's embrace of sustainability has not been extended to include the broad agenda of social, economic, and cultural concerns. Economic problems such as rising unemployment and declining personal income during the 1990s weakened the Swedish commitment to the welfare state and to government regulation; funding for the Swedish EPA, for example, was cut by 25 percent in the late 1990s. Assistance to developing countries, while still at 0.7 percent of GDP and one of the highest percentages in the world, has fallen from a high of 0.9 to 1.0 percent of GDP during the 1980s. Environmental concerns have been replaced by the more pressing problems of unemployment and reduced welfare benefits.[88]

The Netherlands provides a third example of a country that has developed a strong environmental policy infrastructure and has integrated environmental concerns into policy making, has directed considerable public attention toward sustainable development, and has produced a number of sustainable development reports and plans. There is a systematic, integrated plan for sustainable development that includes a number of policy innovations such as tax reform and integrated environmental planning. The Netherlands is particularly vulnerable to environmental problems given its small size, its dense population, and its susceptibility to pollution from neighboring states. But all this activity has not resulted in a transformation to sustainable consumption and production, and the Dutch government has had a difficult time translating the plan into specific policies. In 1989 the government issued its National Environmental Policy Plan (NEPP), designed to produce within one generation (the year 2010) a sustainable society while still allowing for continued economic growth. The NEPP provides a number of targets to be achieved by that date but largely suggests traditional pollution-control measures that extend the existing regulatory system rather than transform policy. The government also issued a white paper to ensure that international aid promoted conservation and did not produce negative ecological consequences. [89] The implementation of the Dutch National Environmental Plan has fallen well behind deadline, and enforcement has been weak. As Anna Bramwell has observed, if consensus over environmentalism cannot be obtained in a consensual society like the Dutch, what chance is there it will occur in more contentious, competitive political systems?[90]

Germany is one of the most densely populated and highly industrialized nations in the world, and those conditions have generated a number of environmental problems as well as a strong policy response. Germany was one of the first countries to develop environmental protection agencies and programs, and it has in place a rather effective pollution-control program. Early on, Germany adopted the precautionary principle to guide policy making, and it has been widely accepted in the nation as the underlying goal of antipollution programs. As global negotiations leading to the 1992 UNCED meeting began focusing on sustainability, Germans argued that they were already ahead of that movement by embracing the precautionary principle, and argued that they had already achieved sustainability in areas such as agricultural production. There has been some acknowledgment, at an abstract level, of the idea of sustainability, but it has not been viewed as a challenge to traditional environmental policy, nor to the broader range of current economic and social policies. One example: When the federal government moved the core government functions from Bonn to Berlin in the late 1990s, it moved the finance, agriculture, economics, and transportation ministries but left the environment ministry in Bonn. As a result, economic and ecological questions have not been regularly connected.[91]

There has been little effort in Germany to assess national progress toward sustainability and little restructuring of government to promote an integration of ecological and other concerns. While environmental groups have developed a number of initiatives to promote sustainability, they have been resisted by industry groups who favor increased efficiency in energy and resource use but argue that customers will not pay higher prices for greener products. Suggestions for changes in lifestyle, consumption, and social norms have attracted little interest. Concerns about the future of the German welfare state, how to reduce unemployment, and other economic issues dominate the political agenda. In one policy area—climate change—Germany has been a leading force for more ambitious reductions in carbon dioxide emissions. Some proponents of cuts in greenhouse gas emissions have argued that Germany's commitment here should be viewed as a significant move to pursue the idea of sustainable development.[92]

Other countries show a pattern of strong interest in and commitment to sustainable development and the implementation of Agenda 21, only to see that commitment dissipate in the face of other concerns, usually economic, that are seen as more important. In Australia, for example, the national government responded to the UNCED conference with detailed initiatives on climate change and biodiversity, reducing waste, and conserving resources; they also have made efforts to link economic development and environmental protection. Governments, business, and environmental groups have worked together to devise plans for implementing sustainable development. There have been some modest policy initiatives such as tax incentives and user charges to promote conservation and clean technologies. The Labour Party fostered constructive dialogue between environmental and industry groups, but the Liberal government that took power in the mid-1990s emphasizing economic values, fears of unemployment, competitiveness in the global economy, and the importance of Australia's exports of minerals and fossil fuels have weakened environmental protection commitments. While there is a framework in place in Australia that could be used to promote sustainability, the national government seems content to delegate some of that responsibility to local governments, and there are conflicts between environmental groups and the federal government over policy priorities. Most of the progress in responding to sustainability actually occurred before UNCED; there has been little progress since 1992 in pursuing sustainable development—and even some retreat in commitment.[93]

The pattern diverges somewhat in Japan. The Japanese government embarked on an ambitious set of environmental policies in the late 1980s,

with a strong emphasis on technological developments and energy efficiency. It seeks to be an international leader in environmental issues, in
part at least to remedy its history of environmental inaction. NGOs are encouraged to participate because that is viewed as an international expectation, but their influence is slight. Business interests are systematically
involved in policy-making decisions. Some argue that Japan has been
quite successful in institutionalizing energy conservation and pollution
reduction. As the Japanese economy grew rapidly, policy makers began to
recognize the seriousness of environmental problems as well as the importance of conserving energy costs. These two goals were very compatible, and industry and government have worked together very closely to
integrate conservation and pollution-reduction goals. Energy policy was
consciously and expressly used to address air pollution problems, and is
now at the heart of the nation's climate change efforts. All of this has been
rather independent of direct political activity by citizens, as the Japanese
government pushed through energy and environmental laws. While industries were recalcitrant in the 1960s, they have become quite cooperative in response to low- interest loans, preferential taxing and subsidies,
and other incentives to encourage conservation and reduced emissions.
One study concluded that, "very explicitly now, energy policy is having
to address environmental issues, and energy conservation has come to be
regarded as an important element of environmental policy."[94]

Many Japanese companies have developed conservation programs that
also promise to reduce greenhouse gas emissions. The aggressive role of
the Japanese government in subsidizing and regulating energy conservation has been successful in getting industries committed to conservation
and pollution-reduction goals, but energy consumption in the transport
and consumer sectors is increasing as consumers demand larger, more en-
ergy-consuming products. There is some evidence that consumers have
become more interested in conservation efforts. But much more important
has been the development by industries of new technologies to reduce
energy costs during the past three decades, and those efforts have expanded tremendously as Japanese technological advances in conservation
are marketed worldwide. As these efforts by industries and government
continue, they are also being championed as aggressive steps to reduce
climate change threats. However, faced with scarce resources and a
densely-populated island, Japan's extensive import of natural resources
such as timber from old growth forests in Asia and North America reflect
a commitment to pursuing sustainability as a domestic imperative but not
as a global commitment.[95]

Finally, it should be noted here that despite the many limitations, the
advanced industrialized nations have considerable governmental capacity, scientific infrastructure, and political stability, and are in a position to

devise and implement ambitious policies aimed at ecological sustainability if they choose to do so. That capacity is lacking in the developing countries, where there is relatively little scientific and technical expertise, where environmental ministries are underdeveloped, where there is little tradition of design and implementation of effective regulatory programs, and where political instability and conflict make policy making particularly difficult. As discussed above, indigenous environmental groups in some countries have linked with international environmental groups. But for most of these countries, sustainability will require considerable assistance from the developed countries and from international organizations, as discussed in the next chapter.

Conclusion

Environmental politics throughout the world have been quite successful in transforming the environmental movement to organized interest-group politics. While there are major differences between these political relationships across the industrialized democracies and across democracies in emerging and developing nations, environmental politics have placed many issues on the public agenda and effectively lobbied for changes. Even in some nondemocratic countries, environmental groups have arisen to challenge existing practices and pressure governments and businesses to be more responsive to environmental concerns. The agenda for environmentalism is changing and becoming much more ambitious than in the past, but environmental politics and public opinion have not caught up to those changes. The most vibrant politics is at the grass-roots level, and while some communities are becoming more sustainable, that kind of politics is, for the most part, not reaching national policy makers. Local efforts are essential, but it is not enough to think globally and act locally— many problems are global in origins and implications. Acting nationally and internationally is just as important.

4

The Global Environmental Movement

A tremendous amount of global activity has focused on environmental issues since 1970. The 1992 Stockholm and 1992 Rio de Janeiro earth summits were major gatherings of national leaders; a host of more specialized meetings on population, social development, climate change, biodiversity, forests, and other issues also have directed a great deal of attention toward ecological problems. The World Bank and other multilateral institutions have committed to reorient their lending to reduce adverse environmental consequences and to fund conservation projects. At the beginning of the twenty-first century, there were more than one thousand international legal instruments aimed at environmental protection.[1] Major agreements address global commons such as Antarctica, the global climate, the stratospheric ozone layer, and the oceans as well as regional commons such as seas and regional air pollution problems like acid rain. Hundreds of agreements regulate transboundary pollution and the sharing of water and air sheds across national boundaries. Other international efforts have encouraged voluntary acceptance of policies promoting sustainability, such as the 1992 Rio Earth Charter and Agenda 21.[2] Thousands of governmental and nongovernmental organizations have formed to help protect the global environment. Environmental issues are at the heart of interactions between the developing and developed nations over how to reduce poverty in the world. Regional and global trade accords include, or are under pressure to include, environmental provisions.

What does all this interest in global environmental issues mean in terms of the transformation to ecologically sustainable development? This chapter explores three areas that illustrate the nature of ecological politics: the rise of nongovernmental organizations in global politics dedicated to preserving the environment, the role of sustainability in North–South relations, and the interaction of environmental and trade values in the context of sustainability. These three topics represent only a part of the total

105

activity that comprises global environmental politics but are logical topics for emphasis. Nongovernmental organizations (NGOs) play a key role in getting environmental issues on the global policy-making agenda, pressuring governments to implement agreements they have signed, and encouraging individuals and businesses to take voluntary action to reduce environmental risks. Global environmental politics cannot be separated from the broader issue of how the interests of the developing countries (the South) and the wealthy world (the North) interact. Finally, the growing globalization of economic activity places international trade policy in the middle of any debate over sustainability.

As the discussion of developments in these areas will emphasize, sustainability has been institutionalized at the global level, but the form of sustainability commonly invoked is economic sustainability, calling for only modest changes in practices and priorities. In many ways, the interest in and commitment to sustainability peaked in 1992 at the United Nations Conference on Environment and Development or UNCED, where the developing countries' concerns with reducing poverty seemed to be linked with the industrialized world's commitment to reduce pollution in ways that seemed to reflect the interests of both. Looking back on the past two decades, environmentalism does not appear to have strengthened its grip on global politics during the past several years. Particularly significant is the lack of progress in strengthening the global governance required to address global environmental problems; this will become increasingly important in the future.

NGOs and the Global Environment

Robert Keohane and Joseph Nye define globalism as a "state of the world involving networks of interdependence at multicontinental distances." They identify four different forms of globalism:

- **Economic globalism**—long-distance flows of goods, services, and capital, as well as the information and perceptions that accompany market exchange.
- **Military globalism**—long-distance networks of interdependence in which force, and the threat or promise of force, are employed.
- **Social and cultural globalism**—the movement of ideas, information, images, and people (who, of course, carry ideas and information with them).
- **Environmental globalism**—the long-distance transport of materials in the atmosphere or oceans, or of biological substances such as pathogens or genetic materials, that affect human health and well-being.[3]

Changes in these different dimensions do not necessarily occur at the same time. Environmental globalism, for example, has occurred much later than economic or military interdependence. Globalism can either be relatively thin or thick depending on the density of the networks, the level of participation, and the velocity with which information is exchanged. Keohane and Nye argue that globalism at the beginning of the twenty-first century is best described as "complex interdependence," where there are high levels of economic, social, and environmental interaction, and low levels of military activity.[4] What is really new about these forms of globalism is the systemic effects this interdependence produces and the difficulty in predicting what those effects will be. NGOs play an increasingly important role as global networks become more pluralistic. A key question is whether they will form a "coherent and credible coalition" that is able to effectively shape these global trends in ways that are compatible with the health of the biosphere.[5]

An Overview of International NGOs

International environmental NGOs have grown from a handful of conservation groups formed in the 1890s to important actors in global environmental politics. Many international NGOs—or INGOs—have very broad portfolios. In 1948, 68 NGOs formed the International Union for the Protection of Nature, which later became known as the World Conservation Union. It functions as a kind of UN for nature, with countries, government agencies, and NGOs as members, and forums to debate and implement global actions. There was a lot of activity around the formation of NGOs in the 1970s and 1980s. In the late 1990s, environmental NGOs found powerful allies. Some 600 NGOs joined forces to block the closed-door meeting of representatives of the world's 29 wealthiest nations in Paris in 1998 to negotiate a Multilateral Agreement on Investments (MAI). The goal of the MAI talks was to reduce national barriers to the flow of investment funds throughout the world. Protestors feared that an MAI agreement, like free-trade accords, weaken the ability of nation–states to establish environmental and labor standards. Activists explained that they "honed their skills on MAI," and that contributed to their ability to challenge the World Trade Organization.[6]

A host of nongovernmental actors are pieces of the patchwork of global environmental institutions. NGOs are enormously important to the implementation of global environmental accords. There is tremendous variety among NGOs. Some are grass-roots organizations that work in villages and urban communities in the less developed nations. Others are service organizations that provide support for grass-roots groups. Some NGOs have grown into regional or national federations, and some form

international networks and coalitions. Many NGOs focus on particular issues such as development, the environment, human rights, relief, and
women's issues, while others provide services such as policy research, financial and technical assistance, and training to grass-roots groups.[7] International associations of scientists support research that triggers demand for global action and provides a basis for shaping policies.
Environmental and other coalitions can focus considerable public pressure on environmental problems through publicity, supplying information to governmental bodies, and facilitating environmental activism in
various nations. Media decisions concerning what issues to address and
how to depict them significantly shape the global policy formulation and
implementation. A few bodies, such as the World Conservation Union
(IUCN) and the Ecosystem Conservation Group (ECG), combine national
governments, international agencies, and NGOs.[8]

One of the best known NGOs is Greenpeace, which has offices in 30
countries and an annual budget of $130 million, down from a peak of $179
million in 1991. Despite the downturn in support, Greenpeace is widely
viewed as an effective voice for the environment, and even businesspeo-
ple have come to admire its ability to be both centralized and decentralized. National offices plan their own campaigns and make decisions, but
all offices have been wired to an international computer network since
1986, and local campaigns must be consistent with Greenpeace policy positions. When offices in several countries mount a campaign, one staff
member is placed in charge. Greenpeace takes a long perspective and in-
vests in campaigns that take years to come to fruition. But one-half of the
international office's budget and one-fourth of the local budget is also set
aside to respond to emergencies. One of its most difficult challenges is expanding its efforts into the developing world. There are few donors—
some accuse Greenpeace of colonialism, others demand that poverty be
viewed as an environmental problem, and many supporters in the
wealthy world want the organization to continue to focus on traditional
environmental issues.[9]

Western environmental groups and foundations have become increasingly active in Eastern Europe. The U.S. National Academy of Sciences
has organized workshops with Polish and Romanian scientists on energy
efficiency and natural resources management. A number of other groups,
including the Institute for European Environmental Policy, Friends of the
Earth International, World Environment Center, Management Sciences for
Health, Environmental Law Institute, Rockefeller Brothers Fund, World
Conservation Union, Ecological Studies Institute, and the International
Institute for Applied Systems Analysis, are involved in a variety of envi-
ronmental protection projects. The International Council of Scientific
Unions has established a number of programs and task forces to explore

climate change, ocean circulation, global atmosphere, and satellite cloud climatology.[10]

A variety of NGOs focus on sustainable development. The Earth Council, created in late 1992 by Maurice Strong, secretary general of the Earth Summit, and others, for example, is located in Costa Rica. It is working with other NGOs to publicize and assess national efforts to achieve sustainable development goals. The Committee on International Development Institutions on the Environment, which is made up of UN and non-UN agencies and other global and regional bodies, was established in 1980 to review UN agencies' efforts to promote sustainable development.[11] The Stockholm Initiative on Global Security and Governance led to the creation of the Commission on Global Governance, another organization that is exploring options for improving the functioning of international environmental organizations.[12]

Multinational corporations and large banks, although not environmental NGOs, make decisions that have enormous consequences for environmental quality and resource preservation as well as economic growth and development, and deserve a brief mention here. By the end of the century, there were, according to one estimate, some 60,000 transnational corporations that controlled 25 percent of the global economic output.[13] The impacts of multinationals on the global environment is complex. In some cases, such as whaling, deforestation, and biodiversity, they have been rather successful in blocking, delaying, and weakening global environmental agreements. But some industries have recognized the opportunities created by the commitment to sustainable development and are taking advantage of emerging markets in Green technologies. The World Business Council for Sustainable Development, for example, formed in 1995, has a membership of some 120 companies in 34 countries. The council works with the United Nations Environment Program (UNEP) on pollution projects, issues reports on sustainable industry practices, and is involved in efforts to devise Green certification programs for industries.[14] Given the power of multinationals in terms of their influence in policy making and their impacts on the environment, their participation is essential in building global environmental commitments and capacity. As important as groups like the World Business Council are, they still only reach a fraction of companies that affect the health of the environment.

NGOs are part of a fragmented, complex set of international organizations that play a role in international environmental policy. They are intertwined with other efforts, particularly those aimed at fostering development in poorer countries. International development and environment protection efforts are closely related: Development projects may exacerbate environmental problems or contribute to their resolution, and environmental improvements are often prerequisites to improving health, agricultural output, and economic activity. As a result, both development and environmental organizations are part of the institutional infrastructure for dealing with global environmental problems. One study identified more than 120 such agencies and programs that interact with NGOs.[15]

The Strengths and Weaknesses of NGOs

NGOs mobilize collective action and render important economic and other services such as providing sources of credit, access to marketing services, technical support, educational programs, and health care. NGOs give voice to grass-roots concerns and become effective political and economic forces. Studies of NGOs involved in development have found them to be "relatively effective at reaching the poor, mobilizing local resources, delivering services, and solving problems." NGOs have generally been more effective in helping poor individuals who have some resources rather than those who have few or no assets, and "administrative flexibility, small size, and relative freedom from political constraints make it easier for successful service organizations to try innovative solutions to problems."[16]

Grass-roots organizations are invaluable in mobilizing local energy to address pressing problems. They can pressure government officials to support international agreements and pursue additional domestic initiatives. Local support is essential for the long-run sustainability of policy efforts. NGOs increase the range of interests that are included in policy making and play a particularly important role in ensuring that local concerns and interests are reflected in policy deliberations. The involvement of local groups greatly increases the likelihood that programs will be sustained over the long run. NGOs, working together in local networks, can ensure that concerns that are relevant to development, environmental quality, public health, literacy, justice, and culture are integrated into public policies and community efforts. National, regional, and international NGOs can spread knowledge and help compensate for differences in the distribution of wealth, resources, and technologies.[17]

As discussed in chapter 3, grass-roots environmental groups have sprouted in many parts of the developing world. Southern NGOs participated in the unofficial, NGO-based conferences at both the 1972 and 1992 UN environmental summits, and several were accredited by the UN to participate in the preparatory meetings leading up to the Earth Summit. One of the most promising developments is the creation of network organizations, which bring together NGOs to exchange information and coordinate activities in the South. One such organization is the Indonesian Environmental Forum—made up of more than 400 smaller environmental organizations—which organizes conservation education programs, sponsors training programs on assessing environmental impacts or environmentally appropriate technology, and provides technical assistance for issues such as fund-raising, lobbying government officials, and bringing lawsuits, including Indonesia's first suit against a corporation for violating environmental laws.[18]

International environmental organizations can play key roles in expanding the capacity of national governments, and their motivation and commitment, to help preserve environmental quality and natural resources. As international agreements are made through the sponsorship of international organizations, then domestic environmental and other groups can help hold accountable national governments for their global commitments. International environmental organizations have been able to increase the level of concern about environmental threats, facilitate the negotiating of global accords, and help build national governmental capacity while still respecting the integrity of nation–states. These regional and international institutions—such as UNEP and commissions and secretariats responsible for implementing regional environmental agreements for acid rain and protection of oceans—create networks that transfer technical and managerial expertise, information, and funds. The value of international environmental institutions lies not in their direct exercise of authority but in their role as catalysts: They link environmental issues with other concerns, create and disseminate scientific information, and facilitate the application of domestic political pressure on governments. They provide forums for negotiations that reduce transaction costs and facilitate decision making, and they monitor compliance and related environmental quality. [19]

David G. Victor and Eugene B. Skolnikoff's study of the implementation and effectiveness of international environmental agreements found that while there has been a high degree of compliance with these agreements, it likely linked to the modest requirements they have imposed on participating nations. Agreements have become more ambitious, largely due to the role of environmental NGOs, and most of the issues on the international environmental agenda are there because of the efforts of NGOs. The challenge of implementation is increasingly difficult as agreements require more from parties. NGOs played an indispensable role in designing and implementing effective environmental agreements, primarily because of the information they provided. This is particularly true of industry groups that participate in developing regulatory programs because the information they bring can be used to devise more realistic and effective programs. Victor and Skolnikoff concluded that "the most successful efforts to engage stakeholders have been those that have altered the incentives for them to participate—for example, by making useful

environmental data available so that public interest groups could participate on an equal footing with private firms and governments."[20] They
also warned that NGOs are rarely in a position to perform independent
oversight of compliance efforts because they usually lack the resources to
obtain the information required. As regulatory regimes begin to embrace
market-based approaches to regulation, such as emissions trading, monitoring and enforcement are critical in ensuring that these innovations
produce real reductions in emissions and protection for resources. Governments need to have realistic expectations of what NGOs can and cannot do in contributing to the enforcement and, ultimately, the effectiveness of global environmental accords. Fostering NGO participation must
be combined with strong incentives such as financial assistance and sanctions such as trade penalties for noncompliance.[21]

The great diversity of environmental NGOs and the energy and dedica-
tion they bring to international negotiations, global consciousness-raising,
and the monitoring of compliance with treaties and agreements is impressive. Their participation in international negotiations has had a major impact on the direction of talks and the agreements fashioned. They have
provided strong voices to hold international institutions accountable for
the environmental impacts of the projects they fund. They have played a
critical role in putting a number of issues on the agenda, such as persistent
organic pollutants. They foster the sharing of information and the empowering of citizens worldwide. They supply the political pressure to link
global obligations with domestic laws and programs. But they are fragmented. There are major divisions between NGOs in the North and South
that parallel the differences between the two regions: They have different
priorities, they struggle with different problems, and they have greatly uneven resources. Some coalitions have formed, and some groups have
broadened their vision to recognize that the interests of rich and poor are
closely intertwined, but as Philip Shabecoff recently wrote, "It would take
a great leap of faith to speak of a coherent global movement."[22]

While NGOs have played and will continue to play a major role in environmental cleanup and preservation efforts, many problems remain.
Some service NGOs have been criticized for failing to reach the poorest in
less developed nations, for becoming as inflexible as traditional governmental bureaucracies, for lacking the necessary technical expertise and organizational skills, for being unable to replicate successful projects, and
for not sustaining their efforts after initial assistance from outside groups
is withdrawn. Long-term planning is often lacking in NGO efforts, largely
because of the instability of funding. There is often little coordination
among NGOs that operate in the same geographic areas because of competition for scarce resources, government support, and local allegiances.
There is usually little coordination with government programs, and some-

times there are conflicts between NGO and government programs. Some NGOs fail to invest in the development of administrative infrastructure and the institutional capacity building necessary for the long-term viability of their efforts. Local grass-roots organizations may find it difficult to expand their activities or influence broader governmental efforts. Technical expertise is often scarce. Efforts that remedy one problem, such as reducing emissions from one local source, may not be able to prevent other problems, such as pollution from other areas.[23]

The global environmental movement faces tremendous challenges. It has become increasingly fragmented (but also energized) by the rise of grass-roots groups. Decentralization or devolution of policy in the United States and the principle of subsidiarity in Europe means that more and more policies are implemented at local levels, compounding the challenge of developing coordinated and comprehensive policy solutions. At the global level, the growth of transnational corporations made it more difficult to devise national policies to preserve environmental quality. The flow of private capital to developing areas is more than 50 times the level of governmental development assistance, and that ratio is increasing, making it more difficult to ensure that economic development is responsive to sustainability norms.[24]

NGOs have been increasingly effective in international forums such as UN conferences as well as in local, community-based efforts. Kumi Naidoo, secretary general and CEO of CIVITUS: World Alliance for Citizen Participation, argues that environmental activists who may not be able to make much progress in changing national policy have had more success in demanding global changes as they have worked in concert with other activists. International NGO networks are increasingly able to check the power of national governments and the wealthy nations in particular. But they have not created a "global civil society": There is no strong global institutional infrastructure in place to support NGOs, and it is not clear how local activists can be connected with global civil society. Nor is civic globalism a substitute for democratic government, but it can contribute to improving and strengthening it.[25]

Sustainability and North–South Politics[26]

The 1992 United Nations Conference on the Environment and Development, or Rio "Earth Summit," was an extraordinarily ambitious undertaking to integrate efforts to protect the planet's ecosystems with the economic development of the poor nations of the world. Its roots were in the 1972 United Nations Conference on the Human Environment in Stockholm, where delegates from 113 countries met in the Stockholm Opera House to examine the ecological health of the planet. The conference produced a declaration of principles to guide a new era in global environmental cooperation and an action plan for forming a new generation of global, national, and nongovernmental institutions dedicated to improving environmental quality. A 1987 report issued by the World Commission on Environment and Development, entitled *Our Common Future*, renewed the promise of the Stockholm meeting, arguing that economic growth and the production and consumption of goods could be done in ways that were consistent with limited global resources. "Sustainable development" promised to improve the quality of life of current residents without compromising the resource base on which future generations will depend.[27] In 1989, the United Nations General Assembly called on leaders from the nations of the earth to meet in three years to explore what was required to shift the planet toward sustainable development.

The Earth Summit was the first global meeting to expressly link the plight of the planet's ecosystems with the poverty that plagues so many of its inhabitants. More than 30,000 government officials, environmental activists, corporate officials, religious leaders, and others gathered in Rio for 12 days of speeches, demonstrations, and negotiations. Delegates from 178 countries gathered, the largest collection of national political leaders ever assembled, to debate and ratify a number of agreements. The earnestness of the negotiations over the conference's documents and treaties was matched by the energy and exuberance of the Global Forum, a festival dedicated to the earth and its citizens, where members of 7,892 NGOs from 167 countries made their own case for protecting the earth's ecosystems. More than 1,000 women held an all-night vigil on the beach near the park in which the Forum was held to focus attention on lack of representation of women in the official delegations. Each day speeches, dances, and concerts took place under a large bronze statue, the Tree of Life, and some 1 million paper leaves had been sent from people throughout the world as an expression of hope and solidarity.[28]

The Rio Declaration, or "Earth Charter," adopted by consensus by the delegates to the conference, is a brief statement calling the world to action and outlining the broad responsibilities of the rich and poor nations. It recognizes a "right to development" for the poorer nations and calls on all nations to commit to assisting with the "developmental and environmental needs of present and future generations." While the Rio Declaration itself is non-binding, it was a symbolic effort by the leaders of most of the nations of the earth to make at least some commitment to sustainable development and environmental preservation.[29] The declaration reaffirmed that states have "the sovereign right to exploit their own resources pursuant to their own environmental and development policies," although they also have the "responsibility to ensure that activities within their jurisdiction or control do not cause damage to the environment of other states or of areas beyond the limits of national jurisdiction."[30] The Earth Summit culminated in two important global agreements: (1) a climate convention aimed at encouraging nations to reduce emissions of greenhouse gases, and (2) a convention aimed at protecting the world's biodiversity by having the wealthy nations fund efforts to protect endangered species and ecosystems by regulating biotechnology, and the formation of a program to protect forests.[31]

Defining Sustainability

The Stockholm and Rio declarations both affirm the power of sovereign states to control the use of their own resources, but nations have also agreed to an ambitious set of principles to govern their behavior, as shown in Table 4-1. In addition to doing no harm to others or to global commons, there are other modest limitations on sovereignty, largely limited to notifying other states of transboundary environmental problems and eliminating and resolving environmental disputes peacefully. A number of principles in the Rio Declaration suggest that states cooperate in protecting the environment, work to eradicate poverty, promote the internalization of environmental costs, require polluters to pay the cost of pollution, assess environmental impacts of actions within their borders, and eliminate unsustainable patterns of production and consumption. But the principles also call for economic growth and deference to global trade agreements. Many principles are vague statements that do not identify the parties responsible for their achievement. Most importantly, only a few of these principles are institutionalized in global environmental accords and there is no effective mechanism to apply them to specific disputes.

The UNCED conference also produced and adopted by consensus Agenda 21, a 500-page document divided into 40 chapters that outlined what nations and international organizations agreed to do to protect the environment and promote sustainable development in the developing world.[32] The various chapters required participating states to make a number of commitments, including:

- Develop ways to achieve sustainable levels of consumption in the industrialized nations.
- Address population growth "where appropriate."
- Consider market-oriented reform of their economies.
- Encourage prices to be set that incorporate and internalize the environmental costs of production and disposal.
- Ensure increased participation by women in development and environmental policies and programs.

TABLE 4-1
Principles of International Environmental Law and Policy:
The Rio Declaration on Environment and Development

Rights of individuals:

- Human beings are entitled to a healthy and productive life in harmony with nature.
- The right to development must be fulfilled so as to equitably meet developmental and environmental needs of present and future generations.
- At the national level, each individual shall have appropriate access to information concerning the environment that is held by public authorities and the opportunity to participate in decision-making processes.
- Women have a vital role in environmental management and development; their full participation is therefore essential.
- The creativity, ideals, and courage of the youth of the world should be mobilized.
- The environment and natural resources of people under oppression shall be protected.

Sovereignty of nation—states:

- States have the sovereign right to exploit their own resources pursuant to their own environmental and developmental policies.

Duty of states to do no harm to others:

- States have the responsibility to ensure that activities within their jurisdiction or control do not cause damage to the environment of other States or of areas beyond the limits of national jurisdiction.
- States should discourage or prevent the relocation and transfer to other States of any activities and substances that cause severe environmental degradation.
- States shall immediately notify other States of any natural disasters or other emergencies that are likely to produce sudden harmful effects on the environment of those States.
- States shall provide prior and timely notification and relevant information to potentially affected States that may have a significant adverse transboundary environmental effect.

(continued)

- Support the creation of a new agency, the UN Commission on Sustainable Development, to collect data on environmental and development activities and monitor implementation of the provisions of Agenda 21 by participating states through "national action plans."
- Facilitate the transfer of technologies from the developed to the developing world.
- Take actions to maintain or increase biodiversity.
- Eliminate subsidies for harvesting of natural resources that "do not conform with sustainable development objectives."

TABLE 4-1 *(continued)*

Collective duty of states:

- States shall cooperate in the essential task of eradicating poverty.
- States should reduce and eliminate unsustainable patterns of production and consumption.
- States shall facilitate and encourage public awareness and participation.
- States shall enact effective environmental legislation.
- States should promote a supportive and open international economic system that would lead to economic growth and sustainable development to better address the problems of environmental degradation; unilateral actions to deal with environmental challenges outside the jurisdiction of the importing country should be avoided.
- States shall develop national law regarding liability and compensation for the victims of pollution and other environmental damage.
- The precautionary approach shall be widely applied; where there are threats of serious or irreversible damage, lack of full scientific certainty shall not be used as a reason for postponing cost-effective measures.
- States should recognize and duly support [the] identity, culture, and interests [of indigenous peoples and their communities] and enable their effective participation in the achievement of sustainable development.
- National authorities should endeavor to promote the internalization of costs and the use of economic instruments, taking into account the approach that the polluter should bear the cost of pollution.
- Environmental impact assessment shall be undertaken for proposed activities that are likely to have a significant adverse impact on the environment.
- States shall respect international law providing protection for the environment in times of armed conflict.
- States shall resolve all their environmental disputes peacefully.
- States shall cooperate in good faith and in a spirit of partnership.

General values:

- Peace, development, and environmental protection are interdependent and indivisible.

Source: The text of the declaration is reprinted in David Hunter, James Salzman, and Durwood Zaelke, *International Environmental Law and Policy* (New York: Foundation Press, 1998): 307–08.

- Expand their institutional capacity to encourage sustainable development.
- Increase access to natural resources by indigenous peoples and expand agricultural training and assistance in rural areas.
- Strengthen governmental capacity to assess forest resources.
- Support completion of studies of ocean disposal of radioactive wastes.
- Support a ban on the export of hazardous wastes to countries that do not have the technological capacity to manage them.

- Encourage the formulation of new regional agreements to protect the marine environment.
- Participate fully in the UN program of "prior informed consent" for international shipments of toxic chemicals.[33]

While Agenda 21 did not establish priorities or provide funds (its estimated cost was $125 billion) and is not legally binding, it represents a long list of what delegates considered the most pressing global problems.[34] The Earth Summit culminated in two global conventions and two other agreements: a climate convention aimed at encouraging nations to reduce emissions of greenhouse gases; a convention aimed at protecting the world's biodiversity by having the wealthy nations fund efforts to protect endangered species and ecosystems and by regulating biotechnology; an agreement to limit deforestation and logging in tropical forests; and an agreement by the wealthy nations to provide $2 billion in additional assistance to the poorer nations. Despite the expansive agenda, however, the Earth Summit failed to address a number of major issues. Little discussion focused on direct efforts to address global hunger, malnutrition, poor health, poverty, drought, and agricultural problems, for example.[35]

The Earth Summit and Agenda 21 in particular reflected the view that achieving the global agenda of environmental sustainability requires the participation of the developing countries as well as that of the industrialized nations, and that the North must play a major role in funding investments in sustainable development. That view is based on at least three major arguments that are central to understanding and assessing Agenda 21 and the Earth Summit itself. First, the countries of the South play a key role in accomplishing the goals of these and other global environmental accords, such as the Montreal Protocol to protect the stratospheric ozone layer. They are a growing source of greenhouse gas and ozone-layer-depleting emissions, and their forests play an important role in absorbing carbon dioxide from the atmosphere.[36] Their lands are also home to much of the world's biodiversity.[37] Second, the North has a moral obligation to provide financial and technical assistance to the South: The North is the primary source of greenhouse and ozone-threatening gases but also has the resources to mitigate many of the effects of changes to the atmosphere; the South is less responsible for the problem but much more likely to suffer the adverse consequences because its residents lack the resources to mitigate the effects.[38] Industrial nations control the technology that can solve the problem, but cooperation from the developing countries is essential. Third, the interests of the North largely dominate the global environmental protection and economic development agendas; Rio and subsequent meetings have recognized that more of the priorities of the South might be pursued if they are linked to the interests of the North.[39]

Agenda 21 created an expectation of North–South partnership that is critical to the achievement of protecting the global environment and minimizing the environmental impact of economic growth. A key question for both the North and the South is whether that partnership has been firmly established. In 1992, the UN General Assembly endorsed Agenda 21 and promised to convene a special session after five years to review progress. In June 1997, the UN General Assembly Special Session to Review Implementation of Agenda 21 (UNGASS) heard assessments of the progress made toward Agenda 21 by 197 heads of state, ministers, and UN representatives. The General Assembly adopted a "Programme for the Further Implementation of Agenda 21" that began with an assessment of progress made since Rio and painted a pessimistic picture of the lack of progress in achieving the agenda's goals. Globalization has accelerated and foreign direct investment and world trade have increased in a limited number of developing countries, but the impact has been uneven, and many areas continue to be plagued by foreign debt and receive little assistance. Poverty has prevented them from participating in and benefiting from the global economy and require assistance to help them meet basic needs. The total number of poor people in the world has increased since the Rio meeting and the gap between the wealthy and poor countries "has grown rapidly in recent years."[40] While some countries have reduced emissions of pollutants and resource use, and population growth rates have declined in most areas, overall, global environmental conditions have worsened and "significant environmental problems remain deeply embedded in the socioeconomic fabric of countries in all regions." Persistent poverty continues to contribute to ecological decline and threats to fragile ecosystems. Foreign debt remains in many developing countries "a major constraint on achieving sustainable development."[41] In sum, the state of the global environment "has continued to deteriorate . . . and significant problems remain deeply embedded in the socioeconomic fabric of countries in all regions. Overall trends remain unsustainable. As a result, increasing levels of pollution threaten to exceed the capacity of the global environment to absorb them, increasing the potential obstacles to economic and social development in developing countries."[42]

The UNGASS outlined a number of issues requiring urgent attention in order to implement Agenda 21 and urged that "international cooperation be reactivated and intensified" and the "invigoration of a genuine new global partnership, taking into account the special needs and priorities of developing countries."[43] The list of issues to be addressed is daunting. It urged nations to integrate economic, social, and environmental objectives in national policies; foster a dynamic economy "favorable to all countries"; eradicate poverty and improve access to social services; change unsustainable consumption and production patterns; make trade and the environment "mutually supportive"; further promote the decline in population growth rates; enable all people to "achieve a higher level of health and well-being"; and improve living conditions throughout the world.[44] It reaffirmed the goal of official development assistance, encouraged increased private investment and foreign-debt reduction in developing countries, called for more transparency of subsidies, called for increased transfer of environmentally sound technologies to developing countries, and other efforts to build their capacity for effective policy making.[45] UNGASS agreed to again review progress in the implementation of Agenda 21 in the year 2002.[46]

One indicator of the very limited success of Agenda 21 in reshaping our discourse of economic growth and environmental preservation is a comparison of the 1997 UNGASS with the 1992 Earth Summit. The problems confronting the delegates to the 1992 Rio conference largely resurfaced in the 1997 meeting. There was still little discussion in 1997 of regulating private capital flows, corporate behavior, and the impact of trade on environmental quality. On the positive side, there was increasing discussion and monitoring of concrete indicators of reproductive health care and consumption and production patterns. The meeting was a frank assessment of the lack of progress rather than an attempt to "paper over the cracks in the celebrated 'global partnership' for sustainable development and pretend that things are better than they are."[47] Nevertheless, the question of funding for the implementation of Agenda 21 in the developing countries seemed as vexing in 1997 as it was five years earlier. The UN meeting reminded global leaders of the idea of sustainable development but seemed to lack any ability to identify strategic plans or generate commitments to specific actions. UN documents dutifully cataloged the many global environmental challenges but failed to take on the dominant force in economic activity and development—international trade and private investment decisions—and was unable to focus attention on a limited set of actions that deserve priority or even impose some direction to and coordination of the activities that are undertaken under the auspices of the United Nations. Most troubling is the lack of direction for the future: The "question dominating debate at UNGASS," according to one observer, was "where to go from here?"[48]

Assessments of the success of Agenda 21 ultimately depend on how it is understood. From one perspective, it is a catalog of policies that countries can embrace as they seek to become more sustainable. Agenda 21 has clearly triggered some policy innovations in some nations and has served as a vehicle for sharing information and ideas. It can be judged more or less successful depending on the extent to which more and more nations, over time, choose to implement more and more of the policy prescriptions it offers, and the extent to which economic, political, and social goals underlying the policies are achieved. A great deal of activity in these areas has occurred, although it is difficult to know what can and cannot be attributed to Agenda 21. Within the first two years of UNCED, 103 of the 178 nations attending the Rio meeting had established national sustainable development commissions. Many countries reported progress in reducing lead exposures and cleaning up freshwater resources.[49] Agenda 21 will likely become increasingly important in the future as a source of ideas for sustainable development.

From another view, Agenda 21 represents a national commitment to a new set of policies that domestic political groups can use to pressure their governments. The governments that signed Agenda 21 but have failed to implement it can be aggressively criticized by environmental and other groups for failing to keep their pledges. Governments can be nudged and urged from within to make sustainable development a national policy, and Agenda 21 can be a useful vehicle for drawing attention to commitments and suggesting concrete steps.

Perhaps most importantly, Agenda 21 can be viewed as an attempt to change the terms of discourse surrounding economic growth. The key here is whether Agenda 21 has changed the global economic and environmental protection agenda—whether it has reshaped the way we think about economic growth, international trade, and international relations. From this perspective, Agenda 21 has not produced a major commitment to rethinking our approaches to development and to the globalization of the world's economy. It has not become a central idea in international trade agreements and the operation of the World Trade Organization. It was not a major factor in shaping negotiations over the Multilateral Investment Agreement facilitating the flow of capital worldwide.

One of the primary challenges that continues to plague efforts to implement Agenda 21 is the lack of coordination among international agencies that continue to pursue their own agendas and resist efforts to reshape their work. The issues raised in Agenda 21 and sustainable development require a complicated balancing of economic, environmental, and social goals, making difficult tradeoffs, and coordinating disparate efforts. As one study concluded, this requires a "structure which is capable of making complex assessments and reaching carefully calibrated judgments in a manner which is open and accountable. No UN agency meets these criteria."[50] Agenda 21 emphasized the interrelationship between reducing poverty and protecting environmental quality. Reducing poverty is central to the idea of sustainable development. But the implementation of Agenda 21 has focused more on environmental issues than on poverty reduction. The UN Commission on Sustainable Development, the agency responsible for monitoring progress in implementing Agenda 21, for example, has "not made poverty a theme of its discussions."[51] The Global Environmental Facility (GEF) has been the primary mechanism for providing additional funding for Agenda 21 but has not emphasized the connection between environment and poverty. The UN Commission on Social Development, created to monitor implementation of the agreement signed in the 1995 World Summit for Social Development, has not focused on environmental quality. As one UN Development Program (UNDP) report put it, "In the five years since UNCED, the need to contribute to poverty reduction while attempting to apply Agenda 21 has been ignored."[52] The same UN department that provided secretariat services for the Commission on Sustainable Development, for example, also provided it for the 1995 World Summit for Social Development, but the summit made virtually no effort to pursue the agenda of sustainable development. Building institutional capacity is an essential element in pursuing the provisions of Agenda 21, but that task seems to overwhelm the UNEP and other UN and global institutions.[53]

The most troubling conclusion to be drawn from a brief review of the five years since signing Agenda 21 is the failure to establish a new regime of international development—"persistent and connected sets of rules and practices that prescribe behavioral roles, constrain activity, and shape expectations" and bureaucratic institutions created to formulate and implement policies.[54] Relatively little has changed during the five years in the structure and capacity of the global community to organize for sustainable development. A great number of programs are in place but with little coordination, and there does not appear to be the capacity to bring about more fundamental change in economic activity. Trade continues to dominate the global agenda. When attention is briefly directed toward environmental issues like climate change, there is little effort to explore the interaction of free trade and investment agreements with the imperatives of sustainable development.

Financing Sustainable Development

Multilateral institutions, bilateral assistance, and the efforts of national governments, NGOs, and industries have contributed to debt relief and institutional capacity building in the South. The idea of sustainable development has become a part of economic planning in a few nations, and the principles of Agenda 21 are being pursued through local sustainable development programs. Some businesses have become greener. New institutions have been created and public–private collaboration has increased.[55] Progress has been made in implementing the two treaties signed in Rio, particularly the Climate Change agreement, which was strengthened considerably in December 1997 when the industrialized countries agreed to reduce their emissions of six greenhouse gases by an average of 5 percent below 1990 levels during the years 2008–2012.[56]

However, the progress that has been made is dwarfed by the remaining tasks. The goodwill and cooperation that were generated during the 1992 Earth Summit have already dissipated and may deteriorate further without a renewed commitment on the part of the North to work with the South in providing an alternative to traditional economic development. There has been relatively little debate over the idea of sustainable development itself, for example, and whether it is even possible. Skeptics argue that sustainable development is a thinly veiled attempt to justify business as usual—that businesses promise to make minor accommodations to the idea of environmental sustainability while continuing to pursue economic growth. From this view, economic growth is simply not possible because humans have already exceeded the carrying capacity of the planet, and future generations are already destined to have a lower quality of life. Even if this pessimistic view of sustainable development is discarded, it still requires a major shift in effort to reduce the consumption and waste of the developed world and increase economic growth without increasing pollution or resource degradation in the developing countries, and there has been little movement toward that goal during the past five years. It is difficult to envision how the political will for such a shift in priorities could be fostered. There has been little discussion of sustainable development or more precise efforts such as limits on consumption and production, investment in conservation and efficiency, or how to integrate the poor into the global economy.

The argument for providing financial assistance to developing countries seems compelling but has become quite complicated. Since newer technologies are generally less polluting, economic prosperity can also reduce environmental degradation. Increased activity, however, also increases emissions and resource consumption.[57] Nevertheless, providing such assistance is a primary element of the deal struck by the developing and developed countries to work together to reduce global environmental threats. The developing countries require massive amounts of capital to upgrade their industrial infrastructure, but their current external debt is a major barrier.[58] While the developing nations have sought new funds to help them comply with the Rio conventions, the net flow of resources has been from the developing countries to the industrialized nations as a result of large loans granted to the developing nations during the 1970s and early 1980s.[59] Until 1983, the net flow of funds (in assistance and loans) from the North to the South averaged about $40 billion a year. The net flow reversed direction in 1983, and the poorer countries throughout the balance of that decade sent more than $20 billion more per year to the wealthy nations than they received in new assistance.[60] The developing countries owe some $1.8 trillion dollars to banks and international lending institutions, and the debt–GNP ratio—the dollar value of outstanding medium- and long-term debt as a percentage of gross national product—is nearly 40 percent in the developing world, and as high as 80 percent in the poorest African nations.[61]

In 1996, the World Bank and the International Monetary Fund (IMF) proposed a plan to reduce the debt of 20 of the world's poorer and more indebted nations. These countries would first undergo a three-year economic reform program outlined by the World Bank and the IMF, and would then be eligible for forgiveness of up to two-thirds of the debt they owe to the major industrialized nations.[62] After another three years, up to 90 percent of their debt could be forgiven: the World Bank would pay off some of the debts owed to multilateral lending institutions, and the IMF would lend money at a low interest rate ($\frac{1}{2}$ of 1 percent) to the countries to pay off some of their debt.[63] The debt owed by the developing countries would eventually be no greater than 350 percent of their annual export earnings.[64] This proposal, approved by the Group of Seven in September 1996, marks the first time that debts to international lending agencies have been forgiven.[65] Critics argue, however, that the six-year plan will take too long to reduce the crushing burden of debt and does not reach enough needy countries.[66]

One of the most important global agencies involved in environmental protection projects is the World Bank. The 1944 Bretton Woods conference on the global financial system resulted in the creation of the World Bank and the IMF to help finance the reconstruction of Europe that was devastated by World War II and to provide a mechanism for promoting international trade. They both come under the broad UN umbrella because they have established formal, legal relationships with UN agencies, but they are otherwise autonomous bodies. These institutions are dominated by the more developed nations, which contribute funds and have votes in proportion to their contribution. The World Bank is the largest source of funds for development projects. Its projects have been severely criticized as ecological disasters, causing pollution, deforestation, export agriculture rather than domestic food production, and forced resettlement of indigenous peoples.[67] The IMF has imposed economic adjustment programs on less-developed countries as a condition for receiving international financial assistance. These required "adjustments" include decontrol of exchange rates and currency, deregulation of foreign direct investment in less-developed countries, and trade liberalization. Unsustainable harvesting of natural resources, increased pollution, and social disruption have also been a consequence of IMF programs.[68]

In response to criticism, including a major campaign by environmentalists and advocates of the poor to reform its lending policies, the World Bank's procedures began to shift. In the first four years after Rio (FY 1993–1996), the World Bank lent $87 billion; $7.2 billion or 8 percent of the spending was dedicated to environmental projects.[69] The most common type of project is one that seeks to build the institutional capacity of developing countries. The purpose of such projects is to assist the developing countries in monitoring environmental conditions and problems; engaging in resource planning and management; conducting research; and implementing general environmental regulatory and administrative programs as well as those that deal with the particular problems of air and water pollution, hazardous and solid waste, and other threats to public health and natural resources.[70] These efforts at institution-building are often combined with specific projects aimed at addressing particular environmental problems, but the investments in institutional infrastructure go beyond the resolution of these immediate concerns.[71] Approximately one-fourth of the projects are located in Brazil, China, and India,[72] and of course, priorities differ across the various regions. In Africa and the Latin American and Caribbean areas, the typical project seeks to develop the natural resource management capabilities of governments. In Eastern Europe and Central Asia, projects are primarily aimed at improving water quality and energy efficiency. In South Asia, the focus is on protecting forests.[73]

Technology transfer programs promise to play a key role in integrating the environment and development agendas. Energy efficiency is one of the more important investments developing countries can make,[74] but they will need to invest $70 billion a year over the next several years, and twice that amount in the first years of the twenty-first century to meet growing energy demands. This investment represents approximately one-fourth of all the money targeted for their capital investments, thus reducing the resources available for other pressing needs.[75] As discussed in the next chapter, some of the industrial nations favor joint implementation—agreements between the developing and developed countries to transfer technologies in exchange for claiming credits for reducing greenhouse gas emissions—because such promises would favor the most cost-effective solutions for reducing the threat of global climate change.[76]

The World Bank's investments in building the institutional capacity of governments promise to have long-term benefits because they give those countries the tools to effectively design and implement programs that will help them meet international obligations and ensure economic activity is environmentally sustainable. Unfortunately, these efforts face tremendous barriers.[77] Many developing countries lack the governmental, regulatory infrastructure to develop effective regulatory programs, a tradition and culture of compliance with regulatory requirements, as well as the necessary scientific infrastructure to examine the problems they confront. Developing nations must address such issues as "rapid population growth, corruption, inadequate technical and managerial standards of competence, extreme income disparities, and 'unrealistic' official rates of exchange."[78] The World Bank and GEF projects that are aimed at reinforcing institutional capacity for environmental protection projects are important responses to these problems in the South, but the level of funding provided is not sufficient to help build effective governing institutions. Furthermore, even if spending increases, the political instability that has engulfed so many areas prevents progress in environmental protection and development. Wars and other forms of military activity also pose tremendous environmental challenges. Natural disasters further hinder effective programs."[79]

A promising institutional development was the establishment of the Global Environmental Facility, created to channel funds to the developing countries to help them implement programs to reduce pressure on global ecosystems.[80] As part of the 1990 London amendments to the Montreal Protocol, the industrialized countries agreed to pay developing countries' "incremental" costs of compliance with the protocol. These costs are defined as the expenses for the development of alternatives to ozone-depleting substances (ODS) beyond what these countries would otherwise spend to modernize their economies.[81] A $240 million Interim Multilateral Fund was created for these costs. The World Bank administers the trust fund; UNEP provides technical and scientific assistance in identifying and selecting projects, relying on an international Scientific and Technical Advisory Panel; and the UNDP coordinates the financing and managing of technical assistance and pre-project preparations.[82] In 1992, the parties agreed to make the Montreal Multilateral Fund permanent.[83] Between 1990 and 1996, the fund disbursed $540 million to 99 countries for some 1,300 projects.[84]

Grants typically go to private-sector parties for projects like recycling of CFCs and conversion to non-ODS chemicals. These projects are eventually expected to reduce by one-third the contribution of the South to ozone depletion. UNEP also provides information on new technologies and processes to reduce ODS emissions, and some companies have voluntarily shared such technologies with the developing world.[85] The GEF was expanded to fund projects to achieve the goals of the climate change and biodiversity conventions. Managing agencies are charged with ensuring that grants enhance long-term, sustainable development. Projects include a $4.8 million effort to monitor greenhouse gas emission, $10 million for biodiversity protection in East Africa, and $7 million for a biomass gasification project in Brazil. These funds are earmarked for additional programs; they are not to replace existing development funds. The pilot phase of the GEF was completed in March 1995.[86]

The United States and other wealthy nations pledged $2 billion to the GEF in 1994 for a three-year period, and some donors have given additional funds to co-finance GEF projects.[87] In exchange for the new round of financial support, the 80 countries participating in the fund agreed on a restructuring of the governing process: Actions by the governing council now require support from 60 percent of the members who must also have contributed at least 60 percent of the funds.[88] Expenditures are still controlled by the secretariat (comprised of World Bank and UN agency bureaucrats), but any four members of the council can stop projects they find inappropriate and refer them to the entire council for review.[89] In December 1999, the parties of the Montreal Protocol agreed to spend $440 million between 2000 and 2002 for a new round of projects to convert refrigerators, air conditioners, and other consumer goods and industrial processes in developing nations from halons and CFCs. By 2000, the multilateral fund had provided some $1 billion in aid to 110 countries since 1991.[90]

The GEF is an important innovation, but there have been problems.[91] Both the UNCED Climate Change and Biodiversity conventions require that funding mechanisms be accountable to all parties and include an equitable and balanced system of representation and governance. Unfortunately, this has not been enough to ensure that funded projects address the environment and development priorities of the developing world.[92] One study of the GEF argued that the fund generated widespread support initially because there was a strong commitment to the general idea of assisting the developing countries. That consensus collapsed into conflict, however, when specific decisions regarding implementation were made.[93] As a result, during the pilot phase, the GEF failed to have an impact on the environmental policies of the developing countries.[94] The Montreal Protocol Multilateral Fund has operated more smoothly, but project implementation has been slow, as has been progress in reducing emissions in the developing countries.[95] The GEF projects play a key role in ecologically sustainable development, but its funding is miniscule in light of other spending, such as private investments in the developing countries.

The importance of the Rio conference lies in the idea that the future of all of us, rich and poor, is bound together. But in the five years since Rio, the consensus over that idea seems to have come unraveled. The assistance promised by the developing countries has not materialized. The lack of progress in reducing the absolute poverty that afflicts so many, and global inequality in general, is less likely to be linked to international environmental goals than was true five or six years ago. The debate over strengthening the Climate Change Convention at the end of the 1990s showed a yawning gap between the poorer nations to modernize in environmentally sustainable ways, and the developing countries refuse to commit to restraints on their economic growth until the wealthy nations keep their promises.[96] The leaders of the developed world seem unwilling and unable to re-create the consensus that linked the environment and development in Rio. Unless they provide that kind of leadership and keep their commitments that were central to that consensus, future agreements will be all the more difficult to produce, and the goals of the agreements already in place will not be realized.

Agenda 21 and other agreements represent important statements concerning emerging global expectations. Part of their strength comes from the way they represent cooperative efforts on the part of participating countries: that it is in everyone's interest to protect the global environment and promote environmentally sustainable economic growth. But the agreements in place are built on the expectation that the wealthy world will provide major new sources of funding to accomplish these goals, and that expectation has not been realized. Nevertheless, these agreements have overcome significant obstacles. The tension between the developing and developed nations is considerable—rooted in the history of colonialism, economic exploitation, military adventurism, nationalism, and other factors. The tension has become more pronounced as the debate over addressing global environmental problems has evolved during the past two decades. Those in the South fear that their aspirations of economic growth, reduced poverty and starvation, and improved health and education will now be sacrificed in the name of environmental preservation. They worry that global efforts fashioned by wealthy nations will prevent them from harvesting their natural resources and expanding their industrial base. They believe that their dreams of an improved life will give way to a global effort to reverse the excesses of the wealthy nations that have precipitated environmental threats. The agreements in place are not enough to secure our environmental future, and new agreements will need to be negotiated for decades into the future. If commitments already made are not kept, future agreements will be all the more difficult to produce, and the goals of the agreements in place will not be realized. The futures of all the planet's residents, rich and poor, are inextricably intertwined.

Economic Globalization and Environmentalism

One of the most important indicators of the strength of environmental concerns is the extent to which they shape international trade. Globalization—the spread of international commerce, the intertwining of national economies, and the reduction of trade barriers—is for many environmentalists a threat to environmental quality. Some level of globalization is inevitable as technology progresses and communications and transportation systems develop. But it is also a result of policies aimed at lowering trade barriers and other agreements.[97] Trade agreements have come to be important targets for environmentalists who fear the ecological consequences of increased trade.

The General Agreement on Tariffs and Trade (GATT) was one of the global economic institutions created after World War II. GATT agreements to reduce trade barriers among member states have been negotiated since the 1940s. A central provision of GATT is the Most Favored Nation obligation, which prohibits discrimination in favor of or against the imports of member nations. Benefits accorded one member must be extended to all. Members also agree to not discriminate between imported and domestically produced "like products," and to not place quantitative restrictions on exported and imported products. The most recent negotiations, called the Uruguay Round, which were completed in 1993, called for the creation of a new legal structure to implement trade agreements. In 1995, the World Trade Organization (WTO) was created to provide a forum for national trade ministers to negotiate trade agreements and for the resolution of disputes as the agreements are implemented.

Much of the environment-related trade disputes focus on the definition of "like products." Products that are similar in appearance but are produced by different processes that may be environmentally dangerous, for example, are considered like products. Developing countries have insisted on such an interpretation because their generally lower environmental standards allow them to be more competitive in global markets. But environmental groups have argued that this discourages countries from fostering production processes that internalize environmental costs and promote ecologically sustainable industry. In a celebrated trade dispute between Mexico and the United States, the WTO ruled that the United States could not discriminate against Mexican tuna that had been caught using purse seine nets that incidentally kill dolphins, because the tuna caught by Mexican fishers was identical to the tuna caught by U.S. companies that did not harm dolphins.[98] GATT provides that parties are free to adopt measures "necessary to protect human, animal, or plant life or health" or "relating to the conservation of exhaustible natural resources" as long as such measures are made "in conjunction with restrictions on domestic production or consumption." The WTO panel found that the United States could not impose restrictive measures on trade to protect environmental conditions beyond its boundaries.[99]

Critics point to cases such as the tuna–dolphin dispute as evidence that environmental values are sacrificed in trade agreements. They argue that the WTO is preventing the United States from applying conservation laws in order to prevent import of products inconsistent with these laws, only to have the exporting country successfully challenge the U.S. actions as an impermissible restraint of trade. Free-trade agreements, they fear, limit

the ability of the United States and other nations to set more stringent environmental standards than others and limit their ability to devise their
own approach to environmental protection.[100]

Globalization of markets and trade also represents a broader environmental threat. Less developed countries are encouraged to sell off at unsustainable rates their natural resources in order to generate revenues for
imports and payments to meet debt obligations. Globalization may mean
that transnational or foreign-owned companies determine how production takes place, and these absentee owners may be less sensitive to local
environmental conditions and less responsive to local environmental regulations. Even more broadly for the environmental agenda, free trade can
overwhelm communities and cultural practices. It may not make everyone better off, although it may increase consumption as indigenous communities may give up much of their autonomy. And free trade may
thwart democratization, as decisions affecting the use of resources and
production of goods and services are made increasingly outside the community. WTO deliberations are not open to the public, and private individuals and groups have no standing to challenges rules and decisions.
While globalization empowers people and helps them get access to more
goods, services, and information—and the money to buy them—personal
freedom may be enhanced but other values may be constrained. Free
trade clearly increases the movement of goods, services, capital, labor,
and information across borders in ways that are increasingly difficult for
domestic governments to control.

Defenders of free trade argue that the WTO is no threat to the environment and that freer trade does reduce poverty and promote democracy.
The WTO writes rules by consensus, so any party can block adoption of
new rules. WTO rules have no domestic force but must be implemented
through national legislation. If a country loses a dispute over trade and
the environment, it can retain its domestic laws and accept unilateral
trade sanctions from other nations.[101] Cases in which the United States has
lost disputes in the WTO, defenders believe, pose no environmental
threat. In the case of U.S. regulation of shrimp harvesting to protect sea
turtles, for example, the WTO appellate body did not reject the U.S. environmental law in dispute but only its selective enforcement against four
countries that were given only four months to meet the standards, while
other countries were given three years,[102] and the rule's application to
fishers who did not export their catch to the United States.[103] Proponents
emphasize the broader argument that free trade generates wealth and reduces poverty; as the wealth of countries increases and as the income of
people rises, they will have more to spend on environmental protection
and will face fewer pressures to consume resources unsustainably. They
also argue that environmentalists cannot have it both ways, they cannot

condemn the WTO as a threat to national sovereignty and at the same time embrace global environmental accords that also place limits on states' prerogatives.[104]

Trade agreements interact in an important fashion with competing definitions of sustainability. Sustainable development calls for global trade accords that take environment into account—that ensure economic goals will not be pursued without considering their impact on environmental values. The problem here is that this conception of sustainability provides no clear guidelines for dealing with conflicts. The most likely approach is to analyze the costs and benefits of alternatives, and choose options where the economic benefits outweigh the environmental costs; conversely, if some options result in more environmental damage than the costs generated, they should be rejected. But environmental values are difficult to quantify and monetize, and while some promising work is being done to develop such economic measures, there is still great fear that they will be undervalued. In contrast, ecological sustainability places environmental values above economic ones; economic activities are allowed only if their environmental impacts are acceptable. That general principle is also rather vague and requires further elaboration. But cost–benefit analysis is less helpful here; the test is whether the options will lead to sustainability or not. Here, sustainability includes biodiversity, the health of ecosystems, human health, and other related values. There may be room for some balancing; for example, an option that produces a great deal of economic benefit and reduces biodiversity by an insignificant amount might be acceptable under this thick notion of sustainability, but we are still faced with the task of giving more precise meaning to terms like significant and insignificant.

The debate between proponents and opponents of free trade and the WTO cannot be addressed in any depth here. It may be that the freer the trade and the more wealth that is generated, the greater the environmental protection we will be able to buy. It may be possible to have a free-trade-enforcing WTO with lots of environmental safeguards and provisions. Trade sanctions could even be used to enforce environmental treaties. But it is clear that strong sustainability is not likely to be the agenda of the WTO.

As the disruption of the Seattle trade talks in December 1999 demonstrated, there is a growing belief that the WTO is unaccountable to broader political forces and dominated by the agenda of multinationals who simply want to reduce barriers to moving capital and resources throughout the world as they search for profits. Many in the developing world see the agenda of the WTO dominated by U.S. businesses and those in other wealthy countries that are trying to expand their exports. They point to the unwillingness of the WTO to take on issues that would benefit the developing nations, such as antidumping laws, and see labor protests against the WTO and efforts to respond as attempts to insulate the wealthy world from poorer countries' exports.[105] And many developing-country trade ministers fear that attempts to impose environmental limits on trade are nothing more than barriers to importing their products into the United States.[106]

Environmental and labor groups clearly had some momentum at the beginning of the twenty-first century. They generated enough opposition to the proposed Multilateral Agreement on Investment—proposed by multinationals to facilitate the flow of capital throughout the world—that those talks were suspended. In the United States, they convinced Congress to deny presidential power to put trade agreements on a fast track that would allow minimal *congressional intervention, and promise to make ratification* of the Clinton administration's proposal to admit China to the WTO at least very controversial. Defenders of the WTO argue that global environmental accords (and others such as human rights) undermine national sovereignty and autonomy and limit the ability of national policy makers to control what goes on within their country and what crosses their borders. Once we accept global environmental accords, there is no principled argument against other kinds of international agreements based on the idea of sovereignty. Here is how one optimist nicely summarized the agenda that he believes everyone should be able to embrace:

> In a rational world, it would be clear to all that the freeing up of markets around the world is the most powerful engine of economic growth and progress. CEOs would receive full credit for creating trade, investment, and jobs around the world. They would be praised for helping people from Boston to Beijing to lead better and freer lives. Advocacy groups, for their part, would be applauded for pointing to serious abuses of corporate employment practices and calling attention to egregious environmental conditions. Global capitalism would evolve with companies and public-interest groups working cooperatively, united in their conviction that market-oriented growth is the precondition for better lives everywhere.[107]

The policy implications that arise from different versions of sustainability are significant. For example, the agenda for free trade, from the perspective of minimal sustainability, might require trade agreements that expressly provide that domestic environmental laws and regulations are not violations of free-trade agreements unless applied in a discriminatory manner, (such as having different standards for imported versus domestically produced goods); that workers who lose their jobs as a result of trade agreements could apply for funds for retraining and other support; and that trade sanctions be used to enforce environmental treaties. Sustainability here requires a balancing of economic and environmental policy goals and some reciprocity in pursuing different objectives. There is no agreement among advocates of free trade for these views. President Clinton, for example, reportedly stunned delegates at the December 1999 WTO Seattle Summit when he suggested that the WTO should use trade sanctions to enforce core labor rights. One delegate responded that, "if you start using trade as a lever to implement non-trade related issues, that will be the end of the multilateral trading system, maybe not this year, but in 10 to 15 years."[108]

Using trade sanctions to enforce environmental agreements would similarly likely be rejected in the United States. House Ways and Means Committee Chair Bill Archer (R–Texas) has warned that, "if we expend our energies on labor and the environment, we may lose opportunities for open market."[109] Or as a Cato Institute analysis put it, "The new round of [trade] talks should avoid entirely competition policy and the enforcement of environmental and labor standards, which could threaten to overwhelm the WTO administratively while broadening the scope for sanctions."[110] The ability of demonstrators to disrupt the meeting is one sign of the strength of environmental and labor coalitions, but the collapse of the Seattle talks was in part a reflection of widespread opposition among trade ministers to expanding the trade agenda to include labor and environmental issues. It may be that the talks will not be resumed until there is some progress in addressing broader issues. Democrats, such as Robert Matsui of California, argued that, "the trade consensus is not unraveling, but there are a lot of frayed ends. The issues of labor and environment have to be addressed in order to get a trade consensus."[111] Both major party presidential candidates in 2000 voiced strong support for more open trade: A key indicator of the prospects for environmental and labor demands being able to shape trade policy will be the composition of the new Congress elected in November 2000.

From the perspective of ecological sustainability, the WTO is simply not the primary global vehicle for advancing sustainable development. The WTO's highest-level decision-making body is the ministerial conference, a meeting every two years of the trade ministers of member countries. The General Council administers the trade agreements negotiated by the conference and makes interim decisions. It includes a Trade Policy Review Body, to review the trade policy of members, and a Dispute Settlement Body. The General Council has established a set of councils to determine policy in specific areas, such as trade in goods, trade in services, and trade-related aspects of intellectual property. Finally, there are committees on trade and environment, trade and development, and working groups on issues like trade and investment and transparency in government procurement.[112] Environmental concerns are clearly peripheral. The Clinton administration proposed, in preparation for the Seattle Summit, to request a working group on labor issues, to press for the elimination of trade barriers to environmentally friendly goods and services, that federal agencies review the environmental effects of WTO agreements, and reforms to make WTO decision making more transparent.[113] In November 1999, the administration issued an executive order requiring analyses of the environmental impacts of trade agreements that could have "significant, reasonably foreseeable environmental effects."[114]

Environmentalists, however, demand much more, including a requirement that the WTO consider assessing the environmental impacts of trade agreements and that it defer to the provisions of all international environmental agreements and to international bodies with ecological expertise. While some environmentalists supported NAFTA, hoping that free trade would improve environmental regulation in Mexico and would help nudge trade policy toward more consideration of Green concerns, they have largely been disappointed by subsequent events. "Unfortunately," said one Natural Resources Defense Council staff member, "the NAFTA package was the high-water mark for environmental reform of trade, rather than the foundation."[115]

The World Trade Organization is the dominant institution in international affairs, and its lack of a formal relationship or even an informal working relationship with UN bodies such as the United Nations Environment Program is evidence of the dominance of open trade as its singular objective. The debate is not over whether the WTO should be the dominant institutional mechanism for managing international interactions, but whether or how the WTO can be broadened to provide a forum for environmental concerns as well. The prospects for forums that advocate for a strong sense of sustainability appear to be weaker now than they were at the 1992 Earth Summit. In many ways, the WTO is the kind of global institution environmentalists want: a body with some authority to get nations to commit to a set of standards that provide for environmental quality for all the world. However, determining the kind of authority that global institutions should possess is a complicated task. Greens have favored the right of countries to set their own standards for genetically altered foods, for example, and also favor agreements such as the Kyoto Protocol, which would require that national policies conform with international norms. The key value here is not preserving or weakening sovereignty but to ensure ecological sustainability. So, for instance, nations should be able to impose domestic standards that are stronger than international ones, but not be allowed to select weaker standards.

One of the paradoxes of international economic and environmental politics is that they both strengthen and threaten national sovereignty as they raise profound questions about the ability of people to maintain some collective control over their lives. Trade and environmental agreements threaten sovereignty by imposing limits on what states can and can't do. But global agreements bring states together in recognition of their legal status and authority. States are the prime governing institutions for enforcing international environmental and economic agreements domestically. Unless national sovereignty is replaced by some supranational authority, the nation–state will be constrained by international agreements, and, at the same time, strengthened by their role in enforcing them. The major task is to increase the level of commitment to environmental values within this framework.

Conclusion

Agenda 21 urged the UN to give greater voice to NGOs in UN agency deliberations—to let them participate in formal meetings and working-group sessions, submit reports and recommendations, and participate in formal country delegations. Agenda 21 also recommended that the United Nations Environment Program be bolstered so that it can play a greater role in global environmental policy making. The United Nations Development Program is focusing on ways to strengthen institutional capacity for sustainable development and has added a new unit, called Capacity 21, to assist less developed countries in related efforts. The United Nations Conference on Trade and Development is expected to focus on the interaction of trade, development, and environmental protection. UN regional economic commissions, regional development banks, regional offices of major UN agencies, and other regional organizations are part of the UN structure for sustainable development and environmental protection.[116]

There is little coordination among these sometimes competing organizations, and there is no overarching body to ensure that environmental concerns are given priority at the highest levels of policy making—no environmental organizations comparable to those for arms talks and international trade, for example. And despite the success of the 1992 Earth Summit in drawing attention to environment and development issues, environmental concerns still lack a central place in international relations. There have been few successful attempts to integrate environmental protection and development; development activities are themselves often plagued by competing and conflicting institutions, overlapping efforts, lack of coordination, and failure to integrate the less developed nations into the world economy.[117] The credibility of global agencies is critical in gaining the largely voluntary support and participation of sovereign states, but the UN is viewed by some in the South as a tool of the wealthy nations. While the General Assembly may provide a forum for speakers from the poorer nations, the wealthy ones control the funding and institutions of real power. But criticism of the UN is also a wealthy-world practice, and the long-running dispute over the United States' failure to pay back assessments has left the UN strapped for funds.

A 1997 UNEP report argued that "significant progress" has been made during the past decade "in the realm of institutional developments, international cooperation, public participation, and the emergence of private-sector action." The report highlighted the spread of new environmental laws, environmental impact assessments, economic incentives, and other policy efforts, and the development of cleaner, less polluting production processes and technologies. These innovations, it argued, resulted in several countries reporting "marked progress in curbing environmental pollution and slowing the rate of resource degradation as well as reducing the intensity of resource use."[118] However, the report concluded that "from a global perspective, the environment has continued to degrade during the past decade, and significant environmental problems remain deeply embedded in the socioeconomic fabric of nations in all regions. Progress toward a global sustainable future is just too slow." The report argued that while technologies are available to remedy environmental problems, a "sense of urgency is lacking" as are the financial resources and the "political will" to reduce environmental degradation and protect natural resources. There is a "general lack of sustained interest in global and long-term environmental issues"; global "governance structures and environmental solidarity remain too weak to make progress a worldwide reality"; and, consequently, the "gap between what has been done thus far and what is realistically needed is widening."[119]

Global environmentalism is a potent political force. It can generate publicity, attention, and interest. Earth Day 2000 celebrations attracted millions of participants worldwide, from a rally at the National Mall in Washington, D.C., to a clean-air fair in Mexico City, a car-free day in Tokyo and Seoul, a bicycle rally in New Delhi, and a solar-cooking workshop in Burkina Faso, as events occurred in 185 countries.[120] But concerns of national security, economic growth, and trade still dominate the global political agenda.

5

Climate Change: A Case Study
of Environmental Politics

Global climate change is the most serious, long-term environmental issue confronting the world. Climate change—because it is such a broad problem, and because actions required to minimize the threat implicate such a wide range of activities—provides a useful case study of the nature of environmental politics and the extent to which it is undergoing a transformation to ecological sustainability. The politics of climate change is also a useful window into the nature of the environmental movement in the United States and elsewhere for a number of reasons. Climate change is closely related to sustainability because greenhouse gases result from such a wide variety of sources. Many of the options for pursuing sustainability are the same as those to prevent or minimize the likelihood and effects of climate change; a more sustainable world includes, at its core, a world less likely to suffer from global warming and climate disruptions. Both issues call for a transformative politics that reorients humankind's interaction with natural systems. The agenda for reducing the threat of climate change is clear but challenging: There is much more agreement over the changes required to reduce the threat of climate change than there is over the demands of sustainability.

A Brief Overview of Climate Change

Human activities such as the burning of fossil fuels have increased the concentration of carbon dioxide (CO_2) and other gases that help trap heat in the atmosphere. The accumulation of these gases threatens to magnify the planet's natural greenhouse effect and to disrupt and change current climate patterns. There is much uncertainty about the magnitude of the changes, when changes might take place, the nature of the changes, and their geographic distribution. There may be some benefits in some areas: Increased levels of CO_2 and warmer temperatures,

137

for example, might stimulate plant growth in areas that are now colder and less productive. However, climate disruption is likely to have adverse impacts, such as increased flooding, in some areas; more frequent and more disruptive storms; new forms of pests and other threats to agriculture; and loss of biodiversity. The areas that are most likely to suffer from these adverse impacts are often in developing countries, where residents have contributed relatively few greenhouse gases and lack the resources to mitigate the adverse effects. The magnitude and extent of the disruption that might result from climate change, and the grossly unfair distribution of the burdens of dealing with it, are compelling reasons to take precautionary actions to reduce the threat of climate change by reducing greenhouse gas emissions.

The four most important greenhouse gases (GHGs) are carbon dioxide, methane, nitrous oxide, and chlorofluorocarbons or CFCs. Most of the attention has focused on carbon dioxide, but the other gases are becoming increasingly important.[1] In the United States, carbon dioxide is not currently regulated under the Clean Air Act, but other GHGs are. CFC emissions, for example, are regulated under the Clean Air Act as part of the U.S. implementation of the Montreal Protocol on Substances that Deplete the Ozone Layer. Methane is released during the production and use of oil and natural gas (as well as when anaerobic bacteria break down dead organic matter). Nitrogen oxides result from the burning of biomass and coal (and from the breakdown of nitrogen fertilizers in soil and water).[2]

Global trends show modest progress in reducing the amount of carbon dioxide emitted in the production of energy: In 1985, the carbon emitted per unit of oil-equivalent energy was about 1.1 tons; a decade later, it had fallen to about 0.8 tons. Oil currently accounts for the largest amount of energy consumption, followed by coal and natural gas. As the use of wood and coal has fallen, they have been replaced by lower carbon fuels like oil and natural gas. Some energy experts project that the use of natural gas, the cleanest fossil fuel, is about to peak, and that a carbon-free, hydrogen-based energy supply lies ahead. The use of coal is on the way out virtually everywhere in the world except in the United States and China. Because energy consumption continues to grow, the total amount of carbon dioxide emissions continues to grow.[3] Greenhouse gases have a long atmospheric lifetime, so even if emissions are reduced, the concentration of gases in the atmosphere may continue to rise. U. S. Greenhouse gas emissions increased on average by 1.2 percent a year during the 1990s; by 1998, greenhouse gas emissions were about 10 percent above 1990 levels.[4]

Studies released in late 1999 reported that the global climate warmed by 0.7–0.8 degrees C during the twentieth century. Scientists, industry officials, environmental advocates, and political leaders are vigorously debating the extent to which there is evidence the climate is dangerously warming. Much of the controversy focuses on alternative explanations for the warming trend; whether the trend is statistically significant or within the natural range of temperature variation; how elements of the global climate such as oceans and ice caps interact; and how soils, forests, and other ecosystems interact with the atmosphere as they store and release carbon. Researchers at the Naval Research Laboratory and the National Oceanic and Atmospheric Administration, for example, concluded that natural climate variability "cannot explain the magnitude of the observed warming over the twentieth century." Other explanations, such as variations in solar radiation, "are large enough to shape, but not dominate, the observed warming." Greenhouse gases "provide, by far, the most plausible hypothesis for explaining the warming of the twentieth century."[5]

There is little disagreement surrounding the existence of the greenhouse effect, the rise in carbon dioxide levels from human activity, the likelihood that if this continues it will lead to a warming of the earth's surface, and that climate changes will vary across the planet's regions. But a number of issues concerning the causes and impacts of climate change are disputed. There is a strong level of agreement among scientists throughout the world that climate change is occurring as a result of human activity,[6] but the fossil-fuel industry and some scientific skeptics have aggressively challenged the global consensus reflected in the Framework Convention on Climate Change and subsequent agreements.[7] The disagreements focus on the consequences of the earth's natural feedback systems (such as the hydrologic cycle) and other human effects (such as the emissions of other air pollutants) and the impacts climate change will produce (such as droughts, storms, forest fires, heat waves, and flooding). Critics of studies that warn of climate change include those who censure the elements of climate change models; proponents of alternative theories to explain warming trends; those who argue that warming has not actually occurred and will likely not; and those who argue that even if warming does occur, it will produce more benefits than problems. Many critics seek to defend the use of fossil fuels as the cheapest way to produce energy and fuel economic growth or oppose more government regulation or intervention in the economy in response to climate changes.[8]

Climate change research as early as the 1820s suggested that greenhouse gases warmed the earth's atmosphere, but it was not until the 1957 International Geophysical Year that scientists began developing a global monitoring network to better understand the impact of human behavior on the biosphere. By 1970, the threat of a "catastrophic warming effect" was included in the UN General Secretary's report on the environment. The first World Climate Conference was convened in 1979 and led to climate workshops throughout the world in the 1980s. The

Intergovernmental Panel on Climate Change (IPCC) was established in 1988, and its work provided the scientific base on which the 1992 Framework Convention on Climate Change and subsequent protocols rest. The IPCC's first report, published in 1990, concluded that rising carbon dioxide levels, and those of other greenhouse gases, were caused by human activity, and would result in a rise in global temperatures and related climatic changes.[9] The Second Assessment Report, published in 1996, also concluded that greenhouse gas levels had continued to rise as a result of human activity, but went further, in determining that the global average temperature had risen and the balance of evidence pointed to a discernible impact from humans on the global climate. The report identified "no regrets" policies that nations could undertake, at no net cost, that would reduce GHG emissions, and also called for reductions beyond the no regrets proposals because of the potential risk climate change posed.[10] The Third Assessment Report, due in 2001, will provide additional data on the causes and consequences of climate change.[11]

While the scientific debate continues, what is striking about the actual weather events during the past decade is how disruptive storms, droughts, and heat waves are. They wreak tremendous havoc on human beings and natural systems. And these massive disruptions have occurred while temperature changes are still quite modest. Given the response so far, if the planet does actually experience the several-degree temperature increase forecasted, given the tumult that has already occurred, climate change could prove calamitous. The question clearly becomes, how much are we willing to risk these changes, and what are the costs and benefits of acting now to decrease their likelihood?

The Evolution of the Politics of Climate Change Policy in the United States

The policy of the U.S. government toward climate change poses a puzzling paradox. U.S.-funded research has played a major role in identifying the threat of climate change and in developing climate models, and American scientists have been among the leading voices in drawing attention to the challenges it poses to the global community. Al Gore, who enjoyed unprecedented power and influence for a vice president, focused on climate change in his 1992 book, *Earth in the Balance*, calling it the most important environmental problem we face. But U.S. policy commitments addressing the threat of climate change have been quite weak. The United States fell far short of its goal of reducing greenhouse gas emissions to 1990 levels by the year 2000, as agreed to in the Framework Convention on Climate Change, and it led the initial opposition to binding commitments for reducing emissions. Even though the Clinton–Gore administration agreed to a 7 percent reduction in greenhouse gas emissions by 2008 in the Kyoto Protocol, there has been great opposition to binding emission reductions in Congress.

The Rise of Climate Change Politics

Climate change first surfaced as a significant political issue in congressional hearings in 1987 and 1988, led by the efforts of then Senators Al Gore (Tenn.) and Tim Wirth (Colo.), both Democrats who later came to work on climate change issues in the Clinton administration (Wirth was appointed assistant secretary of state for international environmental issues), and Republican John Chafee (R.I.). In the summer of 1988, an important breakthrough in political discourse occurred during the record-breaking heat wave, when NASA scientist James Hansen argued before a congressional panel that the warming period was the first sign that global warming had begun.[12]

Research by Hansen and other U.S. scientists contributed to demands for action that led to the first climate change meeting, in Toronto, in 1988, where scientists called for a 20 percent reduction in greenhouse gas (GHG) emissions by the year 2005. The United States, however, was not a major player in the Toronto conference, although the threat of global warming was briefly raised in the 1988 election. Candidate George Bush was initially interested in the problem, telling voters worried about the greenhouse effect that he would as president launch the "White House effect" to solve the problem. In 1989, Secretary of State James Baker, in one of his first speeches, suggested that the United States respond to the threat of climate change through a "no regrets" policy. Given the scientific uncertainty surrounding the issue and the seriousness of the potential threat, said Baker, the United States and others should take actions to reduce the threat of warming that would produce other benefits that were more certain: "While scientists refine the state of our knowledge, we should focus immediately on prudent steps that are already justified on grounds other than climate change."[13] Investments in emissions reduction and energy efficiency, for example, would reduce local air pollution and save money, and should be pursued even if the additional contribution they made to reducing the threat of global warming turned out to be unnecessary. The Bush administration also led the way in addressing acid rain in 1989: Its proposal to reduce sulfur dioxide emissions from power plants by 50 percent was much more ambitious than any plan offered by members of Congress, and became the key provision in the 1990 Clean Air Act Amendments.[14]

By 1990, however, the Bush administration looked much less Green. The 1990 White House International Conference on Scientific and Economic Issues Related to Global Climate Change concluded with a call for more research before taking any action to reduce GHG emissions. The administration opposed the development of a global climate change agreement, as Chief of Staff John Sununu and other senior officials warned that limits on emissions would require major changes in Americans' way of life and would threaten an already weak economy.[15] During the 1992 United Nations Conference on Environment and Development, the Bush administration opposed any agreement that imposed binding limits on GHG emissions and was successful in ensuring that the Framework Convention on Climate Change (FCCC), signed by the United States and other countries at the Earth Summit, called for only voluntary reductions. The U.S. Senate gave its advise and consent to the convention in May 1992, committing the nation to the non-binding goal of limiting greenhouse gas emissions to 1990 levels by 2000.

The Clinton Administration and Climate Change

In the spring of 1993, one of the first policy initiatives announced by the newly elected Clinton administration was a BTU tax, aimed at raising the price of gasoline, electricity, and other forms of energy in order to raise new revenue and encourage conservation. But opposition to the proposal from senators representing energy-producing states killed the proposal, and the administration could only salvage a 4.3 cents per gallon gas-tax increase as part of its deficit-reduction plan.[16] The rapidity of the administration's retreat in the face of congressional opposition was clear evidence of its unwillingness to take on an ambitious and politically controversial response to the threat of climate change. In October 1993, the Clinton administration released its Climate Change Action Plan, as required by the FCCC.[17] The plan promised to reduce levels of greenhouse gas emissions to 1990 levels by the year 2000, a reduction of some 110 million tons (out of a total of some 1.5 billion tons). The Climate Change Action Plan became the basis for the National Action Plan the United States submitted in 1994 to the secretariat of the FCCC. Under the plan, U.S. emissions for 2000 were to be about 100 million tons lower than if no plan were implemented. The plan called for a gradual shift from coal and oil to natural gas, and, because energy consumption is growing fastest in transportation and industrial uses, the plan proposed a modest effort at conservation of energy across the major sectors, with a smaller reduction in transportation than in other areas.[18] The plan was a smorgasbord of some 50 new and expanded programs, largely voluntary, that sought to (1) promote energy efficiency among commercial, residential, and industrial users (through demonstration projects for emerging technologies, incentives for industrial equipment efficiency, upgrading of energy-efficiency standards, funding for investments in energy efficiency in government buildings, and revisions to tax expenditures for expenses such as employer-provided parking); (2) promote use of natural gas and other cleaner fuels; (3) increase the efficiency of hydroelectric and other energy production; and (4) reduce emissions of CFCs, nitrous oxide, and other greenhouse gases.[19]

The United States adopted the Berlin Mandate in March 1995, at the First Conference of the Parties to the climate change convention in Berlin, Germany—an agreement that structured future negotiations and provided that developing countries would not be required to make binding greenhouse gas-reduction commitments.[20] The release of the Intergovernmental Panel on Climate Change's Second Assessment Report in December 1995 prompted U.S. officials to accept the idea of new, binding commitments to reduce the threat of global climate change. Many scientists had believed that there would be no definitive links found between human activity and climate change until the twenty-first century, but the 1995 report, involving some 2,500 scientists worldwide, concluded that the "balance of evidence suggests a discernible human influence on global climate."[21] The United States rejected as too ambitious the proposal from the small island states to reduce greenhouse gas emissions by 20 percent by the year 2005 but also conceded that voluntary commitments to reduce emissions were not working.[22] In July 1996, at the Geneva Climate Summit, the United States announced a shift in policy and committed to legally binding targets and timetables for reducing greenhouse gas emissions in the more developed world.[23]

The Clinton administration's Climate Change Action Plan was primarily a set of voluntary actions that industries, commercial establishments, energy companies, and consumers were encouraged to take. However, by 1994, carbon dioxide emissions in the United States exceeded the levels to be achieved by 2000, and in that year Congress approved only half the funds requested to comply with the convention.[24] Within a few years of issuing the plan, the Clinton administration acknowledged that the goal of reducing greenhouse gas emissions to 1990 levels by the year 2000 would not be met. In late 1997, the U.S. Department of Energy reported that emissions in 1996 were 7.4 percent above 1990 levels, and the administration estimated that emissions would be 13 percent higher in 2000 from 1990 levels. Strong economic growth, unusually severe weather, increased coal use by electric utilities, growing popularity of less-efficient sport utility vehicles and light trucks all combined to increase carbon emissions. Energy efficiency actually declined by one measure in 1996, when energy use increased by 3.2 percent while the economy grew by only 2.4 percent.[25]

Critics of the administration's 1993 plan argued that its refusal to pursue mandatory measures such as higher fuel-efficiency standards or increased taxes doomed the plan, but congressional reductions in spending for energy conservation, Congress's opposition to new energy-efficiency standards for household appliances, the failure of the Department of Energy to issue new standards for electricity transformers on power lines, and lower-than-anticipated energy prices also contributed to the failure of the plan. Tax provisions for employer-provided parking were not revised by Congress, and new tree-planting goals were not met. While 70 percent of the projected reductions in emissions were achieved, those savings were simply overwhelmed by economic growth and increased use of energy. The greatest progress in slowing the growth of emissions (but not actually decreasing them) occurred in the utility industry, mainly through shifts in fuel from coal to natural gas (which likely would have occurred even without a climate change plan), and through increased reliance on nuclear power. Only 7 percent of the reductions in emissions came from investments in renewable energy. One of the most glaring shortcomings of the plan was its failure to offer any significant program to reduce emissions from transportation sources, which are responsible for about one-third of emissions. Despite the overall failure of the plan to achieve its goals, the experience in voluntary efforts was not really ineffective; it simply was not balanced with some mandatory measures and more powerful incentives. In an area where traditional regulatory power was used, the EPA's regulation of methane releases from landfills produced 60 percent more reductions than anticipated.[26]

The new Republican Congress, elected in 1995, expressed great hostility toward environmental regulation in particular—singling out the U.S. EPA for budget cuts and restrictions on regulatory authority—and sought to weaken most environmental laws. It opposed new energy-efficiency standards and cut spending for conservation and the development of alternative fuels. It tried to impose new procedural requirements on rule making such as new cost–benefit analyses and increased opportunities for judicial challenges that would have made the process even more cumbersome.[27] Congress took on the administration's climate change policies directly in July 1997 when the Senate unanimously passed Resolution 98, aimed at ensuring that the United States and other developed countries not sign a climate change agreement that did not impose on developing countries at least some (if not a similar) commitment to reduce greenhouse gas emissions.[28] The resolution specified two key conditions required for Senate approval: The treaty "should include commitments for countries with developing economies (termed non-Annex I countries under the existing UN Framework Convention), and should not result in serious harm to the economy of the United States." The resolution also requires that the president, when submitting any climate change agreement to the Senate, provide two additional documents: (1) a detailed explanation of legislation or regulations that would be required to implement the agreement, and (2) a detailed analysis of the financial and economic costs incurred by the United States in implementing the agreement submitted to the Senate. The resolution also included an unusual oversight provision, recommending that a bipartisan group of senators be appointed "to monitor the status of negotiations on climate change and report periodically to the Senate."

In October 1997, the Clinton administration announced that it would support in the Third Climate Summit (held in December 1997 in Kyoto, Japan) a requirement that developed countries commit to reduce greenhouse gas emissions to 1990 levels between the years 2008 and 2012 and reduce emissions to an unspecified amount below those levels by 2017. The administration also stated that it would not "assume binding obligations unless key developing nations meaningfully participate in this effort" but offered no precise explanation of what that required. Other industrialized countries have pushed for much more ambitious reductions: Japan proposed a 5 percent reduction below 1990 levels by 2012, and the European Union (EU) proposed a 15 percent reduction.[29] The administration announced that it would not accept binding reduction commitments unless the developing countries also agreed to take such actions and as long as countries have flexibility in implementing agreements, including the creation of an emissions budget that would allow participating nations to trade emission allowances in order to meet targets, and bank or save allowances to meet obligations in future years.

Strong lobbying by environmental groups and the intervention of Vice President Gore resulted in the shift in policy, and the United States agreed to reduce greenhouse gas emissions by 7 percent in the Kyoto Protocol it signed in December 1997.[30] However, the prospects in the United States for ratification of this Protocol seem bleak because of the failure to gain binding commitments from the developing countries to reduce their emissions. Industry representatives charge that this failure will unfairly advantage developing-country industries in global markets. The Clinton administration also announced it would not submit the treaty to the Senate for ratification until there was both "meaningful participation" from developing nations, and a clear agreement that flexible measures (primarily market-based mechanisms such as GHG trading and Clean Development Mechanisms that allowed industrial countries to offset their emission reductions with investments in energy efficiency and other projects in emerging countries) could be used to demonstrate compliance.[31] In November 1998, during the Buenos Aires talks on climate change, the Clinton administration signed the Kyoto Protocol in an effort to boost the flagging negotiations, but repeated its position that it would not submit the treaty to the Senate until the meaningful participation and flexible measures conditions were met.[32] The Buenos Aires meeting concluded with the industrialized and emerging countries agreeing to a two-year plan of action aimed at producing binding agreements on flexibility measures, technology transfers, and limits on GHG emissions from all nations.

Negotiations continued in 1999 in Bonn, Germany, as delegates from 166 countries focused on how to implement agreements in ways that would minimize compliance costs, and how to get meaningful participation from the developing countries. There was some agreement over the details of implementation, such as the preparation of reports on greenhouse gas emissions, but strong differences continue to divide the United States and European countries over the use of flexible or market-based regulatory approaches in achieving goals. Contentious issues—for example, what kind of emissions trading might be allowed in pursuing national emission goals, how to determine the baseline of emissions used to assess what level of cuts are required, and how to increase the technical and regulatory capacity of developing countries—were set aside until the next meeting of parties to the agreement, scheduled to be held in The Hague, in November 2000.[33]

While international negotiations were proceeding globally, U.S. policy making moved along in fits and starts. In October 1997, the Clinton administration issued another plan to combat climate change. It called for a five-year, $5 billion program of tax incentives and research and development aimed at reducing CO_2 emissions to 1990 levels by the year 2008, and reducing emissions below that level in the future. The plan would eventually initiate an emissions trading scheme for greenhouse gases that would cut emissions by 30 percent from projected levels in 2008. Sources that moved early to reduce emissions would get credits that they could use later when pollution permits are issued. The trading system would eventually expand internationally, so that U.S. companies could buy and sell the allowances given them to emit greenhouse gases and encourage the most cost-effective ways of reducing emissions. Some industry officials welcomed the proposal because of its incentives for early reductions in emissions, while others warned that greenhouse gas-reduction efforts would be costly and disruptive to the economy.[34] To achieve the plan's goal, the United States will need to reduce emissions by an average of about 1 percent a year for the next decade.[35]

In March 1998, the Clinton administration released its budget for the Climate Change Technology Initiative, which included $2.7 billion for increased research and development spending and $3.6 billion in tax credits to encourage energy efficiency. It also estimated that the cost of implementing the Kyoto agreement would be $7–12 billion a year between 2008 and 2012, in contrast to an industry estimate that the cost would be about $50 billion a year. The chair of the White House Council of Economic Advisers estimated that compliance with the treaty would mean an increase in costs of from $70 to $110 a year for the average American family; an estimate from Wharton Econometric Forecasting Associates concluded that implementing the agreement would cost each family some $2,700 a year, including increasing the cost of gas by 65 cents a gallon, and resulting in 2.4 million lost jobs.[36]

Members of Congress focused on the industry projections of costs and rejected the administration's estimates. Senator Chuck Hagel (R–Neb.) complained that the treaty is "unfair to the United States." Representative Joe Kollenberg (R–Mich.) charged that the treaty is "based on immature science. And it would have a chilling effect on the American economy." His colleague, Representative Henry Bonilla (R–Texas) claimed that the treaty was an "anti-American effort."[37] Republicans in Congress pursued numerous paths in 1997 and 1998 to ensure that the treaty was not ratified nor its provisions implemented by the federal government. The Senate Budget Committee's FY'99 budget resolution provided no money for the climate change initiative, as Republican leaders promised to block any new spending on climate change until the treaty is submitted to the Senate.[38] Several House appropriations bills for FY'99 included deep cuts in spending for climate change-related programs. The House 1999 appropriations bill for the EPA and other agencies included a ban on spending for any effort to implement the Kyoto agreement, including meetings aimed at educating the public on climate change issues, and that measure was overwhelmingly passed by the House in July.[39] Other bills made major reductions in spending on solar and renewable fuels research and energy-efficiency programs. The administration also asked for $300 million to meet U.S. commitments to the Global Environmental Facility, but the House bill provided only $42.5 million as Republicans charged that the funds could be used to implement the Kyoto accord.[40] The restriction on public education and information was eventually dropped, but Congress did enact in its fiscal year 1999 appropriations a ban on any effort to formulate and issue regulations or any other action to implement or prepare for the implementation of the Kyoto Protocol until it has been ratified by the Senate.

Members of Congress repeated their attacks on the Kyoto Protocol in late 1998 and throughout 1999. When the Clinton administration appeared to be ready to sign the agreement, a number of members of Congress quickly warned against it. Senate Foreign Relations Chair Jesse Helms (R–N.C.) wrote to the Secretary of State that the Protocol should not be signed, but if the administration did so, it should "quickly submit the treaty for Senate advise and consent so that the Senate may reject [it] and scrap the Kyoto Protocol process altogether." Opposition was bipartisan: Representative Ron Klink (D–Penn.) warned that the treaty "would be the first major step toward the de-industrialization of this country."[41] When the administration announced that it would indeed sign the Protocol, critics swiftly responded: "The administration has chosen to ignore economic realities and pursue this misguided political agenda," complained Senator Larry Craig (R–Idaho). "It appears the president and vice president want to shove this protocol down the throats of the American people."[42] In 1999, Congress again passed a rider to a FY 2000 appropriations bill that prohibited the use of any funds for implementation of the Kyoto Protocol before it is ratified.[43]

Despite the weakened position of the Clinton administration resulting from the president's impeachment and Senate trial, the administration was surprisingly successful in warding off many of the more extreme congressional attacks aimed at its support for the Kyoto agreement but still was sufficiently wounded such that it could not provide much leadership on the issue even if it decided to do so. The administration decided not to submit the treaty to the Senate for approval; this jeopardizes the entire ratification effort because at least 55 countries, representing at least 55 percent of total GHG emissions, must ratify before the treaty takes effect. Other countries that are major sources of GHG emissions may not ratify if their leading competitor does not. Climate change was one of the issues dividing candidates in the 2000 presidential election, although both Gore and George W. Bush said they believed that global warming was a problem. In his January 2000 State of the Union address, President Clinton raised the issue by proposing a new round of funding for measures to reduce greenhouse gas emissions through improved energy efficiency and the use of cleaner fuels, but members of Congress quickly retorted, as they have in the past, that his budget was dead on arrival.

Assessing the Politics of Climate Change in the United States

The level of congressional hostility to the Kyoto Protocol is surprising, given the rather modest commitments reflected in the accord. Many scientists have argued that the Kyoto agreement was much too weak. Bert Bolin, former chair of the UN Intergovernmental Panel on Climate Change, for example, warned that "the Kyoto conference did not achieve much with regard to limiting the buildup of greenhouse gases in the atmosphere. If no further steps are taken during the next 10 years, CO_2 will increase in the atmosphere during the first decade of the next century essentially as it has done during the past few decades."[44] The 5.2 percent reduction in GHG emissions below 1990 levels among the industrialized nations falls far, far short of the 60 to 80 percent cuts recommended by many groups. If developing countries do not reduce their emissions, total global GHG emissions, despite cutbacks in the industrialized world, will actually grow from 1990 levels by 2008.[45]

The demands by the United States for flexible mechanisms also weaken the prospects for addressing the threat of climate change. What little interest there has been in Congress in responding to the international agreement over the threat of climate change has focused on establishing a system to ensure credits to sources that reduce their greenhouse gas emissions ahead of mandates. In 1997, a bipartisan group of senators introduced legislation, S. 2617, that would have amended the Clean Air Act to allow the president to make binding agreements with U.S. businesses that reduce their greenhouse gas emissions to get credit for those reductions if and when a mandatory program is devised. Industry groups sent conflicting signals to Congress: Some opposed the early-credit scheme because it might actually encourage the ratification of the Kyoto Protocol, while others favored it as a useful protection for companies that make early reductions voluntarily in case binding reductions are later mandated.[46] A bipartisan group of senators, led by Senator John Chafee (R–R.I.) reintroduced the bill, S. 882, in 1999, but Senator Chafee's untimely death in October 1999 clouded the future of the bill. Opponents of climate change policy also introduced legislation in 1999, H.R. 2221, that would prohibit the executive branch from implementing the Kyoto Protocol until it is ratified, and would bar any federal agency from regulating CO_2 emissions.

Much of the controversy surrounding the lobbying in Congress for climate change focuses on the science of modeling the problem—predicting the magnitude, timing, consequences, and other issues of atmospheric science.[47] Some congressional interest in this scientific debate is to be expected, but the Republicans who have led the charge against the climate change accord have chosen to listen to a small minority of scientists involved in this debate and embrace their views without question. A handful of scientists, including Patrick Michaels, Robert Balling, S. Fred Singer, and Richard Lindzen, have been regularly invited to congressional hearings organized by Republican committee chairs, and whose views outweigh, in the minds of members of Congress, the thousands of scientists who have endorsed the basic conclusions of the Intergovernmental Panel on Climate Change and other reports issued by scientists in the United States and elsewhere. These members of Congress have been untroubled by the level of funding from fossil-fuel industries that has been channeled to these opponents of climate change policy making and by the lack of peer-reviewed research to support their claims.[48]

The debate over the policy responses necessary to reduce the risks resulting from climate change is in many ways less contentious than the predictions of warming and climate disruptions. It is true that some economists warn of the economic costs and disruptions that might come from a dramatic shift away from fossil-fuel use, and that industry has invested millions of dollars in a campaign to challenge the conclusions of most climate change scientists. And given the uncertainties surrounding the consequences and impacts of climate change, it is not clear what the best policy responses are in every area. But the policy prescriptions suggested to reduce the risks and impacts of climate change are rather straightforward. There is great potential for improving energy efficiency. Technologies exist to reduce resource consumption and emissions of air pollutants that directly threaten health and ecosystems as well as greenhouse gas emissions. These investments also are economically rational and promise to reduce costs in the long term.[49] For two decades, engineers—Amory Lovins, for example—have been demonstrating the technological and economic opportunities for energy investments.[50] Congress has considerable experience in legislating for energy efficiency and alternative sources of energy, and is in a position to provide some leadership in creating incentives for a shift away from fossil fuels.

Despite the considerable evidence of the economic and environmental advantages of energy efficiency, however, there is still a debate in Congress over what, if any, public policies are appropriate for encouraging shifts to more energy-efficient products and activities even apart from climate change controversies. There are some barriers to investment in energy efficiency technologies—they require upfront investments that take years to recover. Some energy consumers may be unaware of new technologies. Legislation can respond to both of these concerns. Many conservatives in Congress warn that government programs are so prone to rent-seeking and inefficiencies that it is much better to rely on markets to encourage energy-efficiency investments. That debate will likely continue in Congress because of the central role energy-efficiency policies play in a host of areas: traditional air pollution regulation, national security, the importation of oil, and climate change.[51]

The "no regrets" principle, championed briefly during the Bush administration by Secretary of State James Baker and others (see chapter 4), is a very attractive option for devising a political compromise for climate change in Congress—it pursues only the policies aimed at reducing greenhouse gas emissions that also promise more certain, immediate benefits. It is a moderate step, not enough for those who demand immediate and dramatic actions to reduce climate change threats, and too much for those who oppose any kind of public investment, subsidy, or tax break. It might be sufficient to produce a reduction in the order of 20 percent of 1990 level greenhouse gas emissions, no small feat and a major first step for the United States, but would likely not be enough to produce the 50–60 percent reduction in emissions some have called for.[52] Nevertheless, despite its Republican pedigree, the no regrets policy has been rejected by the Republican leadership in Congress. The demands of many members to not even allow the federal government to spend any money talking about climate change, and the overwhelming support for cuts in climate change research, is remarkably extreme, hostile to scientific research, and, given the threat posed by greenhouse gas emissions originating in the United States to less wealthy nations, quite arrogant.

Several theories of policy making help explain congressional recalcitrance in facing heat on the global debate over climate change and the inability of the environmental movement to counter the opponents of climate change action in Congress. First, as many scholars have argued, the separation of powers and the division of authority between the president and Congress for making foreign policy commitments, giving advice and consent, enacting implementing legislation, and establishing regulatory programs pose tremendous barriers to effective policy making. The division of power between the president, who negotiates international treaties and accords, and Congress, which must pass legislation to implement them, is a recipe for deadlock. The president, and the United States as a whole, cannot assume effective leadership in global environmental issues as long as Congress remains at home and willing to block commitments from being made in response to narrow interests and constituencies.[53] Presidents must make policy in a kind of two-level chess game—they must interact with Congress at one level and with other nations at another. This poses challenges for any administration, even a politically adept and popular one, to anticipate how international agreements will be viewed by domestic actors.[54] Presidents and members of Congress represent different kinds of constituencies, and the broad, national scope of presidential elections aggregates national interests much differently than the decentralized system of congressional representation that gives great deference to those representing local interests. Congress and the White House remain distrustful of each other and largely unable to move forward in dealing with new environmental problems and concerns. That distrust has roots in the 1980s and the Reagan administration's assault on environmental laws and its conflicts with Congress over what kind of environmental policy should be pursued.[55] Even though the roles are now reversed—Congress is the recalcitrant partner in responding aggressively to environmental problems—the mistrust continues to make policy making difficult.

The Clinton administration was so weakened by scandal and impeachment that nothing more from it should be expected. But it was rather successful in achieving many of its economic policy goals—such as increased spending for education—and received much of the credit for a robust economy in the late 1990s. In contrast, the administration was largely willing to use its political resources to make the case for a strong climate change agreement. Part of that hesitancy in Congress to be more precautionary is certainly due to a strong campaign by the fossil-fuel industry. Industry lobbying against climate change agreements has been quite effective: It has skillfully manipulated scientific debate over the timing, magnitude, nature, distribution, and consequences of climate change to one that questions whether the threat is actually very serious. It has capitalized on the national preoccupation with economic indicators and the political importance of protecting economic growth at all costs in ways that have diminished the discussion of competing policy concerns. Unions also have effectively raised fears about the loss of U.S. jobs, even though the number of jobs lost in implementing the Kyoto Protocol would be offset by new jobs in other industries, let alone the number of jobs created and lost due to market forces that simply dwarf the results of public policies.[56] Conversely, environmental groups in the United States have been less successful than their European counterparts in focusing attention on the threat of climate change. There is no equivalent U.S. effort, for example, to develop a "Sustainable Europe" plan introduced by the Friends of the Earth. The lesson of the late 1990s is sobering: If the United States cannot act in response to a major global environmental threat when its economy is unusually strong, how will it respond when its economy is in a recession?

Second, the decentralized and fragmented structure of Congress and the challenges this poses for addressing issues like environmental policy and climate change that cut across traditional jurisdictions and sectors is daunting. The U.S. EPA, for example, is subject to oversight hearings and investigations by dozens of congressional committees, placing a heavy burden and time constraint on senior administrators, and subjecting the agency to conflicting demands and instructions. Congress as an institution has not kept up with changes in technologies, environmental problems, and policy options, and its policy efforts are mired in political gridlock. The fragmentation of Congress is also manifest in environmental laws that are poorly integrated and often result in pollution being transferred from one medium to another—rather than pollution prevention efforts that are, in the long run, more efficient and less costly.[57] Members of Congress are so jealous of their committee jurisdictions and so anxious to expand the number of subcommittee chairs and staffs available to members that the institution regularly becomes bogged down in duplicative and conflicting legislative efforts.[58] This fragmentation poses major problems in effectively regulating problems like air and water pollution. The problems are orders of magnitude worse when Congress tries to deal with an issue like climate change that cuts across so many economic sectors and is affected by the vast scope of economic, commercial, and personal activity.

The third and most important explanation of congressional response to climate change is rooted in the ideological differences among members of Congress—differences that have shaped the debate over environmental and other policies and that are part of broader debates over the role of government in regulating industry and individual behavior. Climate change is part of the next generation of environmental challenges facing the United States and the world that fall within the broad context of sustainable development. While many are debating the kinds of actions needed in designing a new generation of policies to promote sustainability, Congress is still mired in the debate over whether there should be more or less environmental regulation. As discussed in chapter 2, when the Republicans took control of Congress in 1994, the Republican leadership saw "reforming" environmental regulation as high priority. Their "Contract with America" promised to "roll back government regulations and create jobs."[59] Opposition in Congress and the Clinton administration blocked most of these proposals in the late 1990s. Relief from regulation, rather than reform, has driven Congress's regulatory agenda since 1995 as members have tried to reduce the size and scope of the regulatory state, cutting the costs of compliance, and slowing down the regulatory process. The conflict and uncertainty surrounding environmental law has weakened U.S. leadership in global environmental issues. This weakness is evident not just in climate change, but in the broader agenda of sustainable development. There is a remarkable level of hostility in Congress to the idea of international organizations and to global commitments, as evidenced by continual criticism of the United Nations in Congress and its unwillingness to fund the United States' financial obligations.

While the primary barrier to a reasonable, prudent, precautionary policy response to the threat of climate change is Congress, the Clinton administration has been, on the whole, rather timid in its pursuit of a strong climate change policy. It came on board late in the negotiations leading to Kyoto, and even then only supported a modest reduction in emissions. Clinton administration negotiators must constantly look over their shoulders to assess congressional criticism of whatever measures they support, but they have also been unwilling to take Congress head on over this issue. They have largely failed to make the case that while environmental protection does not need to be equated with economic decline and can be consistent with a dynamic, competitive economy, some practices and approaches will have to be abandoned, and the fossil-fuel industry must be radically downsized.

Policies can be enacted that facilitate this transition and help workers who are displaced, and, in so doing, soften the opposition to change. Promoting efforts by industries to reduce pollution, reforming tax and spending policies to discourage destructive activities such as pollution and resource depletion through taxes and elimination of harmful subsidies, creating new incentives for renewable fuels and conservation, and ensuring that markets include all the costs of production are all promising reforms that have been discussed but not seriously debated in Congress.

Given its critical role in the policy process, Congress will have to join the executive branch in taking sustainable development seriously before major progress will be made. Congress's fragmented and decentralized structure and the access and influence industry enjoys, makes it a conservative, cautious institution, ill-suited for taking the initiative to reconceptualize problems and integrate policies unless there is strong leadership. Executive branch agencies and leaders are structurally better able to devise national strategies and coordinate efforts. But they also need to be nudged forward by public opinion to give priority to designing and implementing the kinds of effective actions required by climate change. This is the paradox in which the United States finds itself in the beginning of the twenty-first century: Reducing the threat of climate change, and pursuing a more proactive, sustainable development policy, requires a comprehensive policy response. But its political system is so divided by federalism, the separation of powers, and other institutional means, that coherent policy efforts seem impossible in the absence of a national crisis.

The Future of Climate Change Politics in the United States

The United States agreed to reduce emissions by 7 percent from 1990 levels during the years 2008–12; industrialized nations as a whole agreed to an average reduction of 5 percent. However, emissions increased by 10 percent between 1990 and 1997 and by 0.4 percent in 1998. Emissions may increase by 1 percent a year or more; according to the U.S. Department of Energy, if trends in production and consumption continue, carbon emissions in the United States will be some 34 percent higher in 2010 than in 1990.[60] It is highly unlikely that the United States can reduce emissions by one-third, in getting back to 1990 levels, let alone reduce emission by an additional 7 percent.

The agenda for making immediate and long-term changes in policies and practices to reduce the threat of climate change are straightforward. Much as proponents of the "no regrets" policy have argued, there are steps we can take now to minimize the dangers posed by climate change and produce other, rather certain benefits. Reducing the use of and emissions from fossil fuel, particularly coal, is the most important action we can take to minimize the likelihood of climate change. There is a compelling case for conserving energy use and shifting to cleaner, renewable sources for energy production. Such changes would reduce local air pollution and improve public health, protect biodiversity, and reduce energy costs. Policy choices for reducing fossil-fuel emissions, encouraging clean renewable sources, and promoting conservation include ending subsidies for fossil-fuel development and use, enacting new energy taxes and other disincentives for fossil fuel use, and creating new subsidies and other incentives for the development and dissemination of cleaner technologies for producing energy; devising new regulatory mandates for emissions reductions, tighter efficiency standards, and changes in fuels; increasing the Corporate Average Fuel Economy (CAFE) standards for motor vehicles and increasing incentives for mass transit and reductions in vehicle miles traveled; and restructuring the electric utility industry to reduce GHG emissions. These policy choices can largely be pursued under existing energy, transportation, and other related laws.

A recent study of greenhouse gases and other air pollutants by the State and Territorial Air Pollution Program Administrators and the Association of Local Air Pollution Control Officials (STAPPA/ALAPCO) identified a number of strategies for reducing GHG emissions and other pollutants regulated because of their impacts on human health. These strategies included switching to cleaner fuels, using renewable sources of energy, increasing efficiency, and reducing motor vehicle use—all actions that can be undertaken with existing technologies. The study concluded that the 7 percent reduction in GHG emissions provided for the United States in the Kyoto Protocol "is well within the reach of most states and localities," and that those actions would also help achieve U.S. clean air goals aimed at protecting human health.[61]

There have been some modest but promising steps at the state and local level. In 1993, for example, Minnesota's Public Utilities Commission began requiring power companies to assign a dollar value to the environmental impact of each ton of CO_2 their plants emit and add that amount to their estimate of the total cost of operating their plants. This effort to deal with power plant externalities was a planning tool rather than a regulatory requirement. Minnesota industries that burn coal sued the commission, challenging the science behind climate change fears and warning of economic collapse. The judge ruled in favor of the commission but ordered it to value the CO_2 at $0.30 to $3.00 a ton; advocates of the tax had pushed for a tax range an order of magnitude higher. Industry groups unsuccessfully appealed the decision, claiming the commission's policy impeded interstate commerce.

The Minnesota state legislature considered a bill in 1997 that would have cut income and payroll tax and imposed a new carbon tax, but opponents successfully blocked action, claiming that it was a tax increase rather than a tax shift. In some states, climate change efforts are a tool used by industries to protect themselves against greenhouse gas agreements. In 1991, Illinois, a state responsible for 1 percent of global greenhouse gas emissions, established a climate change task force to make recommendations to state policy makers. The task force was pushed by the coal industry who saw it as a way to monitor efforts to reduce greenhouse gases that might adversely affect the state's economy, which is heavily dependent on coal. The task force recommended, for example, that the cheapest way to reduce CO_2 was to plant trees, ignoring the state's power plants, which are among the dirtiest in the nation.

In Oregon, a new electric power deregulation law, enacted in 1997, requires utilities to offset 17 percent of the CO_2 they emit, based on emissions when operating at full capacity; if they operate below capacity, they must still offset 17 percent of the maximum CO_2 they could generate. New plants must also emit 17 percent less CO_2 than the cleanest facility in the nation, creating an ongoing incentive to develop cleaner technologies. Utilities can offset the CO_2 themselves or give money to the Oregon Climate Trust, a nonprofit organization responsible for seeing that offset projects actually reduce CO_2 levels. Vermont officials have proposed a carbon tax, to be offset by income-and sales-tax cuts. Wisconsin is exploring options for a major transition to energy efficiency and shifting from coal to natural gas. Much of the impetus for change comes from state officials who see the possibility of federal greenhouse gas controls and prefer to develop their own plans rather than have them imposed by Washington.

Some 23 states, according to one count, have developed action plans for reducing greenhouse gases.[62] State decisions concerning the restructuring of the electric energy industry are critical. The way in which deregulation is pursued in states (and, eventually, nationally, if Congress decides to act) will have a major consequence on levels of coal combustion and the resultant carbon dioxide emissions. If deregulation results in incentives for producing electricity the cheapest way possible, then coal use will increase because, in many areas, it is the cheapest form of power. In contrast, if deregulatory policies include provisions aimed at ensuring that prices include environmental costs, or if there are effective greenhouse gas restrictions, then at least some coal-burning plants will close down.

As discussed earlier, the Clinton administration's initial Climate Change Action Plan was primarily a set of voluntary actions. The plan included nearly 50 new and expanded initiatives. Some 18 actions promised to promote energy efficiency among commercial, residential, and industrial users, including devising demonstration projects for emerging technologies, creating incentives for industrial equipment efficiency, upgrading energy-efficiency standards, and funding investments in energy efficiency in government buildings. Four programs would reduce energy consumption in transportation by reforming tax expenditures for employer-provided parking, promoting telecommuting, reducing the number of motor vehicles traveled, and developing fuel economy labels for tires. Nine programs were aimed at increasing the supply of energy, promoting use of cleaner fuels, developing new technologies, and increasing the efficiency of energy production. Eight initiatives would reduce methane production or increase its recovery, primarily through research and development programs and regulation of landfills, coal mining, and livestock production. Four programs promised to reduce use of CFCs, HCFCs, nitrogen oxide, and other emissions from industries and fertilizer use. Four efforts called for accelerated tree planting and reduced loss of forests.[63] Several policies were aimed at increasing the use of natural gas through promoting the commercialization of high-efficiency gas technologies and through improving the efficiency of hydroelectric generation at existing dams.[64] These initiatives could be made mandatory rather than voluntary. This modest effort is not enough according to some who have called for much more ambitious reductions. For example, in October 1999, the Sustainable Energy Coalition, an organization of business, environmental, consumer, and energy groups, called on the United States to reduce GHG emissions by 50–80 percent over the next half century by funding renewable energy sources and energy efficiency in development projects, setting higher fuel-efficiency standards for motor vehicles, phasing in a revenue-neutral fossil-fuel tax, tightening emission limits on power plants, increasing efficiency standards for buildings and appliances, shifting to renewables producing at least 10 percent of total electricity demand, and creating incentives for "next-generation," more-efficient industrial processes.[65]

Public-opinion data paint a discouraging view of the public's understanding of energy and environmental issues. Views are inconsistent: People tend to oppose new energy development efforts—such as offshore drilling and nuclear power plants—but also oppose mandatory conservation programs that they fear will reduce their energy use and quality of life. The public as a whole is poorly informed about energy policy issues and fails to grasp the basic nature of the debate and understand the major issues.[66] This is part of the broader nature of public opinion on environmental issues that is superficial and poorly formed. This is likely a result of a number of factors. The issues are complex and require some technical expertise to understand, and political leaders have not engaged the public successfully. Jimmy Carter tried but was not effective; Ronald Reagan was more politically successful in arguing that there was no problem if we just increased production and reduced environmental protections.

Environmental protection advocates can make climate change a higher priority issue and mobilize the kind of grass-roots lobbying campaigns they have been able to generate so successfully in other areas like the new national air-quality standards issued in 1997. Industries can make the economic case for a much more aggressive shift to energy efficiency and renewable energy sources. Rather than allowing the fossil-fuel industry to dominate the debate, other industries involved in the creation of new jobs and opportunities can help shape

U.S. policy.[67] As the United States deregulates the production of electricity, it can resist the temptation to encourage increased coal burning as the cheapest source of electricity, and ensure that environmental costs are included in the way energy costs are calculated.[68] The projections about the eventual decline in oil can be taken seriously and the transition to renewable energy pursued more aggressively.[69] The path to a sustainable economy, one that contributes fewer greenhouse gases, requires difficult choices and decisions that will impose burdens and losses on some industries and workers. But the overall distribution of benefits and burdens is compelling. If Congress does not become engaged in policy making to reduce the threat of climate change, it will make it more difficult for Americans and U.S. businesses to be part of the global shift to more sustainable economies. It will also reaffirm our responsibility to remedy the unconscionable distribution of global risks, where those who are least responsible for the threat of climate change are most likely to bear its consequences and least likely to have the resources to mitigate its effects.

Climate Change and Environmental Politics in Other Countries

The politics of climate change in other nations confirms the conclusion based on a review of the U.S. experience that the threat of climate disruptions has not prompted a major rethinking of environmental policy or a shift toward more ecologically sustainable energy production. The Framework Convention on Climate Change was adopted in 1992 and entered into force in 1994. Some 179 countries and the EU have ratified it.[70] In contrast, the Kyoto Protocol, which sets binding reductions for the industrialized nations of 5.2 percent from 1990 levels during 2008–2012, was adopted in 1997, but at the end of 1999 only 16 countries had ratified it. The Protocol must be ratified by 55 nations that account for at least 55 percent of emissions from industrial nations before it takes effect, and the hope expressed at the 1999 Bonn climate change meeting was that it could be in force by 2002.[71]

There is some hope that Kyoto will lead to reductions in emissions. A coalition of environmental groups in Europe has called for the Protocol's entering into force on Earth Day 2002, and Japan and the EU have announced their intention to ratify by 2002.[72] Germany, the United Kingdom, and the Netherlands have developed plans to achieve their goals. Industry opposition to climate change agreements has fractured, as Ford and DaimlerChrysler withdrew in late 1999 and early 2000 from the Global Climate Coalition that is made up of industries fighting the Protocol and controls on GHG emissions. Optimists believe that the Kyoto Protocol will come to be seen as the turning point when humanity began to reverse its environmentally damaging actions.[73]

The Framework Convention on Climate Change has resulted in most nations developing inventories of, and reporting on, their greenhouse gas emissions, but it has had little impact on actually reducing discharges. Most parties are emitting more gases now than they were in 1990. It is too early to tell whether these countries will achieve the 5 percent reduction from 1990 levels by 2008, but signs are not promising. The Kyoto Protocol only requires GHG reductions from the industrialized nations, but the Group of 77 developing nations (G77) and China remain distrustful of the agreement. Their position is that developing countries need help with capacity building—developing regulatory agencies, transferring control and emission prevention technologies, human resources development, communications facilities, and the capacity to participate in implementation programs such as the Clean Development Mechanism—but they fear that emissions trading schemes are little more than plans to help the wealthy countries escape responsibility for reducing their greenhouse gas emissions.[74]

Only a few countries are on track to achieve greenhouse gas-reduction goals. The health of national economies will play a major role in determining compliance. Japanese officials, for example, reported that CO_2 emissions fell in the late 1990s as a result of an economic downturn, although some energy-efficiency improvements were made. Japan will not achieve its Kyoto goals unless it can gain credits from improvements it helps fund in developing nations.[75] France released its plan to meet its Kyoto obligations in early 2000, including an energy-consumption tax and emissions trading, but environmentalists warned that the measures might not be implemented. Prime Minister Lionel Jospin's commentary accompanying the announcement of the plan demonstrated that his government was far from committed to a new way of thinking about the environment and the economy: He promised the climate change policies would not "compromise the pursuit of strong growth."

Climate change and other global environmental issues are typically discussed in terms of North–South divisions, but climate change issues (as well as most others) are more complicated. Countries vary considerably in terms of their responsibility for GHG emissions; expected future emissions; susceptibility to climate change consequences; financial and technological resources available to prevent or mitigate effects; and the cultural, political, and social context in which environmental issues are understood and addressed. One study, by Michael Grubb and colleagues, provides a helpful demarcation of the major divisions among nations that surfaced in the 1980s and have been quite resilient as policies have evolved.[76]

The members of the EU have been among the leading voices for action to reduce the threat of climate change, particularly the Northern nations that traditionally have a strong internationalist bent and deep commitment to environmentalism. They champion the precautionary principle as a basic guideline for action. They are largely energy importers, and emphasize the value of developing (and exporting) conservation and renewable energy technologies. They have been at the forefront of support for the adoption of GHG emission reduction targets, although some of the poorer Southern countries are more interested in finding ways to expand their economies than to restrict growth.[77]

Japan's interface with climate change is one of the most complex. Japan is already one of the most energy-efficient nations, and the Japanese are concerned about the impacts of demands for additional conservation efforts. Its technological prowess also gives it the opportunity to provide some global political leadership on environmental protection issues and opens up opportunities for leading export markets of new technologies. Canada is caught between the competing pressures of a sprawling geography that consumes large quantities of energy, like its neighbor to the South, and the cultivation of a Green global reputation. Other industrialized countries like Norway, Switzerland, and New Zealand rely heavily on hydroelectric power, making carbon reductions more difficult. Australia is very dependent on fossil-fuel use and the revenues from exporting its coal, but also feels particularly vulnerable to the consequences of climate change. All of these nations face more technological difficulties than the EU and the United States in reducing GHG emissions.[78]

The third group of nations, comprising the transitional economies of central and eastern Europe, largely developed highly-energy-intensive industries by the 1980s, only to see their economies collapse. They can easily accomplish Kyoto's emission reduction goals. Their interest in joining the EU has also created incentives for them to support the Union's position.[79] Table 5-1 shows the positions countries took throughout the 1990s on binding reductions in GHG emissions:[80]

TABLE 5-1
Positions on Reductions in GHG Emissions

Country	Base Year	1995 (% change from base year)
USA	1,348	+5
EU	907	-3
Japan	307	+9
Canada	126	+7
Russia	647	-30
Poland	130	-22
Romania	53	-36
Czech Rep.	45	-22

The developing countries—G77 plus China—include as many as 120 nations who often unite to try and challenge the power of the industrialized nations. But three subgroups are evident. First, the Alliance of Small Island States are particularly vulnerable to the impacts of climate change, such as sea-level rise, and have been very vocal proponents of aggressive preventative actions. Second, the Organization of Petroleum Exporting Countries (OPEC) fear a decline in their economic clout and income if oil use is reduced, and have called for more research, more investment in sinks, and compensation if their oil revenues fall. The third and largest group comprises nations that are primarily concerned about economic development. They insist that they be able to develop their natural resources in ways benefiting their citizens, and that developed nations provide financial assistance to help them meet global commitments. China is large enough that it occupies a distinct category in the developing-country universe. Sometimes the developing countries act in concert, and other times the OPEC and island state subgroups have clashed.[81]

China is the second-largest source of greenhouse gas emissions, after the United States, and by the year 2015, producing electricity could consume as much as 1 billion tons of coal a year and produce more than 300 million additional tons of carbon released into the atmosphere each year. However, one study found that energy use in China has only grown half as fast as the economy, and that it has been much more successful than the United States in improving energy efficiency. Because of its great dependence on coal, China has a number of technological options open to it to reduce its carbon emissions.[82] Another risk of increased greenhouse gas emissions comes from Brazil. Brazil currently produces relatively few greenhouse gases for a nation its size, because of heavy reliance on hydroelectric power. However, because hydro plants have become increasingly viewed as costly, controversial, and risky, new power plants are expected to use natural gas, resulting in significant increases in emissions.[83] Argentina provides some encouraging news. Argentina was the first country to accept voluntary targets for reducing greenhouse gas emissions and set a goal in 1999 of reducing emissions 2–10 percent during the 2008–2012 period. Despite its major coal resources, carbon emissions are relatively low because of a competitive electricity production sector that favors natural gas.[84] There are hopeful signs that developing countries can pursue economic growth goals without major increases in greenhouse gases.

The participation of developing countries in global accords is critical across environmental issues. Even protection of the stratospheric ozone layer, seen by many as primarily a developed country issue, needs to include the developing world. Klaus Toepfer, executive director of the UN Environment Programme, said in a speech in the summer of 2000 that "for the next few years, the top priority for all governments will be to ensure that developing countries have the technological and financial capacity they need for moving to ozone friendly chemicals."[85]

The most divisive issue in climate change negotiations has been whether to include the developing countries in an agreement that sets binding emission limits. Technology transfer has become a key issue in gaining their support for GHG reductions, and industry groups have been just as adamant that such transfers are a bad idea.[86] But industry is also far from monolithic on this issue. The coal and other fossil-fuel industries in the United States, for example, have fought aggressively against agreements, challenging the scientific underpinnings and emphasizing the costs. Renewable energy and energy-efficiency companies are at the other end of the continuum of interests. Joined by insurance companies who have been hard hit by claims for storm-related damages, they push for more aggressive action.

In the middle are oil companies that sometimes side with coal companies and other times act as if their future lies with the renewables.[87] Like environmental groups, the energy industry got little of what it wanted in climate negotiations, as its primary position was that no agreement was needed. But it was able to accomplish much of its goal through lobbying the U.S. Senate. In contrast to the situation in Europe, many businesses and labor unions continue to oppose the Kyoto protocol. In contrast, non-U.S.-based oil companies such as BP and Royal Dutch/Shell have committed to reduce their in-house GHG emissions by 10 percent and to increase their renewable energy businesses.[88]

The influence of environmental groups in climate change negotiations has grown over time. Greenpeace has worked with the insurance industry to highlight their concern. Other groups have effectively lobbied specific national delegations.[89] Their influence was clearly limited as they have favored much stronger commitments than nations have been willing to achieve.[90] However, their role in forcing negotiations in the first place has been of critical importance. They played a key role in raising public concern through working with the media. They have been particularly important in working with local governments to devise energy-efficiency and renewable energy programs.

The Berlin meeting on climate change was a turning point as the United States was the first major party to support specific, binding, emission-reduction commitments and signaled that the U.S. government was committed to responding to climate change threats.[91] But divisions within the administration during the 1990s complicated negotiations. The EPA and the State Department favored stronger action, while the Commerce, Energy, and Defense departments resisted.[92] The United States has played a dominant role in negotiations, and its position has prevailed on virtually every major issue.[93] The biggest single obstacle to the achievement of Kyoto's goals appears to be the lack of political will in the United States to reduce emissions and participate effectively in the Kyoto process.[94]

A survey of national environmental goals during the year 2000 found only modest commitments to combating climate change, with many countries promising to implement programs that had been proposed, rather than taking on new initiatives. Goals of U.S. agencies are to encourage voluntary partnerships to reduce greenhouse gas emissions, encourage developing countries to link GHG emission reductions with local air-quality goals, and help generate a broader consensus on climate change. Germany's agenda includes the development of a plan to shut down the nation's 19 nuclear power plants, increased support for renewable energy sources, and the publication of a new GHG control strategy to intensify and coordinate existing programs. France announced that energy taxes would be a key element of its climate change efforts. Britain's climate change plan also calls for energy taxes. Italy is focusing on sustainable transportation. The Netherlands is emphasizing voluntary agreements with industrial sectors to improve efficiency and reduce emissions and plans to expand its use of Green taxes, which generated 14 percent of total tax revenue in 1999. Japan's efforts are aimed primarily at energy conservation. South Korea and Hong Kong are giving priority to reducing urban air pollution levels.[95]

Central Europe's efforts to address climate change have been overwhelmed by efforts to modernize the region's economies. The Bank for European Reconstruction and Development (BERD) was created in 1990 to help central European nations protect the environment. The bank has 42 charter members and an initial budget of $12 billion. The European Investment Bank has funded projects in Eastern Europe such as improving domestic gas production in Poland. The World Bank has also loaned money to Poland and Hungary to identify and redress environmental problems, establish a decentralized system for managing environmental problems, reform energy prices, help chemical and energy industries reduce pollution, develop energy conservation projects, and develop new energy sources. Other international organizations funnel financial assistance from the industrialized nations to the less developed countries for environment and natural resource projects.

Europeans have convened focus groups to assess public opinion concerning climate change issues. Group members were given experts' opinions on various climate change issues and access to interactive climate models and alternative scenarios, and were then asked to help write a report summarizing their views on the problem of climate change and policy options. Three conclusions were drawn from focus group observations. First, most people view these kinds of issues primarily in ethical terms rather than economic values. They are concerned about the impacts of climate change on people throughout the world now and in the future. Second, they believe that mitigation measures should be pursued even though there is scientific uncertainty—as suggested by the precautionary principle. Third, they believe that cost considerations in mitigation are very important: They believe that technological innovations can reduce the threats but are opposed to major increases in energy prices. There is some evidence that Americans have roughly similar views; one U.S. focus group also found that ethical considerations were very important and that action should be taken despite uncertainties, but they were opposed to decreasing energy use because they believed that meant decreasing energy services. Uncertainty may not be the barrier to preventative action, but actions are not likely to be supported, at least at current understanding, unless they are low in cost.[96]

The success of climate change policies is so difficult to predict because they are dependent on the interaction of political will, weather, economic activity, and technology. One major problem is that most of the technologies that use fossil fuels have a relatively long lifetime and will not be replaced soon. Complying with the Kyoto Protocol would require that a major part of transportation, energy, and industrial facilities and equipment be replaced soon, and there is little interest in assuming such major expenses. While there is more support in Europe for the Kyoto accord than there is in the United States, those countries are unlikely to impose limits on emissions if the American sources with which their industries compete are doing little to comply with the treaty.[97]

Climate Change Politics and the Importance of "Flexible Mechanisms"

The Clinton administration has directed a great deal of time and energy trying to convince other countries to accept flexible, market-based approaches to achieving greenhouse gas emission goals that are fraught with problems, rather than pursuing actions that will directly reduce emissions. The Kyoto Protocol provides for four flexible mechanisms that are called by different names but are all variants of emissions trading, where parties can meet their obligations by buying, selling, or trading units of emissions or emission credits that represent part of the total emissions allocated to them. Emissions trading can occur either among nations that have accepted legally binding GHG limitations, or between countries that have accepted binding limits and those that have not. Emissions trading could take place in a number of ways; the main goal is to reduce the cost of cutting emissions while meeting the overall targets for GHG emissions reductions.

The Kyoto Protocol provides for a number of flexible mechanisms that might be used in achieving these emission targets:

- Banking and averaging: Emission allowances may be saved during one year and used in subsequent ones. The binding goals are for an average reduction of greenhouse gas emissions (GHGs) over a five year time period; the U.S., for example, need only show an average reduction of 7% over five years to meet its target.
- Emissions target bubbles: Countries can aggregate their targets into one mega-target and reallocate targets to participating nations. For example, the EU committed to reduce emissions by 8% from 1990 levels and have proposed to reallocate targets to member states; Germany has agreed to a 21% reduction and the U.K., 19%; the final allocation must be provided when the EU ratifies the KP.
- International emissions trading: Countries that have accepted binding limits may buy and sell emission allowances across borders and require they hold adequate allowances at the end of each regulatory period to cover their actual emissions. For example, U.S. firms with domestically imposed allowances can trade with Canadian firms that have been allocated their own allowances.
- Allowance Trading: cap and trade programs that allocate allowances to sources and allow them to buy and sell allowances and require they hold adequate allowances at the end of each regulatory period to cover their actual emissions.
- Joint implementation: Trading may occur for projects located in different countries that have accepted binding targets. For example, a firm in Canada may invest in a project in the United States; the governments of both countries must approve of the transaction, the allowances are transferred in exchange for the investment, and the purchaser of the credits may use the credits in meeting its emission limits. Joint implementation projects limited to Annex I parties (industrialized and transitional economies).
- Clean Development Mechanism: Countries with binding limits may obtain credits to use in meeting their GHG allowances by investing in projects in developing countries that produce emission savings. A variety of actors may be involved. National governments or private businesses, for example, could pay for emission reducing projects and claim the credits for use in meeting their own targets. The Clean Development Mechanism evolved from the idea of a clean development fund to be created by fines paid by countries that failed to meet their emission reduction goals to a program where Annex I nations (those accepting binding emission reduction goals) can meet their emission reduction goals by investing in projects in NonAnnex I nations (developing countries) that promote sustainable development.

Joint implementation and clean development mechanism projects may only count emission reductions that are additional to what otherwise might have occurred; and they must be real, measurable, and quantified against a baseline. JI projects generate emission reduction units (ERUs); CDM projects generate certified emissions reductions (CERs), also called CDM credits.[98]

Joint implementation efforts have already been developed to reduce greenhouse gas emissions.[99] In order to meet emission-reduction commitments and to gain some experience with joint implementation projects, several U.S. utilities developed agreements to offset their carbon dioxide emissions with investments in less developed countries.[100] Examples of such joint implementation projects include a program funded by the New England Electric Systems to reduce logging in Malaysia, and also efforts by the Wisconsin Electric Power Company, the Northern Indiana Public Service Company, and the Edison Development Company to assist a Czech Republic power plant convert to natural gas and become more efficient. The AES Corporation, an independent power producer, funds CARE projects to slow deforestation in Guatemala and protect Paraguayan forests.[101]

A successful trading program that reduces emissions and contributes to the achievement of the Kyoto Protocol's goals requires clear rules to govern the exchanges. The trades must be transparent, there must be accountability and enforcement, there must be accurate measurement of emissions, and the entire system must also be flexible enough to encourage buyers and sellers to transact freely and generate the promised economic savings.[102] Developing countries face numerous challenges in developing the capacity to take advantage of the opportunity provided by the CDM to gain financial assistance. They need help determining the baseline of GHG emissions and monitoring emissions; they need institutions to manage the programs; they need educational efforts to explain the opportunities; and so on. More important may be the need to convince these nations that climate change deserves priority and should compete with pressing economic and social problems, and that climate change programs are in their interest even while they appear to be contrary to their short-term goals in economic growth.

Because the primary concern is the total atmospheric concentrations of CO_2, rather than local concentrations, emissions trading can help reduce the cost of achieving the total emissions reductions necessary to meet the acceptable concentration level. A trading program may help reduce the cost of emissions reductions to politically acceptable levels, much as it did for the acid rain program. The Clinton administration has estimated that the cost of reducing emissions from energy-related sources by 31 percent from 1990 levels, as required by the Kyoto Protocol, would be about

$7–12 billion a year; if an "efficient and effective" trading system were used to achieve the reductions, the administration argued, total compliance costs could be reduced by 60 to 75 percent. Costs could be reduced even further, the administration argues, if an effective CDM were in place to reduce emissions in developing countries.[103]

Flexible mechanisms are a key in the United States because they are seen as central to ensuring that GHG-reduction measures do not harm the economy and are pursued at the lowest possible cost. They are, at least for now, a required element of any climate change agreement the United States will participate in. Emissions trading allows the United States (and other nations) to purchase from other nations allowances that are less expensive than the cost of investments to reduce its own emissions. Russia and Ukraine, for example, committed only to keeping their emissions at 1990 levels by 2008, but because their economies were so depressed at the end of the 1990s, they can actually increase their emissions by 50 and 120 percent, respectively, from 1998 levels. And because their economies will not grow by anything close to those levels, the extra emissions will be available for purchase, and actual GHG emissions will not be reduced. The 1998 Clinton plan called for achieving up to 75 percent of the reductions by purchasing allowances from Eastern Europe, and while the proposal was widely criticized and may not be pursued, it illustrates how emissions trading may fail to produce significant cuts in fossil fuel use.[104]

Experience with emissions trading in the United States suggests that emissions trading programs work best—and create more effective incentives to reduce pollution and encourage economic activities that are ecologically sustainable—when they are based on accurate emissions information, are built on emission limits that give adequate protection to environmental quality and natural resources, are stable and predictable, and are rigorously enforced. Many of these conditions simply do not exist for greenhouse gases. There is not yet in place an accurate, comprehensive monitoring system to determine CO_2 emissions and to ensure compliance with emission limits, for example. Nor is there even the basis of an adequate enforcement mechanism.

The politics of the Clean Development Mechanism is even more problematic than for other forms of emissions trading. Getting the developing countries to accept binding reductions is critical to the success of the Kyoto accord, but it is also extremely difficult. Between 1950 and 1995, the developed countries produced a total of some 550 billion metric tons of carbon dioxide; the developing nations produced less than 90 billion metric tons during that same time. Per capita emissions in the industrialized world are about 12 metric tons/person/year, and about 2 metric tons/person/year in the developing countries.[105] If present trends continue, emissions from the developing nations will exceed those from the industrialized world within the next decade or so, according to one projection,[106] and around 2020 by another,[107] so the participation of the South is critical. But there is no mechanism under the Kyoto Protocol for determining binding or even voluntary reductions for developing nations. Many leaders and residents of developing nations argue that development aimed at reducing poverty is their top priority, and are opposed to any global accord that threatens that goal. The threat of climate change pales in comparison with more immediate threats of poverty and local environmental problems such as polluted water, indoor air pollution, and limited fertile lands.

If developing countries do not accept binding GHG emission limits, the Protocol seems destined to fail, because the United States will not ratify and greenhouse gas emissions will not decline. It is difficult to envision a scenario where the South would accept binding limits in exchange for firm commitments from the North to reduce their emissions and fund reductions in the South, but such a deal is fundamental to the future of Kyoto. An example of such a deal might be as follows. Developing countries might agree to put a cap on their emissions of GHGs in exchange for contributions to a fund over which they have control to finance development projects that would contribute to the achievement of the cap. Since the Protocol allows some industrialized countries to increase their emissions (Australia can increase its GHG emissions by 8%; Iceland, by 10%), the developing nations will likely demand at least the same. The problem, of course, is that if their emissions increase by 10 percent and industrialized world emissions decline by 5 percent, we don't actually reduce CO_2 emissions. In 1990, developing country emissions of CO_2 were about 6 billion metric tons; developed nation emissions were about 15 billion tons.[108] The goal under this scenario would be to get industrialized country emissions at about 14 billion and developing nation emissions at about 7 billion, in order for total global emissions in 2008 to return to 1990 levels. These calculations are coarse and incomplete, since they only include CO_2 and ignore other GHGs. But they illustrate the rough parameters of the nature of a possible North-South deal. While the goal of returning to 1990 levels is far from sufficient according to some, who argue that significant reductions from those levels are required to reduce the risks appreciably, success in returning to 1990 levels would be a tremendous achievement, given that GHG emissions have already increased since 1990 and will continue to do so unless dramatic actions are taken

The CDM is the key to get the support of all parties, But there are numerous challenges to be addressed before CDMs are acceptable to both sides and can serve as the basis for making the Kyoto Protocol a reality. First, there are different models for CDMs:[109]

• Government-run: A government agency is authorized to solicit proposals for projects that would reduce GHG emissions or generate credits,

select the projects, oversee the certification, and monitor or even manage the transfer.

- Market-based: Developers and investors would propose projects, raise
funds, manage the project, find a buyer; an independent body would
certify the credits and monitor the process.
- International agencies: The World Bank, the Global Environment Facility, and other multilateral institutions could fund projects that are either proposed by governments or private entities.

Different models could be used in different places. Where markets are
working and governments can oversee transactions, for example, the
market model could be used. Where there is no effective government, the
multilateral lending model might be best. There may be problems of con-
sistency if different models are used. The key challenge is to ensure that
credits are real, measurable, permanent, and additional to what would
otherwise have been done.

A second challenge is determining the number of allowances involved
in trading. From the perspective of economic efficiency, trading should be
as broad as possible and be open to as many parties as possible. But trading also poses the problem of appearing to allow sources to buy credits
from others rather than reducing their emissions. Trading allows polluters
to "escape" the obligation to reduce emissions. Limiting trading to, say, 50
percent of total allowances—permitting nations to purchase no more than
50 percent their emission reduction obligations through trading would
help allay the charge that wealthy sources are not doing their share to
clean up but are simply buying their way out of responsibility. Here, economic and political imperatives clash, and a compromise might be helpful in making trading more broadly acceptable.

A third major challenge in designing and implementing CDMs is that
both parties have an incentive to inflate credits. Unlike in other contrac-
tual agreements, where parties have incentives to enforce the agreements
and ensure the integrity of claims made and the value of goods and services exchanged, here both parties have an incentive to inflate the reductions traded. No one has the incentive to ensure that reductions have really occurred. This makes certification of credits and oversight of the
transactions critical.

Fourth, some governments lack the capacity to implement an emissions
trading system. A number of other global environmental treaties are
plagued by enforcement and compliance problems, and the CDM would
not likely be any different. Enforcement is problematic: will governments (in
nations both developed and developing) have the political will to sanction
locally powerful industries that fail to comply with GHG trading regulations? If there is a perception that cheating is widespread and the credibility
of trading programs damaged, then trading will fail. NGOs will play a key

role in monitoring certification and monitoring, but that requires transparency in the process and the availability of information to them.

A fifth concern is that the generation of GHG reduction credits is based on the calculation of the level of GHGs that would have been emitted in the absence of a project. This is a hypothetical figure that is difficult to calculate. There is a strong incentive for sources and nations to inflate their GHG inventory in order to be in a position to claim more reduction credits. Governments may be hard pressed to be able to calculate accurate baselines. There will be strong incentives to establish generous baselines and credits. The calculation of credits requires certifying bodies to be able to ensure that reductions are permanent and additional. Should projects aimed at reducing local air pollution be eligible for funding as a source of GHG credits? Should projects planned for other reasons be part of the baseline? Should governments be able to claim credits for reducing subsidies, reforming prices, deregulating economic sectors, and restructuring energy production? These policies may be pursued for other reasons, such as reducing costs. And they may not be permanent because they could be reversed by a subsequent administration. Trading may encourage the creation of hot air credits that do not represent real reductions but are a result of declining economic activity.

Sixth, projects aimed at reducing GHG emissions or increasing carbon sinks may create incentives for increased emissions/decreased sinks elsewhere. For example, if some sources shift away from using coal, that might deflate coal prices and stimulate increased use by others. Carbon sequestration may be pursued through investments in plantations that displace farmers and encourage them to move to other areas and cut down trees for crop lands. Some of the cheapest ways of generating GHG credits is to invest in the protection or expansion of carbon sinks, such as planting trees. But this raises numerous problems, such as how to determine what the baseline is of carbon sequestration before a project is pursued, so that credits can be accurately calculated. There are great uncertainties in quantifying credits from carbon sequestration investments and determining their permanency. A 1998 study suggested that the amount of carbon sequestered in U.S. forests is greater than the amount of GHGs emitted by fossil fuel combustion; if so, the United States is not responsible for rising CO_2 levels. Further, the most potent sinks are young forests that are the result of old growth forests being cleared in the eighteenth and nineteenth centuries in the Northeast for farms. Those farms were eventually replaced by the large farms of the Midwest and replanted as forests. The role of the United States as a carbon sink, then, may be a result of deforestation and development rather than policies suggested by environmental protection.[110]

A seventh concern is that effective enforcement that creates incentives for compliance is critical to the success of the CDM. But there are conflicting imperatives to be balanced. Simple rules, minimal transaction costs, and other factors lead to maximizing the volume of trading and the consequential benefits, while effective compliance and enforcement places limits and costs on the process. Sanctions for noncompliance must be developed. Who should bear responsibility for non-fulfillment of conditions—the buyer? The seller? Government? It may be possible to devise insurance schemes, funded by charges imposed on each transaction, that can be used to purchase credits to meet shortfalls. The system could include extra credits to be used for such a purpose. Sanctions for failure to comply with conditions could include a prohibition on future trading and reduction of subsequent allowances by the number of credits in dispute. Generators of credits may be required to demonstrate that real reductions have been produced before trading can occur, as is the case in other commodity markets, where producers must show that the product is available and certify its quality. But, again, this requires strong political will to sanction parties that fail to meet their obligations. Other challenges include how to deal with unanticipated problems such as forest fires that release carbon and destroy sinks?

Finally, the CDM does not offer much promise of helping the poorest residents of the developing countries who do not emit large amounts of greenhouse gases, but rely on low levels of energy from burning wood, crop residue, and animal dung. Reliance on these forms of energy takes considerable time and results in local environmental and health problems such as air pollution—affecting women and children in particular who spend many hours a day indoors cooking—and loss of fertilizer for croplands. Changes in emissions from these sources are not large enough to attract investments to generate emission credits. But their quality of life could be enhanced by the use of improved cooking stoves and renewable energy sources for cooking and heating. Emissions trading offers little hope of benefits to the poorest residents of the earth.[111]

Flexible mechanisms can be part of a political compromise that includes strong, aggressive environmental quality goals with flexibility and reduced compliance costs. Trading can only work when there is an accurate, comprehensive monitoring system so that the allowances can be allocated fairly and emissions monitored accurately; when the cap on emissions is sufficient to protect environmental quality; and when all sources are required to achieve reductions regardless of trading options. U.S. companies can expand their partnerships with developing countries and invest in cleaner technologies and conservation in ways that ensure that emissions from these areas do not increase, while reducing poverty and increasing the quality of life among the world's poorest residents.[112] Given the potential for population growth and increases in greenhouse gas emissions from developing countries, the transfer of cleaner technologies to these countries is critical. Until the problems of emissions trading are solved, much can be done to simply fund programs that transfer technologies to poorer countries that will help them reduce poverty without increasing greenhouse gas emissions.

Business groups seem to be moving to the middle of the debate, while Congress remains clearly on the side of skeptics. The coal industry, oil companies, auto makers, and other heavy industries have pressured Congress to block any action. However, some multinational companies have already begun to calculate their total GHG emissions, set a goal of annual reductions, and allow trading across divisions. The position industries take in the debate is critical, particularly their embrace of flexible mechanisms. The future of the Kyoto Protocol is tied to the ability of nations to come up with an effective CDM program. The CDM may include different models of market/government action, depending on the governing capacity of participating states; sources in the MDCs will fund projects that are of interest to the LDCs and generate high credits; there will need to be developed clear means of certifying the generation of credits, particularly if carbon sequestration projects are included; and the system must be transparent and monitored by NGOs. There are tremendous barriers to overcome, and success is uncertain. A pressing question is to decide whether to continue to work within the Kyoto framework or to begin pursuing an alternative strategy.

The United States and other industrialized nations could choose to make unilateral reductions in GHG emissions for additional economic and environmental reasons. The United States, for example, might set a goal of reducing emissions by 1 percent a year, in order to produce gradual but firm reductions. Carbon dioxide emissions in the United States are roughly distributed equally across three sources: transportation, industrial sources, and residential and commercial sources. A trading program might start with 2000 as a base year, and allocate credits. The major economic sectors could each be given reduction goals, and permitted to buy and sell allowances in meeting those goals. Smaller sources that cannot efficiently participate in trading could be reached through taxes. Alternatively, government agencies could identify the most cost effective measures and subsidize them directly or mandate their achievement. A host of trading opportunities would be created. An owner of a power plant might convert the operation from coal to natural gas, and sell extra allowances to a plant that uses coal to meet peak load demands. A building owner might invest in more efficient energy use, and sell credits to an industrial source that needs credits temporarily for a soon-to-be-closed facility. Credits could be generated from upgrading the fuel efficiency of a fleet or retiring and scrapping old vehicles.[113]

The main advantage of such an approach is that it would encourage investments in conservation, cleaner fuels, and other technologies that can reduce costs, reduce local air pollution and the associated health threats, and generate new technologies that can be exported globally. Such a commitment would be in the economic interest of the nation as well as in improving local air quality. It is rooted in the idea of the "no regrets" policy, articulated by the Bush administration in 1990, as the core of its approach to the threat of climate change. While the policy was never really pursued by that administration, there is ample evidence that such investments are economically quite compelling.[114]

An alternative to the approach taken in the Kyoto Protocol is to pursue a new set of negotiations that focus on actual measures countries agree to take, rather than on goals for reduced emissions. The UN has sponsored other global accords that set goals, such as those to reduce poverty, with similar effects: parties can agree to laudatory goals and then go home and do relatively little to achieve them. Goals have been a central element of environmental laws in the United States, often with similar results. The United States is still far from achieving the goal of zero emissions into navigable waters under the Clean Water Act, and statutory deadlines for achieving goals of the Clean Air Act have been regularly missed. In contrast, parties could negotiate specific measures they promise to take to reduce GHG emissions, such as reducing fossil fuel subsidies, invest in renewable energy sources, restructure the production of electricity, increase forest covers, tax carbon emissions, and other measures. These actions can be monitored through prices, government purchases and spending outlays, and other concrete indicators.

Such an approach is consistent with trade negotiations, the subject of international accords that is for many the most successful. While there is much to question about the environmental consequences of the General Agreement on Trade and Tariffs and its implementation by the World Trade Organization, they have been rather successful in achieving their goal of reducing trade barriers. The approach taken is not for parties to agree to reduce barriers by X percent, but to negotiate specific measures and to back up compliance with sanctions. Governments are responsible for monitoring and enforcing the actions of industries operating within their borders so that they comply with these measures. Such an approach to GHG reducing strategies may be more effective than setting goals.[115]

Another option is to focus on reducing vulnerability to climate-related problems. Sarewitz and Pielke argue that "framing the problem of global warming in terms of carbon-dioxide reduction is a political, environmental, and social dead end" and one that offers "no realistic prospect of a solution." Instead, they argue, efforts would be much more effective, and produce much more human benefit, if they were aimed at reducing society's vulnerability to weather. The goal should not be to prevent humans from disrupting the environment but to "ameliorate the social and political conditions that lead people to behave in environmentally disruptive ways."[116]

Their recipe for action includes three goals: "encouraging democracy, raising standards of living, and improving environmental quality in the developing world."[117] Not only will these efforts help people adapt to changing climates but will also produce real reductions in carbon dioxide emissions. Encouraging democracy in developing countries will foster the development of groups and mechanisms for holding government and business officials for the environmental harms they produce. Raising standards of living will give people more resources to protect themselves against weather and climate. Resources should be channeled towards producing information that can be used in preparing for an preventing disasters and reducing vulnerability to problems when they strike. These actions could be pursued along side other efforts to promote energy efficiency and cleaner fuels and technologies that have clear economic and environmental benefits independent of GHG reduction concerns. Such a reorientation also promises to be politically popular:

> As an organizing principle for political action, vulnerability to weather and climate offers everything that global warming does not; a clear, uncontroversial story rooted in concrete human experience, observable in the present, and definable in terms of unambiguous and widely shared human values, such as the fundamental rights to a secure shelter, a safe community, and a sustainable environment.[118]

It is highly unlikely that the goals of the Kyoto Protocol will be accomplished, but it is possible that some progress might be made in reducing the rate of growth of GHG emissions. A strong commitment to the CDM and emissions trading may encourage investments that reduce emissions and contribute to other environmental goals, such as reducing local air pollution, and may result in investments in developing countries LDCs that improve their material standard of living. But there are alternatives to the Kyoto Protocol that represent some promising options, and debate and analyses of different approaches should proceed vigorously while negotiations for the Protocol continue.

Conclusion

Climate change is an enormously complicated issue. The stakes are similarly profound. Because energy use is at the heart of economies of the industrialized nations, and at the core of solutions to reducing the risk of climate change, solutions will touch virtually every aspect of the economy.

The transition to forms of energy has begun. But the lingering questions are whether the transition will be the result of public policies or of market forces, whether the transition will come soon enough to foster an orderly shift, or whether the path will be disruptive and damaging. Global environmental politics, many believe, will require some kind of major catastrophe before people will be prodded to demand more aggressive political action and change their own behavior. Earth Day Canada coordinator Jed Goldberg observed that "opinion polls all over the place say people are vaguely aware of climate change and global warming, but they're not willing to make the lifestyle changes necessary to deal with the issue."[119] Climate change requires the most ambitious changes in public and private behavior. It is the key to moving toward a more ecologically sustainable society. At the beginning of the twenty-first century, the prospects for an orderly, manageable transition to sustainability through climate change policies seem remote.

6

Environmental Politics, Sustainability, and Self-Interest

Humans are a species that tell stories—they live their lives around stories that give meaning and understanding. The telling of stories is not a simple act, as writer Susan Griffin explains it, but a way of narrating events that gives the listener "a path through those events that leads to some fragment of wisdom . . . by such transmission, consciousness is woven."[1] The stories Americans tell about the land, nature, and the environment are critical in shaping consciousness and, eventually, in determining how people act and how they respond to information and demands for changed behavior.

The story that has dominated environmental politics in the United States, and other high-consumption societies, is that protecting the environment is one of several values we want to pursue and that we are engaged in a continual search to balance competing values and objectives. While environmental politics differ across these nations, environmental voices are among many clamoring for attention and demanding that governments enact and implement policies to protect environmental quality and preserve resources. Environmentalism is a story of the creation of pollution laws that reduce emissions from big smokestacks and pipes that spill their contents into rivers and lakes, lawyers suing recalcitrant industries unwilling to limit their wastes, women organizing their neighbors to demand actions to protect the health of their children, scientists generating findings of emerging problems, engineers designing innovative solutions that reduce wastes, corporate executives promising to improve their companies' environmental image, and politicians assuring that priority will be given to environmental protection.

These stories have accomplished a great deal. In most of the wealthy world, some forms of air and water pollution have diminished. Some sites contaminated by hazardous wastes have been cleaned up. Renewable energy sources are being deployed throughout the world. New technologies

are empowering grass-roots groups, consumers, governments, and businesses to solve pollution problems and use resources more efficiently.
Birth rates have fallen in many developing countries. But every positive
trend can be countered by a negative one. Population growth will continue, primarily in the countries least able to absorb it. The per capita resource base to sustain life, such as topsoil, water, and fisheries, is declining. The global average temperature is rising, the stratospheric ozone
layer over Europe is thinning as it has in other areas, ice caps and glaciers
are melting, coral reefs—the breeding grounds for many species of marine
life—are being destroyed, water tables are falling, the land available to
grow food is shrinking, and the oceanic fish catch is leveling off.[2]

Environmental politics has not been sufficient for two main reasons.
First, despite some progress, environmentalism as just one (albeit, important) interest among many is not enough to encourage the breadth and
depth of changes required to mitigate global environmental trends. Many
of the easiest and cheapest to remedy have been cleaned up, and the remaining problems are more difficult to address. Environmental politics
has led to changes that have allowed us to grow economically and in population without making some problems, such as energy consumption per
unit of economic output, much worse but also without putting us on a
course to reduce the problems. Other problems, such as the threat of climate change and loss of biodiversity, are simply growing.

Second, the story is rooted in individual liberalism, where rights and
liberties are the terms of discourse more than responsibilities and obligations. Environmentalism has enjoyed broad appeal because it promises to
vindicate important rights. People have a right to breathe clean air, drink
clean water, eat food free from dangerous chemicals, and live near land
not contaminated by hazardous wastes, and if those rights are not protected, their government must act to secure them. But the burden of proof
is on governments (or on citizens if their governments are ineffective) to
demonstrate that chemicals are unsafe and pollution exceeds allowable
limits. The reactive mode of environmental regulation is too inefficient
and fails to take advantage of the great potential for reducing problems by
preventing pollution and redesigning processes and products to avoid
producing adverse effects that must then be mitigated. Far more effective
is to shift the burden to producers to show that their actions do not produce any harm, to be members of a community where people do not
dump their garbage into their neighbors' air and water.

Environmental and other social movements are part of a range of phe-
nomena—spontaneous, unstructured responses to public problems; spontaneous and fluid movements with some organization and structure; institutionalized interest groups that participate in established political and
policy making processes but are outside of formal governmental authority;

and advocates who occupy elected or appointed offices. Elements of environmentalism can be found at each entry on the continuum: Some of the environmental policy agenda may be institutionalized, some environmental groups are well integrated into environmental policy making processes, grassroots efforts are closest to the idea of social movement, and some environmental ideas are still at the fad or trend stage. Environmentalism has had a profound impact on economic, political, and personal behavior throughout the world. Yet, despite its considerable successes, it has not transformed these behaviors in ways that are ecologically sustainable.

The kind of environmentalism required to meet the challenges of the twenty-first century is still a social movement, a set of values, attitudes, behaviors, and organizations that are largely outside of government, that seek to mobilize people to change their behavior in ways that are more ecologically sustainable. The challenge for this and any other social movement is to retain its social energy, be a force that engages the public and civil society and provokes policy makers. A social movement that achieves its goals can take several forms. It can remain a social movement and work through private (market and organized group) means, or it can engage policy makers as an influential interest, or it can become part of the government itself. It is far from clear what form will be most likely to contribute to improved environmental quality. Becoming part of the governing structure, as in a green party, is obviously attractive, because of the opportunity to shape public policy. But since private behavior is at least as important a target as public policy, a social movement might be more influential if it remains part of civil society. That debate lies ahead. More immediate is the formulation of the idea of sustainability that will underlie the next generation of environmentalism.

Sustainability as Environmental Worldview

The idea of sustainability is compelling for several reasons. Sustainability is admittedly a broad and vague term. Different people define it differently. It has the potential to aggregate a wide range of interests under its umbrella, but is specific enough to give some direction. Lamont Hempel argues that sustainability, like other transformative ideas, "promises to remake the world through reflection and choice, but its potential to engage people's hopes, imagination, and sense of responsibility may depend more on strategic uses of ambiguity than on conceptual precision and clarity." As argued in chapter 1, sustainability is a powerful concept because it is "sufficiently ambiguous to be embraced by diverse interests, yet coherent enough to inspire movement in a particular direction."[3] Sustainability has the potential to become one of the ideas, like justice, equality, and freedom, that become fundamental expectations for public and private behavior as well as take shape in different contexts in providing specific guidance for action.

Sustainability focuses on comprehensive solutions that reflect the inter-connections of ecology. It respects the maxim, "Everything is connected to everything else," that is at the heart of ecology.[4] It requires that we deal with a broad range of problems that people are concerned about—sprawl, traffic, air pollution, open spaces, access to recreation, overcrowding, and other ills that threaten our quality of life. It suggests that we can do some-thing about these elements of modern life that plague us.

Sustainability compels us to look at the consequences of our actions on future generations. Some critics of efforts toward sustainability and inter-generational equity argue that there is no inherent responsibility to main-tain the human race. Mere perpetuation is not an ethically defensible po-sition. But what makes sustainability politically powerful is not the abstract notion that it will keep humans populating the world for millen-nia, but that we will take actions so that our grandchildren and their chil-dren enjoy at least the same quality of life we do. That is all sustainability needs to accomplish; we cannot anticipate future societies hundreds of years ahead. Making the earth sustainable for the next few generations will be an impressive feat. A millennial year is a dangerous time to think ahead: We are tempted to look far into the past or future—and far beyond our ability to understand—to create unreasonable expectations. Sustain-ability is a powerful idea because it forces us to deal with current prob-lems that are interconnected.

Sustainability is largely a concept of community. The most thriving ex-amples of sustainability seem to be in that context. There is considerable en-thusiasm for the idea of sustainable communities. Sustainability is bound up with notions of strong democracy, participation, and community, and those social characteristics are fostered through a scale of personal interaction. So too is a commitment to a land ethic. As Aldo Leopold de-fined the land ethic, sounding much like a proponent of sustainable com-munities, "An ethic, ecologically, is a limitation on freedom of action in the struggle for existence. . . . All ethics so far evolved rest upon a single premise: that the individual is a member of a community of interdependent parts. . . . The land ethic simply enlarges the boundaries of the community to include soils, water, plants, and animals, or collectively: the land."[5] Dale Jamieson argues that sustainable works in the negative, at the local level. We can agree when local land practices are not sustainable:

> In many specific contexts the language of sustainability can be made more useful by focusing on what is unsustainable rather than on a positive defini-tion of sustainability. Often people who would initially disagree about what sustainability is can agree about when something is unsustainable. Ranchers

and environmentalists (for example) may agree that eroded, denuded land is unsustainable, even if they disagree about what it would be like for the land to be sustainable.[6]

Some argue that sustainability requires the balancing of the "triple Es"— economic prosperity, environmental quality, and social equity. Fairness, ecological health, and production and consumption must be pursued in tandem. For some, economic growth is still the primary value, and sustainability considerations are seen as constraints, just as environmental regulations were viewed in the 1970s and 1980s. Economic and environmental goals are seen as conflicting and requiring tradeoffs. For others, sustainability challenges capitalism and its emphasis on private property rights, corporate structures that are accountable to short-term rate-of-return calculations, competitiveness and the inexorable pressure to externalize and reduce costs, creative destruction and the continual need to generate new demand for consumption, and the incentives that come from unequal distribution of wealth. Sustainability requires new ways of thinking that integrate ideas of individual rights, community responsibility and accountability, material and spiritual well-being, and ecological health. Sustainability requires, from this view, a radical set of changes to ensure fairness in the distribution of benefits and burdens, a perpetual resource base and ecological services, and a social system that secures the interests of all.

Garrett Hardin's 1968 essay, "The Tragedy of the Commons," was a critical element of the ideas that eventually matured into the idea of ecological sustainability. Hardin suggested that either government regulation would intervene to protect the resource or it would be lost. Some have argued that there is a third alternative: The users of the commons can develop a shared set of values and sense of responsibility that encourage them to act in concert to conserve the resource on which they all depend. People act in pursuit of their own best interests; the key is to figure out how to help them see that collective solutions are in their interest and that the depletion of the commons can be avoided if they limit their consumption and resist the temptation to get all they can of a resource before it is gone.[7] Other theorists have posited related theories that suggest why stakeholders in such a situation may make decisions that are not in their best interest (the prisoner's dilemma) because they lack information about what others whose actions affect their interests will do or a means of coordinating their responses, and why agreements are so difficult to fashion when some parties can opt out of constraints but can enjoy the benefits of others' restraints (the free rider). A combination of education—the development of shared values and sense of responsibility—and effective regulation, rather than one or the other, seems to work best. As stakeholders come to see the connection between their use of resources and the consequences that follow, they will come to see that it is in their interest to preserve the common resources. Good data and effective communication are critical. Regulation can reinforce those commitments, create incentives and sanctions to encourage the pursuit of long-term strategies, and reduce the chance that stakeholders will defect from their shared view of common interests to pursue a narrow, unsustainable interest.

There is tremendous interest in community-based, collaborative decision making as a process for making sustainable policies. Some argue that stakeholders should develop their own process; others call for a more structured approach. Some stakeholder groups are established to produce an agreement that everyone embraces and the relevant government agency simply implements, while other forms of participation aim to provide opportunities to respond to proposed decisions and analyses. The U.S. Forest Service and other stakeholders interested in national forest management and planning, for example, have created forestry partnerships to find innovative solutions to the challenges of balancing local economic activities with ecosystem protection, fire management, and other issues. Collaboration seeks to avoid the conflict, litigation, and other problems that have plagued other planning processes, and provide a forum for government officials from different levels of government and overlapping jurisdictions to work together. One of the best-known examples of collaboration is the Quincy Library Group, stakeholders who met in the Quincy, California, town library in the 1990s to devise a management plan for the nearby national forest. National environmental groups opposed the Quincy group's final plan, and Congress eventually intervened by passing legislation to codify the plan. But the idea is not new: Federal public land agencies have convened advisory groups for decades to solve problems and implement policy.[8]

Various forms of collaborative processes are likely to be used by communities as they develop plans and policies for sustainability. A detailed discussion of these processes is not possible here. But a brief discussion is needed to highlight the importance of finding political processes to engage members of a community in devising comprehensive, integrated plans to promote sustainability. Robin Gregory identified some of the problems with the ways in which public participation often takes place in environmental decision making, and argued that "too often decision makers cast a wide net for hearing citizens' views but then disappear behind closed doors to interpret what they have heard and to work out the tough conflicts that inevitably arise across disparate points of view."[9] He suggested five steps that government agencies can take to ensure meaningful involvement in decision-making processes and more effectively incorporate input for stakeholders in deliberations. His structured decision-making approach to public involvement involves five main tasks:

- Framing the decision and identifying the key contextual elements of the decision.
- Defining key objectives of stakeholders.
- Establishing alternatives in light of relevant constraints.
- Identifying consequences and their likelihood of occurring.
- Clarifying tradeoffs and using that knowledge to create new and better alternatives.

Public participation requires the development of a strong foundation; it is not enough for agency officials to "be good listeners" or to "avoid jargon." The goal here is not to produce consensus but information about key constituents—the values to which they are committed and the tradeoffs that are important to them—so decision makers can take those views into account as they decide how to respond to different constituencies. This is a much more modest and realistic expectation than to believe that bringing the stakeholders in one room will produce a consensus.

Proponents argue that successful collaborative processes include the following characteristics: (1) involve the interests of stakeholders who are most affected by decisions, (2) empower local environmental protection groups to advocate for broad environmental values in local decisions, (3) ensure that all interests have adequate resources to represent their views and participate effectively, (4) allow agencies to facilitate participation among stakeholders and develop plans responsive to their concerns, within the constraints of national laws and policies, (5) reduce conflict among stakeholders, (6) generate opportunities to find innovative, and low-cost solutions, and (7) promote partnerships between agencies and stakeholders that promote implementation and foster problem solving and learning by experience. One critical issue here is determining the goal of collaboration: Is it to produce actual decisions and plans that governmental authorities simply adopt, or to assist decision makers in discharging their responsibilities? The more that collaborative groups are seen as advisory, the less concern there is about displacing agency authority. But the more decision-making power collaborative groups have, the more opportunities there are to capture the advantages of collaboration. Collaborative groups have arisen in response to the inadequacies of traditional, agency-based decision making, so there are strong incentives to find new processes and structures.[10]

Critics of collaboration warn that the appeal of a consensus-producing process is illusory. They fear that the benefits of these processes are usually outweighed by serious flaws: (1) the processes exclude national stakeholders' views and weaken national environmental commitments, (2) fragment decision making and reduce the power of national planning efforts, (3) inevitably benefit industry interests that are typically better funded than conservation groups, (4) fail to encourage agencies to make the often difficult decisions mandated by environmental laws, (5) delegitimize the conflict that is sometimes required to move away from unsustainable use of resources and toward their preservation and co-opt the strength of environmentalism as a force rooted in broad public support, (6) increase the costs and time required to make decisions, and (7) fail to recognize that win–win solutions are not always possible as natural resources become increasingly scarce and preservation values fundamentally collide with commodity interests.[11] Part of the evolution of sustainability will be the development of new ways of bringing members of a community together to devise plans that will meet sustainability goals and generate strong commitments to comply with the difficult choices to be made.

Ecological sustainability is admittedly a broad and imprecise term; its vagueness has some political advantages in building support for the concept. But there is sufficient content to provide some direction for policy making. Table 6-1 outlines one way of giving some content to the idea of sustainability. There are elements here of both sustainable development— the thin form—and ecological sustainability—the thick variant. As explained in more detail following the table, the greater the level of commitment to these values and the more of them embraced, the closer a society comes to the goal of ecological sustainability. As these provisions are debated and refined, we can develop a clearer picture of how to achieve that goal.

Table 6-2 seeks to capture the wide range of global environmental problems. Different kinds of environmental problems require different kinds of political solutions. Sustainability promises to address all of these issues but requires different kinds of political responses in different contexts. Some issues require global efforts, while others can be pursued locally. There are at least five major kinds of global environmental problems and concerns that are being addressed in the global environmental movement:

- **Protection of global commons** such as the atmosphere, oceans, and regions such as Antarctica and the Arctic: All countries have a stake in preserving these key elements of the biosphere on which all forms of life depend.
- **Regulating transboundary pollution**: Global treaties and bilateral agreements address water, air, and other forms of pollution that cross national boundaries.
- **Managing environmental threats from global trade**: Globalization of markets and trade has greatly increased the interaction of countries and

TABLE 6-1
Elements of Sustainability

Ecological integrity and services
  Maintain ecological integrity, protect key ecosystem services
  Economic activity within ecological limits
  Intergenerational equity
  Bruntland Commission: meet needs of present without compromising those of future

Natural capital
  Sustainable yield of renewable resources
  Preservation of natural capital base
    Allow substitutes among natural, human, economic, social, cultural capital
    Allow some mixing of capital, but preserve key elements of natural capital
    Maintain each kind of capital—deplete oil but develop other forms of energy
    (Absolute preservation is the extreme but implausible form)
  Regeneration of natural capital

Precautionary principle
  Uncertainty, irreversible impacts, cascading and synergistic effects, cliffs, exponential growth

True-cost prices—internalize environmental costs in market exchanges
  Pollution prevention—redesign of production; life cycle management
  Regulation—emission standards; integration across media and sectors
  Property rights—prices reflect depletion; marketable rights—emissions trading
  Taxes—pollution taxes, fees, and charges
  Reduce subsidies that have harmful environmental consequences—water, energy
  Legal liability; liability insurance
  Economic valuation of natural resources—ecosystem functions

Economic indicators and measures
  Reflect depletion of natural resources
  Count pollution cleanup and illness treatment as costs
  Broader measures of social and economic factors—Genuine Progress Indicators

Wealth, population, and consumption
  Intergenerational: nondeclining per capita wealth
  Intragenerational: social, political, and economic equality and justice
  Bruntland Commission: interaction of poverty and environmental degradation

Technology
  Appropriate technology, super efficiency, technology transfer to South

Politics and government
  Decentralization, community, civil society, and NGOs

---

resulted in agreements to regulate international flows of pollution and wastes as well as chemicals, genetically modified organisms, and other products.

- **Distribution of global resources**, especially those that are scarce, such as biodiversity and fossil fuels, to ensure that there is some fair distribution of access and use as well as preservation for future generations.

- **Regulating essentially local pollution problems** that are found throughout the world and for which cooperation, technology sharing, and other interactions improve efficiency and effectiveness, particularly where more developed nations can assist less developed ones in fostering technical and regulatory capacity to address these problems.

The idea of sustainability may be better suited for some problems than others, as shown in Table 6-2.

Sustainability clearly requires preservation of natural capital—the natural resources that are used to satisfy human needs and wants and make life on the planet possible. But sustainability can mean one of several things here. A weak form holds that the current generation is obligated to pass on to future generations at least the same level of wealth and resources, but the mix of natural, economic, human, social, and even cultural capital is not important. What is important is that the functions performed by these different forms of capital can be maintained. For example, believers in technology may believe that virtual or digital forms of information expression can replace human sensory experience, or that interaction with nature in controlled contexts like zoos are equivalent in function to encounters in nature.

An intermediate position allows for some substituting across different forms of capital but also recognizes that some functions cannot be substituted. Engineers may not be able to design artificial replacements for some ecosystems, such as clean air, or the cost may be so much greater than preserving natural sources that sacrificing those sources to increase income may be irrational. Such a position may also recognize that there are no adequate substitutes for sensory interaction with natural, self-determining systems.

The strong version of sustainability requires that, for precautionary reasons and because we do not know what the desires of future generations (their utility functions, as economists term it) will be, we should ensure that each kind of capital is maintained. For example, we can deplete some nonrenewable sources of energy, such as oil, as long as we invest in new technologies such as solar power, so that future generations have at least the same reserve of energy resources that we have. Finally, the absolutist form of sustainability requires that we not use any nonrenewable resources, but that we limit ourselves to consuming only renewables. We have, of course, long since violated such a proscription, but there is some value here in assessing how far we diverge from this absolute standard. Proponents of preserving biodiversity argue, for example, that because we do not now know how to create or restore extinct species, the genetic

TABLE 6-2
Global Environmental Issues

Type of Issue	Kind of Problems	Global Response	Challenges
Pollution of global commons/resource extraction; regional commons	Atmosphere, oceans, biodiversity, forests, population	Conventions on climate change, law of the sea, and biodiversity; Antarctica; regional seas	Free rider, national sovereignty and enforcement, tragedy of the commons
Transboundary pollution	Air, water, hazardous wastes	Conventions on acid rain, river compacts, international court of justice	Sovereignty, states must consent to be bound; enforcement
Environmental threats resulting from international trade and global markets	Hazardous chemicals and wastes	Agreements on persistent organic pollutants, transboundary movements of hazardous wastes	Knowledge of contaminants, sovereignty, enforcement
Global impact of resource use—intragenerational and intergenerational equity	Consumption of limited resources; exploitation, colonialism, and free trade	Agenda 21, sustainable development	Sovereignty; interaction with economic policy; funding
Local pollution and resource problems that occur worldwide; cooperation, technology transfer, sharing of science and expertise	Air, water, waste, loss of biodiversity and threatened and endangered species	U.S.: Clean Air Act, Clean Water Act, Endangered Species Act, Superfund	Funding, economic competitiveness

pool currently encapsulated within the existing species represents the entire library of genetic material available to us, and that we should strive to preserve as much as possible. Others may argue, in the context of energy, that we should move much more aggressively toward renewable energy forms to reserve fossil fuels for future use.

Underlying this commitment to maintain ecological services and preserve natural capital is the precautionary principle. Given the uncertainty surrounding the consequences of resource use and pollution, we should err on the side of caution by preserving ecosystems and by minimizing pollution and resource use, as the stakes are so high and some consequences are irreversible. Sustainability is rooted in the need to protect against unintended consequences, possible synergistic effects when ecological conditions interact, and cascading effects and feedback loops that exacerbate ecological threats. Global environmental problems may spin out of control and the sheer power of exponential growth belies the belief that ecological change is incremental and predictable.[12]

Sustainability does not call for an end to markets but rather a commitment to make markets work the way they, in theory, are supposed to operate. Poorly functioning markets allow polluters to externalize some of the costs of production and distribution of their products in order to reduce costs, rather than reflecting those costs in prices accurately so that efficient decisions can be made about the allocation of scarce resources and consumers and producers have information about the real consequences of their decisions. The environmental costs of production and marketing can be internalized a number of ways. One of the most effective ways is to prevent pollution from occurring in the first place. Another innovative approach is for manufacturers to retain ownership and responsibility for their products, lease them to consumers rather than sell them, and then take back the used product for recycling and reuse of parts. Sustainability can also be pursued through regulations such as emission standards that go beyond the separate media (water, air, and land) to involve a much more integrated and effective program of reducing emissions. Property rights in resources can be allocated in ways that ensure that any depletion of a resource is reflected in higher prices, and that the most efficient reductions in pollution are made through trading emission rights. Taxes can send strong signals to reduce pollution and conserve resources; taxes on virgin materials can create strong incentives for recycling. Subsidies for water and energy projects that damage the environment and divert resources from more ecologically sound practices are another part of sustainability. Liability rules and the cost of insurance can contribute to conservation.

Adequate measures of the value of natural resources and ecosystem functions are essential in determining true costs and in finding more accurate measures of economic activities. Economic indicators such as the gross national product need to be revised to include measures of sustainability, such as the depletion of natural resources, the cost of cleaning up pollution and treatment for environmentally induced illness, and other broader measures of human well-being.

The distribution of wealth and material resources also is a concern of sustainability, both in terms of intergenerational equity and the wealth-generating opportunities preserved for future generations, and the distribution within the current generation. Wealth matters because the lack of it causes people to engage in ecologically damaging practices in order to survive. Landless farmers cut down rain forests to plant fields only to find in a few years that the lands are exhausted and more forests need to be cut. But sustainability requires also a sense of limits, appropriate scale, and the distribution of resources. The same forces that exploit natural resources also exploit people, and sustainability calls for solidarity and social concern among all human beings. Sustainability also requires that the pressures of human population and consumption growth be moderated. It is not enough to stabilize population growth, but the ecological impact of population is a function of the kinds of technologies that are prevalent, and the level of consumption. One of the fundamental tasks of sustainability is to decrease poverty and increase consumption or access to goods and services, while decreasing the level of pollution produced and the nonrenewable resources used.

Another key factor is technology—the key to decreasing pollution and resource use and increasing wealth and access to goods and services. Technologies can enhance the efficiency by which resources are used, so that fewer inputs are required and fewer effluents are generated. Appropriate technologies that are well suited to the environment in which they operate and to the human community of which they are a part are a key link in building sustainability. The transition is critical: We need to shift from technologies that helped create pollution and unsustainable resource use to those that have the opposite effect.

Finally, sustainability is intertwined with political and governmental renewal that encourages participation of citizens and engages them in identifying problems, designing solutions, and then implementing them. A strong sense of political efficacy encourages people to become involved in devising solutions to environmental problems. A robust commitment to community motivates people to reduce adverse impacts they impose on others and contribute to a shared quality of life. The kinds of changes needed for sustainability require motivation and commitment that are more likely to come from people who feel a sense of responsibility and accountability for how their actions affect the quality of life of others. The changes also require engagement and empowerment, so that participants devise solutions they are then willing to comply with. A spirited, vibrant civil society, composed of effective government and committed non-governmental organizations, works together to ensure that the common interests of all are realized.

These eight factors or variables can each be present in varying levels of commitment. The weaker they are, the closer is a community to the weak or thin form of sustainability, labeled here as sustainable development. The stronger the commitments and their implementation, the closer the community has moved to ecological sustainability, which, in its strongest form, involves the development of a new paradigm for the interaction of humankind with its environment that champions ecological values. Some argue that this is ultimately a transformation from an anthropocentric world view to an ecocentric or biocentric paradigm, where humans are not the primary focus of attention, but all forms of life are valued. Many find such a transformation inspiring, consistent with a commitment to a simpler, less selfish life that acknowledges the inherent value and sanctity of all forms of life and urges a strong commitment to ecological sustainability. But that commitment can also arise within the existing paradigm of self-interested humans: It is simply in our interest to preserve all forms of life, to help other species flourish, because we are all elements of an intricate network of living things—the health of each element of the system strengthens the entire biosphere and the life chances of its most intellectually advanced species.

Sustainability can also be profitably understood as a dynamic concept—a process, a journey, and not a destination or a goal. While Neil Harrison and others argue that sustainable development cannot be defined objectively and understandings of it vary widely, there are principles that can guide policy choices as the process unfolds.[13] Mazmanian and Kraft argue that environmental policy in the United States can be understood as evolving through three epochs or eras. The first era, in the 1970s, built the basic legal and institutional framework for environmental regulation, relying on traditional regulatory approaches of national standards applied throughout the nation. The second epoch, primarily during the 1980s, was a response to the cost of traditional regulation, aimed at reducing regulatory costs. The third epoch is sustainability, beginning in the 1990s, where environmental values are designed into production and distribution processes.[14] This framework is a useful way of theorizing about changes in environmental policy and politics and provides a means of assessing how widespread the commitment to sustainability is, and how far politics and policies have moved from earlier approaches. While the framework is an efficient way to chart the dynamic nature of politics and policy, it can be interpreted in different ways. From one perspective, there has been continual progress from one epoch to the next, and our collective capacity and commitment to preserving the environment have been growing. Epoch two built on the progress made in the first era of environmentalism and made it more sensitive to cost effectiveness in ways that have strengthened efforts. The third epoch is a further strengthening of protection and improvement in efforts. However, there is also ample evidence that epoch two signaled a retreat in environmental commitments and a weakening of governmental capacity, which may be further eroded as sustainable development emphasizes that the economy can grow without damaging the environment.

The idea of a transition from environmentalism to sustainability is attractive because it suggests that gradual, incremental change may be sufficient. But proponents of a thick ecological sustainability call for a new vision of how humankind relates to nature, and fundamental changes are required. Rajni Kothari, for example, suggests that sustainability requires an ethical shift—not a change in the way we employ technology or financial resources, but a shift in viewing nature not in terms of resources to be turned into economic commodities, but nature valued for itself and for the way it supports life. He says, "Respect for nature's diversity, and the responsibility to conserve that diversity, define sustainable development as an ethical ideal. Out of an ethics of respect for nature's diversity flows a respect for the diversity of cultures and livelihoods, the basis not only of sustainability, but also of justice and equity." For Kothari, ecological sustainability is intertwined with social justice: "The ecological crisis is in large part a matter of treating nature's diversity as dispensable, a process that has gone hand in hand with the view that a large portion of the human species is dispensable as well. To reverse the ecological decline we require an ethical shift that treats all life as indispensable."[15]

Self-Interest and Global Environmental Politics

Sustainability seems most promising as an idea for governing a community. The problem is how to extend the idea beyond our community. We may find that our own community is sustainable if we export our wastes or import unsustainable levels of resources. We may find that our own community thrives, while others live lives mired in poverty. How does sustainability guide us in these circumstances? Dale Jamieson argues that, ironically, "the discourse of sustainability is least likely to be useful at the level for which it was originally intended. At the global level there is too little by way of shared beliefs and values to provide enough content to ideas of sustainability to make them effective. . . . The forms of unsustainability and the causal linkages involved are too diverse to command much by way of common responses."[16]

Sustainability, because of its emphasis on community, participation, and integration of economic, social, cultural, and ecological values, seems best suited to guide community-based decision making. Indeed, that is the only level of action that such comprehensive efforts are likely possible. Michael Sandel argues that a commitment to a more engaged local environmental politics may also contribute to a greater sense of global politics required to address problems affecting global commons such as protecting the oceans, stratospheric ozone layer, and climate. "A more promising basis for democratic politics that reaches beyond nations," Sandel believes, "is a revitalized civic life nourished in the more particular communities we inhabit. . . . People will not pledge allegiance to vast and distant entities, whatever their importance, unless those institutions are somehow connected to political arrangements that reflect the identity of the participants."[17] Sandel argues that the republican tradition of government, as articulated by Aristotle and subsequent theorists, is that self-government should be understood as "an activity rooted in a particular place, carried out by citizens loyal to that place and the way of life it embodies." However, self-government now requires "a politics that plays itself out in a multiplicity of settings, from neighborhoods to nations to the world as a whole. . . . The civic virtue distinctive to our time is the capacity to negotiate our way among the sometimes overlapping, sometimes conflicting obligations that claim us, and to live with the tension to which multiple loyalties give rise." Participation and engagement in local political problem solving may engender the kind of commitment and sense of responsibility that might spread to broader, and eventually global issues, that members of Congress would find increasingly difficult to ignore.[18]

Sandel's argument that local civic involvement can lead to global citizenship may prove to be right. A strong commitment to future generations and to the well-being of the global community seems most likely to arise from a people and a political culture who see their future, and the future of their grandchildren, inextricably intertwined with those of their neighbors throughout the world. The way problems are defined is a critical step in the policy process. As long as sustainability is largely viewed as a problem for developing countries to solve, and is not understood as a challenge facing the United States and other high-consumption societies, little progress is likely. But the growing interest in sustainable communities may eventually contribute to the development of a national commitment to sustainability. If such a commitment springs from its people, the nation's policy-making institutions will find ways to devise effective, sustainable, economic, environmental, and social policies. The challenge is in generating the kind of power that other moral imperatives, such as freedom and equality, play in shaping public policy and personal behavior.

Ethicists have suggested a number of alternatives to the pursuit of self-interest that underlies our consumption, production, and economic lives in general, that produces worldwide environmental problems, and that makes international environmental law and cooperation so difficult. Their challenge is to outline a transformation in values that will move from citizens to their governments and the economic institutions that dominate their lives. Some look to religion, given its power to transform individual lives and alter deep-seated commitments, and many religious leaders have become passionate, articulate proponents of a new, ecological ethic consistent with a belief in God and reverence for creation. There is no doubt that such religious fervor can change lives and reshape behavior, but it is less clear that it can bring about a political transformation, particularly in politics that limit the use of spiritual values in shaping public policy. Religious-based politics carries its own threats of intolerance and zeal that can serve as barriers to the development of a new environmental ethic.

Others suggest secular visions of the ethical life. John Rawls's theory of justice as fairness is one of the most prominent efforts. His broad agenda focuses on the question of how human beings with conflicting values and interests can live together in peace and justice. Because the causes and consequences of environmental problems are not distributed equally across humankind, Rawls's theorizing on justice and fairness are quite relevant. Rawls defines the problem of justice this way: Each person's life changes are greatly influenced by the place in which she is born but that is not chosen; it is a question of luck. But the institutions that determine social, political, and economic opportunities are created by humans. How can we create morally acceptable institutions? He argues that inequalities are inevitable, but they must be justified. Justice as fairness, for Rawls, requires "equality in the assignment of basic rights and duties." Equal opportunities must be open to all, and social and economic inequalities are acceptable "only if they result in compensating benefits to everyone, and in particular for the least advantaged members of society."[19] Priority must be given to the status of the least well off, but this cannot be done by violating basic personal and civil liberties.[20]

For Rawls, conflicts among people are to be resolved by giving priority to the less fortunate; improving their status rather than devising a utilitarian measure where we add up the costs and benefits and try to maximize total benefit. To Rawls, cost–benefit analysis is unjust: It doesn't take into account the differences among individuals. People are disadvantaged by social structures for which they are not responsible. Justice is solidarity; the more fortunate can only benefit from social, political, and economic arrangements if the less fortunate benefit more. We may need differential rewards to encourage productivity but only if we see that the less well off would be advantaged by higher productivity and efficiency— those are acceptable goals only if they benefit the disadvantaged. Rawls rejects the idea that people can claim exclusive right to the fruits of their labor and genius as they are a function of chance in their distribution and social investment in their cultivation and development. Rawls calls for strong protection of freedom and for toleration and mutual respect. Some disagreements need to be worked out—we need to determine the basic structure of society; we can leave other issues unsettled, agree to disagree about other things. Freedom and equality take precedence over other conceptions of the human good; this is not neutrality over values but a statement or a belief about the hierarchy of values.[21]

Rawls argues that his theory of justice applies to some extent in international relations, where freedom, equality, and mutual respect should rule. But economic justice requires political institutions with more authority than that possessed by international bodies. The solution is the spread of liberal values, but it cannot be imposed on others. We need to find a way for liberals and nonliberals to live together. Critics argue that individuals rather than peoples are the morally relevant units and that equal respect of societies is less important than justice among individuals.[22]

Peter Singer suggests that our moral intuition, if we listen carefully to it, provides the basis for a global ethic of care. He suggests the following story:

> Bob is close to retirement. He has invested most of his savings in a very rare and valuable old car, a Bugatti, which he has not been able to insure. The Bugatti is his pride and joy. In addition to the pleasure he gets from driving and caring for his car, Bob knows that its rising market value means that he will always be able to sell it and live comfortably after retirement. One day when Bob is out for a drive, he parks the Bugatti near the end of a railway siding and goes for a walk up the track. As he does so, he sees that a runaway train, with no one aboard, is running down the railway track. Looking farther down the track, he sees the small figure of a child very likely to be killed by the runaway train. He can't stop the train and the child is too far away to warn of the danger, but he can throw a switch that will divert the train down the siding where his Bugatti is parked. Then nobody will be killed—but the train will destroy his Bugatti. Thinking of his joy in owning the car and the financial security it represents, Bob decides not to throw the switch. The child is killed. For many years to come, Bob enjoys owning his Bugatti and the financial security it represents.[23]

Singer suggests that our intuition tells us that Bob's conduct is wrong. We might commiserate with him and suggest that he is a most unfortunate fellow to be placed in such a dilemma. But Singer's point is that everyone living in the wealthy world is precisely in Bob's situation. Tens of thousands of children die each day of preventable hunger and disease, and billions suffer from hunger and other wants. If we simply consumed just enough to meet our basic needs and sent the excess—that which we spend on luxuries or to ensure a relaxing and financially secure retirement—to organizations that assist the poor, we could save millions of lives and help billions more reach a decent standard of living.

While Singer and Rawls are both primarily concerned about equality, their arguments are equally applicable to global environmental problems that are a result of inequities in consumption or represent injustices when there are mismatches in the distribution of benefits enjoyed by those who consume goods and services and those who bear the burdens of pollution. Similarly, sustainability-based demands that we forgo the use of some resources so that future generations are guaranteed access to the same level of wealth and ecosystem services are a variant of the idea of distributive justice.

The kind of ethical transformation suggested here seems far beyond the capacity of governments to achieve. One obstacle particularly strong in the United States is the fundamental importance of freedom. Orlando Patterson has argued that freedom is a key idea in Western culture, but actually incorporates three different concepts:

- Negative freedom—Not being under the power of others.
- Positive freedom—The opportunity to exercise power over ourselves.
- Shared freedom of democracy—Sharing in the public power of government.

Until the nineteenth century, Patterson wrote, the three strands were linked; there were disputes over the relative importance of each, but all were important elements of freedom. Liberalism includes only negative freedom, freedom defined as power to resist the encroachments of the state. It means individualism; a separation of the public versus the private; and the renunciation of paternalism, privilege, slavery, and aristocracy. These are considerable accomplishments, and America has made a global contribution to freedom by institutionalizing individual rights as a legal and constitutional claim. But liberalism in America has largely become unidimensional and others see it having little to offer today in dealing with global problems. Social democratic movements throughout the world have tried to reassemble the three strands of liberty. Since 1989, freedom, not libertarianism, has flourished throughout the world, but American political culture is weak, its politics corrupted by wealth and negative political attacks. It seems incapable of producing a vibrant democracy that abolishes want, provides opportunity for all, and preserves the environment on which this and future generations depend. Freedom as sharing in the power of government, in taking responsibility to solve collective problems, is weak.[24]

America's foreign relations are problematic as well. The United States, at the beginning of the twenty-first century, in the words of the editors of *The Economist*, "bestrides the globe like a colossus. It dominates business, commerce and industry; its economy is the world's most successful, its military might second to none." The problem is, however, that with all that power, the colossus "does not know how to behave. Should it act alone and unhindered on the world stage, since it can? Or should it willingly dilute its power in cooperation with others?"[25] While the focus of *The Economist*'s concern was the use of military power, the problem cuts across U.S. foreign policy. The editors rightly observe that, given economic globalism and the interconnectedness of markets and consumers throughout the world, the debate in the United States is not between isolationists and internationalists, but between unilateralists and multilateralists. Some believe that the United States is sufficiently powerful and wealthy to go it alone, to act where and when it wishes, to be independent, to not have to worry what others think or how to work with them. Perhaps nowhere is this position more clearly represented than by the Republican senator from North Carolina and chair of the Foreign Relations Committee, Jesse Helms, who addressed the UN Security Council in January 2000. Helms asserted that he was speaking for the American people in warning the UN to keep its "utopian" ideas off American shores and to respect American autonomy: "If the United Nations respects the rights of the American people, and serves them as an effective tool of diplomacy, it will earn and deserve their respect and support." But, he warned, a UN that "seeks to impose its presumed authority on the American people, without their consent, begs for confrontation and—I want to be candid with you—eventual U.S. withdrawal."[26]

Helms's attack on the UN triggered angry responses and criticism from nearly every member of the Security Council who rejected his view of the UN and blamed the United States for failing in its global citizenship. Even though only a small fraction of Americans have ever voted for Helms, his views appear to be representative of a broad slice of the country, from the nationalism of Pat Buchanan and the Reform Party, to opponents of U.S. troops under UN command. This view of American independence and exceptionalism has deep roots and is a profound barrier to American involvement in collective efforts to reduce global environmental threats. It is not insurmountable, as U.S. involvement in a variety of international settings attests. But that involvement is much more likely to be prompted by a recognition of self-interest than the pursuit of a new global ethic.

Even within the United States, an appeal to a new ethic of sustainability (or other objectives) is problematic. One of the great paradoxes of American political life is that despite a host of impressive collective achievements by its government—such as winning world and cold wars, building transportation and communications infrastructures, transforming the desert West, establishing a strong framework of markets and capitalist investment, and providing a social safety net—Americans still have great mistrust and fear of government.[27] Garry Wills argues that this mistrust of government has been remarkably consistent for more than two centuries of American history.[28] This skepticism makes it difficult to imagine the national government producing a commitment to a radically new and ambitious environmental ethic.

Lynton Keith Caldwell argues that there are four primary causes of these global environmental problems: (1) unrealistic and dangerous assumptions that underlie our thinking, such as a mistaken optimism in growth and progress and an inability to understand and respond to multi-linear and multi-loop feedback systems, (2) a lack of integrative and holistic research and an ignorance of cumulative impacts, (3) the driving forces of population, energy use, and destructive technologies, and (4) an unwillingness to take on difficult questions and to challenge narrow interests and conventions that retard change.

One of the key issues here is whether problems are best characterized as fundamental and conceptual or whether they are really quite familiar and understandable though clearly intractable. Caldwell's diagnosis is of both kinds: The problems are unfamiliar and perhaps unrecognizable to humans who cannot engage in "multi-linear" and "multi-loop" thinking, as well as the result of exponential growth in population, energy use, and industrial and commercial pollution. Caldwell nicely illuminates some of these conceptual dilemmas, such as the way humans have replaced reciprocity with command in their relationship with nature and our unrealistic expectations about growth and consumption.

But there are other ways of characterizing our dilemma in more concrete, familiar terms and concepts. Powerful economic incentives exist to externalize pollution and other costs and consume resources at unsustainable rates. The power of these economic forces poses tremendous barriers to changes in global governance and international law that seek to regulate and limit such actions. Global trade agreements make it difficult for some countries to devise policies aimed at preserving environmental quality and natural resources by making free trade the primary value to be pursued. The pressures on poor countries to generate exports for debt payments, feed burgeoning populations, and improve the quality of life among their citizens often result in unsustainable harvesting of resources. Thinking about global environmental threats in these terms is much different from using a discourse of failed paradigms and lack of multi-linear and multi-loop thinking.

Remedies to the global threats facing humankind, while clearly difficult to pursue, might be more effectively attacked directly and immediately than through the broad prescription Caldwell suggests. In terms of political strategy, are we more likely to bring about change the more the problems are discussed in concrete, familiar challenges? Or are we more likely to generate change if we call for a new way of thinking and a new set of assumptions? More fundamentally, what is the best way to characterize the problem? If we accept as a given the description of the state of the global biosphere provided by, say, the World Scientists' Warning to Humanity that Caldwell cites (see chapter 1), should we understand these problems in the traditional discourse of regulation—externalities, greed, short-term perspectives, pressures to reduce poverty by exploiting resources—or should we describe them in terms of failed paradigms and cognitive pathologies and incapacities?

How should we respond to these threats in ways that significantly reduce or eliminate the threat? Caldwell suggests two major responses: (1) more research on major social and environmental trends that is integrated into national policy making, and (2) development of an ethics of environmental stewardship and sustainability through persuasion and political leadership. This prescription seems best suited for the version of the diagnosis that points to a long-term, chronic problem that we need to gradually work our way through, with more research and plenty of public education and democratic politics. But that seems to be far too modest a response to the seriousness and potentially catastrophic nature of the environmental predicament. We may, for example, not have the luxury of ethical conversion but need to rally support for more coercive policies. Because the health of the environment is a precondition for all human activity, other values, such as individual rights and competing policy goals, may have to be sacrificed. The more the threat is understood in cataclysmic terms, the more radical the remedy required.

A call for a radical change in environmental policy can be effectively made within the context of self-interest. It is more interesting to cast the issue in terms that challenge our conceptual frameworks and paradigms. And it is clearly more consonant with our understanding of ecosystems, biological interconnectedness, and the interdependence of life. A new paradigm that places humans in the context of one of many species—one that consumes less and seeks more for spiritual growth and personal happiness, is more humble and modest in the face of the beauty and power of nature and creation, and reveres all forms of life—is tremendously attractive and compelling. It may be a prerequisite for the flourishing of human communities in the future. It is also a risky way to talk about global environmental risks because it seems so far removed from the possibilities of political change that we may lose the practical, political advantage that comes from concrete, specific, familiar diagnoses and remedies around which we can try to rally support. Our solutions may be inadequate, incomplete, and ultimately insufficient, but we may at least have a chance for some measure of survival if we do some things. If, in contrast, we focus on fostering new ways of thinking and the development of new ethical frameworks and paradigms, we may be mobilized too late for effective responses.

If the global environmental problem can be understood, at least for now, in terms of national self-interest, a final question raised here is the adequacy of current institutions to bring nation–states together to recognize and protect their interests. While there has been a significant amount of international cooperation, many argue that it falls far short of providing sufficient solutions to global environmental problems. One option is to create a stronger, supranational government to devise and implement comprehensive solutions. There are persuasive arguments for global governance. As discussed in chapter 1, a number of observers of global environmental conditions argue that a move to new, powerful, international bodies that can compel compliance with global standards is inevitable. Proposals range from strengthening the UN system of institutions and giving it new enforcement powers,[29] to creating new institutions such as a global legislature for the environment (an Environmental Protection Council), a Global Environmental Organization (to mirror the World Trade Organization), or a Trustee of the Global Commons.[30]

Ecological and political boundaries rarely align, and the connectedness of ecology typically clashes with the territorial autonomy of sovereign nations. Sovereignty poses tremendous challenges to the development and implementation of international environmental law. But the idea of sovereignty has evolved in significant ways, from upholding the rule of monarchs to fostering democratic states. Karen Litfin and her colleagues argue that sovereignty continues to evolve in response to global environmental efforts. While this "greening" of sovereignty is a promising development as the pressure mounts on nation–states to comply with international environmental standards, and some inroads on national autonomy are occurring, "We do not conclude that sovereignty is being eroded in any wholesale or homogenous fashion."[31] Sovereignty can be both a barrier to global cooperation and a key in developing and enforcing binding obligations on companies and citizens within their borders. International law reinforces national sovereignty, as states are the parties to treaties, challenges national autonomy, and seeks to compel unified action. Sovereignty is a bedrock principle in international relations, but there is some evidence that pressures to address environmental problems may alter it in significant ways in the future.

The growth of NGOs challenges traditional views of sovereignty, and they are playing a key role in the evolution of global civic politics and are shaping global civil society. Civil society is the area between the individual and the state, a complex network of economic, cultural, and social practices. States are not the only instruments of social change—activists in civil society are as well. As Paul Wapner puts it, "World civic politics works underneath, above, and around the state to bring about widespread change . . . the state system alone cannot solve our environmental woes nor will substituting it with some other institutional form do the trick." [32] NGOs lobby governments and play key roles in pressuring them to take environmentally sound actions, but their efforts go beyond government to change people's behavior in other ways. Groups like Greenpeace, Friends of the Earth, and the World Wildlife Fund, for example, target the global culture and seek to convince people to care about the planet and shape cultural norms. This is a significant form of world politics even though it does not involve the state. The World Wildlife Fund works with local residents to maintain and restore local ecosystems. Friends of the Earth gives priority to mobilizing civil society to interact with governments and make them more accountable for their environmental actions. Wapner argues that these efforts "actually alter the way people around the globe live their lives." [33]

NGOs play a critical role in keeping alive the idea of environmentalism as a social movement. Public opinion is solidly Green, due in large part to their efforts. Sustainability is becoming more widely used as representing the goal of environmentalism. But it is a weak form of sustainability. It is primarily a localized concept, intertwined with community, a sense of place, a scale of human interaction, public participation, and shared responsibility. It is not yet a global ethic and it may very well be incapable of playing a role. The weakness of Green Parties is a telling indicator: A strong Green Party with an expansive agenda that shows how ecological sustainability is the fundamental public value to pursue and how sustainability includes a broad range of issues would be exactly the kind of integrative function that parties play. Ecological sustainability requires that environmentalism's institutional form shift from interest groups to a party. Some kind of new organization or strengthening of existing ones will likely be required to develop and enforce international environmental standards to preserve global commons and regulate the environmental impacts of international trade. As countries come to see that it is in their self-interest to give up more of their sovereignty to improve their chances of survival, the debate will turn to the creation or strengthening of these institutions. [34]

Until new institutions are formed, we need to think more clearly and accurately about how to characterize global environmental threats and how to prescribe remedies that reflect an understanding of how human societies change their behavior. More than anything else, ecological science should convince us that it is in our self-interest to preserve environmental quality, and to act cautiously and conservatively in the face of global and local ecological risks. Preserving biodiversity, protecting habitat, and ensuring the functioning of ecosystems such as the global atmospheric and oceans are simply matters of self-interest. Transferring the technologies and resources to help poor countries reduce poverty and improve the quality of life for their residents is simply in our own self-interest. Our interests are inextricably intertwined with all those who share the planet. A politics of self-interest may not be enough to achieve an ecologically sustainable global political economy, but, if rooted in strong scientific research that makes our interdependence compelling and clear, it can be a powerful force for good. And it is about all that we are likely to get from a collection of 6 or 8 or 10 billion people who may function as a community among those they come to know, but who are likely to see self-interest and preservation as the value that binds them together.

Kai Bird has written that the beginning of the twenty-first century is in many ways like the era immediately after World War II. In both cases, the United States dominated global affairs and was positioned to address a host of global problems including human rights, self-determination, reducing poverty, and, now, preventing ecological catastrophe. Despite the promise, the United States turned away from a progressive global policy toward a "war economy, and national security state and a foreign policy based on unilaterialism and cowboy triumphalism."[35] Rather than engaging the world today, we dominate it with our exports and equate globalization with Americanization. In 1945 we made a wrong turn in policy and ended up in the Cold War. Can we choose more wisely this time?

The world also looks like it did a century ago, when progressives confronted the growth in industrial power and national markets by championing a shift from strong state to strong national government to match the power of industry and its national reach. Governmental power extends in response to the scope of economic power. Now the challenge is to extend regulatory reach over global commerce through governing institutions of similar scope. International institutions are increasing in power and authority whether they are bodies that enforce trade rules or environmental treaties. Journalist Robert Wright argues that everyone involved in the debate over globalism—"traditional leftists, centrist and right-wing free traders, and assorted single-issue agitators—agree that sometimes nations should surrender an appreciable chuck of sovereignty to a central authority. They just disagree on when."[36] Increased supranational government seems inevitable. Trade liberalization will continue to combine with labor and environmental agreements, so international bodies will have a greater role in regulating commerce and its human and ecological consequences. Poorer countries that, for now, fear global accords as limits on their ability to develop will likely develop their own constituencies that favor stronger global government. Workers in poor nations will find it advantageous to join with workers in the wealthy world to work together for higher wages. While political globalization has been slower to spread than economic globalization, Wright suggests that the two are converging. World government may continue to rely on nation–states to enforce provisions and will likely continue to be fragmented with many overlapping bodies, based on regional, economic, environmental, labor, and other divisions.[37]

Our self-interest compels an ecological reshaping of capitalism. Bruce Cumings summarizes the main characteristics of capitalism that pose such tremendous ecological challenges. Capitalism is driven by spending and consumption. It thrives on cheap credit, cheap energy, and new technologies. As the markets of developed countries become satiated, there is great pressure to expand markets into developing countries. Global capitalism relies on the nation–state to enact rules to foster global trade. Western notions of the rule of law—property rights, contract enforcement, and other policies—are critical in developing the legal framework in which capitalists can operate. Corporations are convenient legal devices for shielding decisions from scrutiny. Markets create inexorable pressure to reduce costs by channeling them to third parties. It places tremendous faith in the idea that self-regulating markets can be the basis of global peace and prosperity.[38] Critics of those who oppose globalism pretend that there are only two choices: global commerce driven by the interests of multinational corporations or right-wing nationalism and protectionism. To oppose one is to embrace the other. But that choice is a false one.[39] There are a host of options for building a world order that is aimed at restraining the recklessness of global financial markets, requiring more accountability of corporations, giving developing countries more power to determine what kind of economic decisions they will make to reduce poverty, reshaping global institutions to serve the interests of all nations not just the wealthy ones—a world order that is fundamentally committed to ecological sustainability. Our self-interest suggests what Mark Hertsgaard has called a Global Green Deal, a program "to renovate our civilization environmentally from top to bottom in rich and poor countries alike . . . [to] do for environmental technologies what government and industry have recently done so well for computer and Internet technologies: launch their commercial takeoff." He argues that the technologies needed have largely already been developed to begin the transformation. Just as important, he argues that such an effort can be politically feasible as well. "It would stimulate both jobs and business throughout the world in the name of a universal value: leaving our children a livable planet."[40]

Conclusion

The term "environmental crisis" is widely used and appears to mean a number of different things to different people. People may understand the global environmental situation to be a crisis—an immediate threat of calamity—or a long-term problem that will never be resolved but will challenge future generations. Four scenarios capture much of the debate over the nature of the environmental crisis that confronts us. First, trends may continue and the ecological consequences will be linear, predictable, and manageable. As threats increase, our technological capacities will expand as well, and the environmental crisis will be an enduring feature of human life. Second, we may make tremendous breakthroughs in technologies: pollution will become less important, critical resources plentiful, and environmentalism less of a concern. Third, environmental consequences may not be linear but erratic—with dramatic changes and turning points, acute crises, and collapses—and humankind will mobilize in the face of disasters to find solutions. Adaptive, flexible, effective responses will be developed by necessity. A fourth scenario also suggests great uncertainty and unpredictable changes, but instead of engendering responses, they overwhelm regions and fundamentally disrupt life for large segments of the planet. In its extreme form, human life as we know it is dramatically reduced.

These four scenarios illustrate what might happen, and some combination of developments may occur over time. We might have linear ecological change for several decades then hit a precipitous decline. There is little agreement over which, if any, of these scenarios, or any close approximation, will occur during this century. How should we act in the face of such uncertainty?

Ecological sustainability provides some goals and guidelines for communities and regions to pursue. It requires a reinvigorated politics of deep public participation and integration of social, economic, ecological, and cultural efforts, with ecological values providing the overriding priorities. There is much to learn about how to give more specific content to sustainability, how to measure progress and monitor results, how communities can learn from one another, and how sustainability efforts in one area can be effectively meshed with those in surrounding areas. For some, it is motivated by fear and dread of catastrophe; for others, it is an exciting, liberating venture that promises to preserve environmental quality and enhance human happiness and fulfillment. The success of the spread of sustainability will shape the world of the twenty-first century.

The global environmental agenda of strong agreements that protect global commons and limit the environmental effects of global-wide practices, and effective institutions that implement and enforce these agreements to achieve their goals, will also shape that world. But the arguments and ideas that drive global efforts will likely be different. Our self-interest compels us to be cautious and prudent. We cannot escape the environmental consequences of humankind's collective actions. It is clearly in our own interest to work together to minimize the threats to our well-being.

Notes

Introducton

1. Peter Waldman, "An Anarchist Looks to Provide Logic to Coterie at Core of WTO Vandalism," *The Wall Street Journal* (December 6, 1999): A17.

2. Helen Cooper, Bob Davis, and Greg Hitt, "WTO's Failure in Bid to Launch Trade Talks Emboldens Protestors," *The Wall Street Journal* (December 6, 1999): A1.

3. "The Non-governmental Order: Will NGOs Democratize, or Merely Disrupt, Global Governance?" *The Economist* (December 11, 1999) http://www.economist.com/editorial/justforyou/19991211/index_sa5268.html.

4. Anne Silverstein, "Gathering of Scientists Leads to Indictment of Humans for Drastic Changes on Earth," *The Earth Times* (August 29, 1999) http://www.earthtimes.org/aug; "Leading Enviros Paint Daunting Picture of 21st Century," Environment and Energy News—e-mail sent to author on December 7, 1999.

5. Silverstein, "Gathering of Scientists."

6. William K. Stevens, "Conservationists Win Battles but Fear War Is Lost," *The New York Times* (January 11, 2000), http://www.nytimes.com/library.

7. Chris Bright, "Anticipating Environmental 'Surprise'" in Lester R. Brown, et al., *State of the World 2000* (New York: W. W. Norton, 2000): 22–38.

8. For a discussion of Pascal, see Frederick Copleston, *A History of Philosophy*, vol. 4 (Garden City, N.Y.: Image Books, 1984): 153–73; quote at 170.

9. See Mark Hertsgaard, "A Global Green Deal" *Time* (Special edition, Earth Day 2000, Spring 2000): 84–85; Paul Hawken, Amory Lovins, L. Hunter Lovins, *Natural Capital: Creating the Next Industrial Revolution* (Boston: Little, Brown, 1999); Curtis Moore and Alan Miller, *Green Gold: Japan, Germany, and the United States and the Race for Environmental Technology* (Boston: Beacon Press, 1994); Joseph J. Romm, *Cool Companies: How the Best Businesses Boost Profits and Productivity by Cutting Greenhouse Gas Emissions* (Washington, D.C.: Island Press, 1999).

10. J. E. Lovelock, *Gaia: A New Look at Life on Earth* (Oxford, England: Oxford University Press, 1979): xii.

11. Lovelock, *Gaia*, 9.

12. Lovelock, *Gaia*, 11.

13. Gary C. Bryner, *From Promises to Performance: Achieving Global Environmental Goals* (New York: W. W. Norton, 1997).

14. Robert L. Heilbroner, *An Inquiry into the Human Prospect* (New York: Norton, 1991): 110.

15. Heilbroner, *An Inquiry*, 134, 139.

16. Heilbroner, *An Inquiry*, 156, 158.

17. William Ophuls and A. Stephan Boyan Jr., *Ecology and the Politics of Scarcity Revisited* (New York: W. W. Freeman, 1992): 3.

18. Ophuls and Boyan, *Ecology*, 278.

19. Ophuls and Boyan, *Ecology*, 311–12.

20. Ophuls and Boyan, *Ecology*, 314.

Chapter 1

1. *Which World? Scenarios for the 21st Century*, "Social and Political Trends," http://mars3.gps.caltech.edu/whichworld/explore/trends/trendssoc.html.

2. "The Next Millennium," *The Wall Street Journal* (January 1, 2000): R28.

3. Julian Simon, *The Ultimate Resource 2* (Princeton, N.J.: Princeton University Press, 1996): 12–13.

4. Associated Press, "Globe Said More Democratic in '99," *The New York Times* (December 21, 1999), http://www.nytimes.com/aponline/a/AP–World–Freedom.html.

5. Bill Emmott, "On the Yellow Brick Road," *The Economist* (September 11, 1999), http://www.economist.com/editorial/freeforall/19990911/su3796.html.

6. "The Next Millennium," *The Wall Street Journal* (January 1, 2000): R28.

7. *Which World? Scenarios for the 21st Century*, "Demographic Trends," http://mars3.gps.caltech.edu/whichworld/explore/trends/trendsecon.html.

8. United Nations Development Program, *Human Development Report 1997* (New York: Oxford University Press, 1997): 2.

9. UNDP, *Human Development Report 1997*, 3. See also, Robert Pear, "New Estimate Doubles Rate of H.I.V. Spread," *The New York Times* (November 26, 1997): A8.

10. The World Bank, *Advancing Sustainable Development* (Washington, D.C.: The World Bank, 1997): 3.

11. UNDP, *Human Development Report 1997*, 5.

12. James Gustave Speth, "The Rich Are Getting Richer While the Poor Waste Away," reprinted in the *Deseret News* (August 25, 1996): A20.

13. UNDP, *Human Development Report 1997*, 9–10.

14. UNDP, *Human Development Report 1997*, 27.

15. UNDP, *Human Development Report 1997*, 13–14, 27.

16. World Resources Institute, *World Resources 1990–91* (Washington, D.C.: World Resources Institute, 1990): 256–64.

17. Jodi L. Jacobson, "The Forgotten Resource," *World Watch* (May–June 1988): 35, 36–38.

18. Ann Misch, "Lost in the Shadow Economy," *World Watch* (April 1992): 18–19.

19. UNDP, *Human Development Report 1997*, 128.

20. *Which World? Scenarios for the 21st Century*, "Demographic Trends." http://mars3.gps.caltech.edu/whichworld/explore/trends/trendsdem.html

21. *Which World?*, "Demographic Trends."

22. *Which World?*, "Demographic Trends."

23. Emmott, "On the Yellow Brick Road."

24. For more on the interaction of population, consumption, and technology, see Paul Harrison, *The Third Revolution: Population, Environment and a Sustainable World* (London: Penguin Books, 1993): 236–55.

25. Lester R. Brown, Michael Renner, and Christopher Flavin, *Vital Signs 1997* (New York: W. W. Norton, 1997): 27.

26. The World Bank, *Advancing Sustainable Development: The World Bank and Agenda 21* (Washington, D.C.: The World Bank, 1997): 35

27. Brown, Renner, and Flavin, *Vital Signs*, 29.

28. Brown, Renner, and Flavin, *Vital Signs*, 32–33.

29. *Which World? Scenarios for the 21st Century*, "Environmental Trends."

30. *Which World? Scenarios for the 21st Century*, "Environmental Trends."

31. *Which World? Scenarios for the 21st Century*, "Environmental Trends."

32. The World Bank, *Advancing Sustainable Development*, vii, 3.

33. The UN Food and Agriculture Organization defines deforestation as depletion of crown cover to less than 10 percent; even if 10 or more percent of crown cover remains, however, significant damage to forests ecosystems may occur. Brown, Renner, and Flavin, *Vital Signs*, 96.

34. World Resources Institute, *World Resources: A Guide to the Global Environment* (New York: Oxford University Press, 1996): x.

35. World Resources Institute, *World Resources*, xi.

36. World Resources Institute, *World Resources*, xi–xii.

37. World Resources Institute, *World Resources*, xiii–iv.

38. "Leading Enviros Paint Daunting Picture of Twenty-First Century," *Environment and Energy News* (December 7, 1999)—email listservice.

39. "World Scientists' Warning to Humanity" (1993), distributed by the Union of Concerned Scientists (April 1993).

40. David W. Orr, *Ecological Literacy: Education and the Transition to a Postmodern World* (Albany: State University of New York Press, 1992).

41. Caldwell, "Is Humanity Destined to Self-Destruct?" *Politics and the Life Sciences*, forthcoming.

42. See Gregg Easterbrook, *A Moment on the Earth: The Coming Age of Environmental Optimism* (New York: Viking, 1995).

43. Jo Freeman and Victoria Johnson, *Waves of Protest: Social Movements Since the Sixties* (Lanham, Md.: Rowman & Littlefield, 1999): 3.

44. Freeman and Johnson, *Waves of Protest*, ix.

45. Freeman and Johnson, *Waves of Protest*, 1–2.

46. Luther P. Gerlach, "The Structure of Social Movements: Environmental Activism and Its Opponents," in *Waves of Protest*, 85–97.

47. Gerlach, *Waves of Protest*, 95–96.

48. David S. Meyer and Sidney Tarrow, "A Movement Society," in Meyer and Tarrow, *The Social Movement Society* (Lanham, Md: Rowman & Littlefield, 1998): 1–28, at 4.

49. Meyer and Tarrow, "A Movement Society," 4.

50. Meyer and Tarrow, "A Movement Society," 25.

51. Meyer and Tarrow, "A Movement Society," 25.

52. Meyer and Tarrow, "A Movement Society," 25.

53. Meyer and Tarrow, "A Movement Society," 23.

54. Meyer and Tarrow, "A Movement Society," 15.

55. See Jeffrey M. Berry, *The New Liberalism: The Rising Power of Citizen Groups* (Washington, D.C.: Brookings Institution, 1999): 7–8.

56. For an engaging history of this issue, see Charles F. Wilkinson, *Crossing the Next Meridian: Land, Water, and the Future of the West* (Washington, D.C.: Island Press, 1992).

57. James N. Rosenau, "Environmental Challenges in a Global Context," in Sheldon Kamieniecki, ed., *Environmental Politics in the International Arena: Movements, Parties, Organizations, and Policy* (Albany: State University of New York Press, 1993): 257–74.

58. Edith Brown Weiss, "Our Rights and Obligations to Future Generations for the Environment," *American Journal of International Law*, vol. 84 (1990): 198–204.

59. See Joseph G. Morone and Edward J. Woodhouse, *Averting Catastrophe: Strategies for Regulating Risky Technologies* (Berkeley: University of California Press, 1986).

60. Aaron Wildavsky, "The Secret of Safety Lies in Danger," in Gary C. Bryner and Dennis L Thomson, *The Constitution and the Regulation of Society* (Albany: State University of New York Press, 1998): 43–62.

61. Wildavsky, "The Secret of Safety Lies in Danger," 44.

62. Rosenau, "Environmental Challenges in a Global Context," 257–74, especially 271.

63. "Ex uno, plures," *The Economist* (August 21, 1999), http://www.economist.com/archive/view.cgi.

64. Jonathan Rauch, *Demosclerosis: The Silent Killer of American Government* (New York: Times Books, 1995).

65. Mancur Olson, *The Logic of Collective Action: Public Goods and the Theory of Groups* (Cambridge, Mass.: Harvard University Press, 1971, revised ed.).

66. G. Tyler Miller, Jr., *Living in the Environment* (Belmont, Calif.: Wadsworth Publishing, 1996): 13, 618–19.

67. Dennis Pirages, *The Sustainable Society* (New York: Praeger, 1977).

68. International Union for the Conservation of Nature, "World Conservation Strategy: Living Resource Conservation for Sustainable Development (Gland, Switz.: IUCN, United Nations Development Programme, and World Wildlife Fund, 1980), cited in John Kirby, Phil O'Keefe, and Lloyd Timberlake, ed., *The Earthscan Reader in Sustainable Development* (London: Earthscan, 1995): 1.

69. World Commission on Environment and Development, *Our Common Future* (New York: Oxford University Press, 1997): 43.

70. For discussions of the Rio Summit, see Adam Rogers, *The Earth Summit* (Los Angeles: Global View Press, 1993); Daniel Sitarz, ed., *Agenda 21: The Earth Summit Strategy to Save Our Planet* (Boulder, Colo.: EarthPress, 1993).

71. Kirby, O'Keefe, and Timberlake, *Earthscan Reader in Sustainable Development*, 1.

72. Executive Order 12852, June 29, 1993, amended on July 19, 1993, 42 U.S.C. 4321.

73. The President's Council on Sustainable Development, "Sustainable Development: A New Consensus" (Washington, D.C.: U.S. Government Printing Office, 1996): iv.

74. For an exploration of these views from an economics perspective, see Todd Sandler, *Global Challenges* (Cambridge: Cambridge University Press, 1997); for a broader ecological and political debate over sustainability, see Dennis Pirages, ed., *Building Sustainable Societies* (Armonk. N.Y.: M.E. Sharpe, 1996).

75. See William Lafferty, "The Politics of Sustainable Development: Global Norms for National Implementation," *Environmental Politics*, vol. 5 (1996): 185–208.

76. Carolyn Merchant, *Radical Ecology* (New York: Routledge, 1992).

77. Bill Devall, "The Deep Ecology Movement," in Carolyn Merchant, ed., *Ecology* (Atlantic Highlands, N.J.: Humanities Press, 1994): 125–39.

78. Arne Ness, "Deep Ecology" in *Ecology*, 120–24.

79. Ynestra King, "Feminism and the Revolt of Nature," in *Ecology*, 198–206.

80. See Christopher Manes, *Green Rage* (Boston: Little, Brown, 1990).

81. See Julian Simon and Herman Kahn, *The Resourceful Earth: A Response to Global 2000* (New York: Basil Blackwell, 1984).

82. Martin W. Lewis, *Green Delusions* (Durham, N.C.: Duke University Press, 1992): 2–14.

83. Lewis, *Green Delusions*, 19–20.

84. Kai N. Lee, *Compass and Gyroscope: Integrating Science and Politics for the Environment* (Washington, D.C.: Island Press, 1993): 200–01.

85. Dale Jamieson, "Sustainability and Beyond," Natural Resources Law Center Discussion Paper Series PL 02 (Boulder, Colo.: University of Colorado School of Law, 1996).

86. Robert W. Kates, "Population and Consumption: What We Know, What We Need to Know," *Environment*, vol. 42 (April 2000): 10–19, at 12.

87. Kates, "Population and Consumption," 12–13.

88. Kates, "Population and Consumption," 18.

89. Neil E. Harrison, *Constructing Sustainable Development* (Albany: State University of New York Press, 2000).

90. Daniel A. Mazmanian and Michael E. Kraft, eds., *Toward Sustainable Communities: Transition and Transformations in Environmental Policy* (Cambridge, Mass.: MIT Press, 1999).

91. Dennis C. Pirages, *Building Sustainable Societies: A Blueprint for a Post–Industrial World* (Armonk, N.Y.: M. E. Sharpe, 1996): 4–5.

92. Pirages, *Building Sustainable Societies*, 12.

Chapter 2

1. Richard A. Epstein, "Too Pragmatic by Half" (a review of Daniel A. Farber, *Eco-Pragmatism: Making Sensible Environmental Decisions in an Uncertain World*, University of Chicago Press, 1999) *The Yale Law Journal* 109 (2000): 1639–1667, at 1639.

2. Philip Shabecoff, *Earth Rising: American Environmentalism in the 21ˢᵗ Century* (Washington, D.C.: Island Press, 2000): 32.

3. Shabecoff, *Earth Rising*, 32–34.

4. Shabecoff, *Earth Rising*, 35.

5. Michael Cohen, "Origins and Early Outings: A History of the Club's Birth and Its Early Wilderness Travels," http://www.sierraclub.org/history/origins. html.

6. Cohen, "Origins and Early Outings."

7. "Sierra Club Timeline—A Proud History, 1892–1996," http://www.sierra-club.org/history/timeline.html.

8. http://www.tnc.org/.

9. http://www.tnc.org/.

10. http://www.edf.org/.

11. http://www.lcv.org/.

12. http://www.enviroweb.org/ef/primer/WhyEF!.html.

13. http://www.enviroweb.org/ef/vail-elf.html.

14. http://www.greenpeace.org/report98/index.html.

15. Robert Cameron Mitchell, Angela G. Mertig, and Riley E. Dunlap, "Twenty Years of Environmental Mobilization: Trends Among National Environmental Organizations," in *American Environmentalism: The U.S. Environmental Movement 1970–1990* eds. Riley E. Dunlap and Angela G. Mertig (Washington, D.C.: Taylor and Francis, 1992); cited in Jacqueline Vaughn Switzer with Gary Bryner, *Environmental Politics: Domestic and Global Dimensions* (New York: St. Martin's Press, 1998): 25–26.

16. Christopher J. Bosso, "Environmental Groups and the New Political Landscape," in Norman J. Vig and Michael E. Kraft, eds., *Environmental Policy* (Washington, D.C.: CQ Press, 2000): 55–76, at 73–74.

17. See Robert D. Bullard, ed., *Confronting Environmental Racism: Voices from the Grass Roots* (Boston: South End Press, 1993); Bunyan Bryant, ed., *Environmental Justice: Issues, Policies, and Solutions* (Washington, D.C.: Island Press, 1995).

18. Sheila Foster, "Justice from the Ground Up: Distributive Inequities, Grass Roots Resistance, and the Transformative Politics of the Environmental Justice Movement," *California Law Review* 86 (July 1998): 775.

19. Herger–Feinstein Quincy Library Group Forest Recovery Act, P.L. 105–277 (October 1998).

20. Quincy Library ROD Draws Criticism from Environmentalists," *Public Lands News* 24:18 (September 17, 1999): 7–8.

21. Judy Christrup and Robert Schaefer, "Not in Anyone's Backyard," *Greenpeace* (January/February 1990): 14–19.

22. See Sharon Begley and Patricia King, "The War Among the Greens," *Newsweek*, (May 4, 1992): 78; Switzer and Bryner, *Environmental Politics: Domestic and Global Dimensions*, 27–28.

23. Switzer and Bryner, *Environmental Politics*, 29–30.

24. See Gary C. Bryner, *Blue Skies, Green Politics: The Clean Air Act of 1990 and its Implementation* (Washington, D.C.: CQ Press, 1995), for development of this argument within the context of the Clean Air Act.

25. See Frederick H. Buttel, Charles C. Geisler and Irving W. Wiswall, eds. *Labor and the Environment* (Westport, Conn.: Greenwood Press, 1984): 1–2.

26. Samuel P. Hays, *Beauty, Health and Permanence: Environmental Politics in the United States 1955–1985* (Cambridge: Cambridge University Press, 1987): 295.

27. Jacqueline Vaughn Switzer, *Green Backlash: The History and Politics of Environmental Opposition in the U.S.* (Boulder, Colo: Lynn Reinner, 1997): xi–xiii.

28. Keith Schneider, "A County's Bid for U.S. Land Draws Lawsuit," *The New York Times* (March 9, 1995): A1.

29. Switzer and Bryner, *Environmental Politics*, 32–33.

30. See the exchange between Phil Brick and others, "The Wise Use Challenge," *Environment* vol. 37 (November 1995): 3–5, 43.

31. Switzer, *Green Backlash*, 10–11. See John Kingdon, Agendas, Alternatives, and Public Policies, 2nd ed. (New York: HarperCollins, 1995).

32. Mark Dowie, *Losing Ground: American Environmentalism at the Close of the Twentieth Century* (Cambridge, Mass.: MIT Press, 1995): x.

33. Dowie, *Losing Ground*, x.

34. Dowie, *Losing Ground*, xi.

35. Dowie, *Losing Ground*, xi.

36. Dowie, *Losing Ground*, xi.

37. Dowie, *Losing Ground*, x–xii.

38. Hays, *Beauty, Health and Permanence*.

39. Robert C. Paehlke, "Environmental Values and Public Policy," in Norman J. Vig and Michael E. Kraft, eds., *Environmental Policy* (Washington, D.C.: CQ Press, 2000): 77–97, at 79.

40. 16 U.S.C. 1536(a)(2); see *Tennessee Valley Authority v. Hill*, 437 U.S. 153 (1978).

41. P.L. 104–6.

42. 104th Congress, H.R. 3019, P.L. 104–134, April 1996: omnibus FY '96 spending bill for the Interior Department and other agencies.

43. 42 U.S.C. 7412; see Bryner, *Blue Skies, Green Politics*, 52.

44. Food Quality Protection Act of 1996, PL 104–170.

45. Safe Drinking Water Act Amendments of 1996, P.L. 104–182.

46. See Ed Gillespie and Rob Schellhas, eds., *Contract with America* (New York: Times Books. 1994), 125–41.

47. Jeffrey Berry, *The New Liberalism: The Rising Power of Citizen Groups* (Washington, D.C.: Brookings Institution, 1999): 3–4.

48. Berry, *The New Liberalism*, 112–13.

49. Berry, *The New Liberalism*, 170.

50. Berry, *The New Liberalism*, 111–12.

51. David Rogers, "Bliley's Pro-Business Reputation, Stock Portfolio Symbolize Postelection Strength of Corporations," *The Wall Street Journal* (December 23, 1994): A14.

52. Associated Press, "A Lobbyist's Perk Will Die," *The New York Times* (May 25, 1995): A13. Jane Fritsch, "Securities-Bill Staff Has Ties to the Industry," *The New York Times* (May 25, 1995): A1; David Maraniss and Michael Weisskopf, "Cashing In: The GOP Revolutionaries Have a Sure-fire Way of Telling Friend from Foe," *The Washington Post National Weekly Edition* (December 4–10, 1995): 6–7.

53. See Deborah Stone, *Policy Paradox* (New York: Norton, 1997).

54. Michael E. Kraft, "Environmental Policy in Congress: Revolution, Reform, or Gridlock?" in Norman J. Vig and Michael E. Kraft, *Environmental Policy in the 1990s* (Washington, D.C.: CQ Press, 1997): 119–43.

55. Several authors have analyzed the initiative, one of the most highly publicized in U.S. electoral history. See Bradley Johnson, "Big Business Attacks Big

Green," *Advertising Age* 61 (October 22, 1990): 4; "Black Day for California's 'Big Green'" *New Scientist*, (November 17, 1990): 20; Richard Lacayo, "No Lack of Initiatives," *Time* (September 3, 1990): 52; and Elizabeth Schaefer, "A Daunting Proposition," *Nature* 347 (September 27, 1990): 323.

56. Switzer and Bryner, *Environmental Politics*, 31–32.

57. http://www.greenparties.org.

58. http://www.greens.org/colorado/.

59. James Dao, "Nader Runs Again, This Time With Feeling," *The New York Times* (April 15, 2000) http://nytimes.com/library/politics/camp/041500wh-green-nader.html.

60. Riley E. Dunlap, "Public Opinion in the 1980s: Clear Consensus, Ambiguous Commitment" Environment 33 (October 1991): 32.

61. Everett Carll Ladd & Karlyn H. Bowman, *Attitudes Toward the Environment: Twenty-Five Years After Earth Day* (Washington, D.C.: American Enterprise Institute for Public Policy Research, 1995): 7.

62. Ladd and Bowman, *Attitudes Toward the Environment*, 10.

63. Ladd and Bowman, *Attitudes Toward the Environment*, 12–14.

64. Ladd and Bowman, *Attitudes Toward the Environment*, 15–16.

65. Ladd and Bowman, *Attitudes Toward the Environment*, 29.

66. Ladd and Bowman, *Attitudes Toward the Environment*, 50.

67. Gregg Easterbrook, *A Moment on the Earth: The Coming Age of Environmental Optimism* (New York: Viking, 1995).

68. Eckerly and Ferrera, "Regulation," in *Heritage Foundation, Issues '94* (Washington, D.C.: Heritage Foundation, 1994): 87.

69. Michael E. Kraft and Norman J. Vig, "Environmental Policy from the 1970s to 2000: An Overview" in Norman J. Vig and Michael E. Kraft, eds., *Environmental Policy* (Washington, D.C.: CQ Press, 2000): 1–31, at 9–10.

70. Will Lester, "Poll: Environmentalists Supported" *Star Tribune* http://ww2.startribune.com/stOnLine/cgi-bin/article?this Story=8157412.

71. Source for all Gallup Poll data (tables 2-4–2-8): Gallup Organization, "Poll Releases" (April 18, 2000) http://www.gallup.com/poll/releases/pr000418.asp.

72. Executive Order 12852, June 29, 1993, amended on July 19, 1993, 42 U.S.C. 4321.

73. President's Council on Sustainable Development, *Sustainable Development: A New Consensus* (Washington, D.C.: U.S. Government Printing Office, 1996): iv.

74. PCSD, *Sustainable Development*, 7.

75. PCSD, *Sustainable Development*, 7.

76. PCSD, *Sustainable Development*, 177–84.

77. U.S. Agency for International Development, http://www.info.usaid.gov/about, accessed September 1999.

78. President's Council on Sustainable Development, "Building on Consensus: A Progress Report on Sustainable America" (Washington, D.C.: PCSD, January 1997): 10–11.

79. PCSD, "Building on Consensus," 13.

80. "Cities to Report Success to COP3," *Initiatives* (International Council for Local Environmental Initiatives), number 17 (November 1997): 1, 3.

81. For a discussion of these efforts, see DeWitt John, *Civic Environmentalism* (Washington, D.C.: CQ press, 1994).

82. U.S. Environmental Protection Agency. "Community Partnerships for Environmental Action: A New Approach to Environmental Protection." (Washington, D.C.: U.S. EPA, Office of Pollution Protection and Toxics, 1996).

83. See, for example, Dennis Pirages, *Building Sustainable Societies: A Blueprint for a Post–Industrial World* (New York: M. E. Sharpe, 1996); Lester Milbraith, *Envisioning a Sustainable Society* (Albany: State University of New York Press, 1991).

84. Paul Hawken, *The Ecology of Commerce* (New York: Harper Business, 1993).

85. U.S. Office of Technology Assessment. *Environmental Policy Tools* (Washington, D.C.: U.S. Government Printing Office, 1995).

86. David M. Roodman, Worldwatch Paper 134, Getting the Signals Right: Tax Reform to Protect the Environment and the Economy (Washington, D.C.: Worldwatch Institute, 1997).

87. John Dernbach, "U.S. Adherence to Its Agenda 21 Commitments: A Five-Year Review." *Environmental Law Reporter*, vol. 27 (October 1997): 10504–25, at 10506.

88. Michael Keating, *The Earth Summit's Agenda for Change* (Geneva: Centre for Our Common Future, 1995).

89. Susan Dentzer, "R.I.P. for the BTU tax," *U.S. News and World Report* (June 21, 1993): 95

90. Howard Gleckman, "Gas Pump Politics," *Business Week* (May 13, 1996): 40–41.

91. "Resource Facts," *Resources* issue #124 (Summer 1996): 4; U.S. Department of Commerce, *Statistical Abstract of the United States 1997* (Washington, D.C.: U.S. Bureau of the Census, 1997): 638.

92. U.S. Environmental Protection Agency. *Unfinished Business: A Comparative Assessment of Environmental Problems* (Washington, D.C.: U.S. EPA, 1987): 96.

93. Terry Davies, ed. *Comparing Environmental Risks: Tools for Setting Government Priorities* (Washington, D.C.: Resources for the Future, 1996).

94. U.S. Environmental Protection Agency, Science Advisory Board. *Reducing Risk: Setting Priorities and Strategies for Environmental Protection* (Washington D.C.: U.S. Environmental Protection Agency, 1990): 22.

95. Shabecoff, *Earth Rising*, 7–38.

96. Quoted by Shabecoff, *Earth Rising*, 27.

97. David Orr, *Ecological Literacy: Education and the Transition to a Postmodern World* (Albany, N.Y.: State University of New York Press, 1992): xi.

98. William Ophuls and A. Stephen Boyan, Jr., *Ecology and the Politics of Scarcity Revisited: The Unraveling of the American Dream* (New York: W. H. Freeman, 1992).

99. Shabecoff, *Earth Rising*, 113.

100. Shabecoff, *Earth Rising*, 113–19.

101. Sherle H. Schwenninger, "Seeking a Stable World," *The Nation* 270 (May 8, 2000): 30–32.

102. Mark Hertsgaard, "A Green Foreign Policy" *The Nation* 270 (May 8, 2000): 32–34.

103. See William Greider, "Time to Rein in Global Finance" *The Nation* 270 (April 24, 2000): 13–20.

104. Shabecoff, *Earth Rising*, 170–75.

105. Shabecoff, *Earth Rising*, 129.

106. Shabecoff, *Earth Rising*, 78–79. For more on the environmental justice movement, see Gary Bryner, Douglas Kenney, and Kathryn Mutz, *Justice and Natural Resources* (forthcoming).

107. For an optimistic view of charting the next industrial revolution along ecological sustainability principles, see Paul Hawken, Amory Lovins, and L. Hunter Lovins, *Natural Capital* (Boston: Little, Brown, 1999).

108. Shabecoff, *Earth Rising*, 179.

Chapter 3

1. Curtis Runyan, "Action on the Front Lines" 12 *World Watch* (November/December 1999): 12–21.

2. Runyan, "Action on the Front Lines," 21.

3. David Vogel, *National Styles of Regulation: Environmental Policy in Great Britain and the United States* (Ithaca, N. Y.: Cornell University Press, 1986): 191.

4. Rob Coppock, *Regulating Chemical Hazards in Japan, West Germany, France, the United Kingdom, and the European Community: A Comparative Examination* (Washington, D.C.: National Academy Press, 1986): 97.

5. George Hoberg and Kathryn Harrison, "It's Not Easy Being Green: The Politics of Canada's Green Plan," *Canadian Public Policy* 20: 2 (1994): 119–37, at 124–25.

6. Hoberg and Harrison, "It's Not Easy Being Green," 135.

7. See Gary C. Bryner, *Bureaucratic Discretion: Law and Policy in Federal Regulatory Agencies* (New York: Pergammon Press, 1987).

8. Vogel, *National Styles of Regulation*, 192.

9. Alan Peacock, ed., *The Regulation Game: How British and West German Companies Bargain with Government* (New York: Basil Blackwell, 1984): 158.

10. Susan Rose-Ackerman, *Controlling Environmental Policy: The Limits of Public Law in Germany and the United States* (New Haven: Yale University Press, 1995): 2.

11. J. Clarence Davies and Jan Mazurek, *Pollution Control in the United States: Evaluating the System* (Washington, D.C.: Resources for the Future, 1998): 287. See also Walter Rosenbaum, *Environmental Politics and Policy* (Washington, D.C.: CQ Press, 4th ed., 1998): 283–85.

12. Jacqueline Vaughn Switzer with Gary Bryner, *Environmental Politics: Domestic and Global Dimensions* (New York: St. Martin's Press, 1998): 37.

13. Runyan, "Action on the Front Lines," 14.

14. David Hunter, James Salzman, and Durwood Zaelke, *International Environmental Law and Policy* (New York: Foundation Press, 1998): 424.

15. Runyan, "Action on the Front Lines," 13.

16. Switzer and Bryner, *Environmental Politics*, 37–38.

17. Robert Livernash, "The Growing Influence of NGOs in the Developing World," *Environment* 34 no. 5 (June 1992): 12–20, 41–43.

18. See Vladimir Kotov and Elena Nikitina, "Russia in Transition: Obstacles to Environmental Protection," *Environment* 35, no. 10 (December 1993).

19. Yohei Harashima, "Effects of Economic Growth on Environmental Policies in Northeast Asia," *Environment* (July-August 2000): 29-40.

20. Matt Forney, "Environmentalism by Ordinary People Is Perilous in China," *The Wall Street Journal* (July 20, 2000): A22.

21. Harashima, "Effects of Economic Growth," quote at 33.

22. For more on China, see Mark Hertsgaard, *Earth Odyssey: Around the world in search of our environmental future* (New York: Broadway Books, 1998).

23. Harashima, "Effects of Economic Growth," 38-39.

24. Anna Bramwell, *The Fading of the Greens: The Decline of Environmental Politics in the West* (New Haven, Conn.: Yale University Press, 1994).

25. See Dick Richardson and Chris Rootes, eds. *The Green Challenge: The Development of Green Parties in Europe* (London: Routledge, 1995), and Sara Parkin, *Green Parties: An International Guide* (London: Heretic Books, 1989).

26. Switzer and Bryner, *Environmental Politics*, 38.

27. Michael G. Renner, "Europe's Green Tide," *World Watch* (January–February 1990): 23–27.

28. See Richardson and Routes, *The Green Challenge*, and Parkin, *Green Parties: An International Guide*.

29. Roland Roth, "Local Green Politics in West German Cities," *International Journal of Urban and Public Policy* 15: 1 (1991): 75–89, at 79.

30. "Germany. Such a Kindly Foe," *The Economist* (March 14, 1998). http://www.economist.com/archive/view.cgi

31. Roth, "Local Green Politics in West German Cities," 75.

32. "Soft Hearts, Hard Heads in New Germany," *The Economist* (June 29, 1996).

33. Roth, "Local Green Politics in West German Cities," 83.

34. Roth, "Local Green Politics in West German Cities," 85–86.

35. "Joshka Fischer, a Sterner Shade of Green," *The Economist* (May 15, 1999).

36. "Greens Grow Up," *The Economist* (August 7, 1999).

37. "German Greens May Put Anti-Car Policy in Reverse," Environmental News Service (May 30, 2000) http://ens.lycos.com/ens/may2000/2000L-05-30-02.html.

38. "German Nuclear Phaseout Deal Near, Gaps Remain," Environmental News Service (June 12, 2000) http://ens.lycos.com/ens/june2000/2000L-06-12-04.html.

39. "The Right Rejected in France," *The Economist* (June 7, 1997).

40. "Greens Grow Up."

41. "Greens Grow Up."

42. http://www.greenparties.org.

43. "Greens Grow Up."

44. "Poland, Germany, Czech Republic Claim 'Black Triangle' Transformed to Green Land," *International Environmental Reporter* 22:21 (October 13, 1999): 846.

45. Murray Feshback and Alfred Friendly, Jr., *Ecocide in the USSR* (New York: Basic Books, 1992).

46. Barbara Jancar–Webster, ed., *Environmental Action in Eastern Europe: Responses to Crisis* (Armonk, New York: M. E. Sharpe, 1993).

47. Associated Press, "Globe Said More Democratic in '99," *The New York Times* (December 21, 1999) http://www/nytimes.com/aponline/a/AP-World-Freedom.html.

48. "A Grubby Spectacle," *The Economist* (December 18, 1999) http://www.economist.com/editorial/justforyou/19991218/sa8212.html.

49. Celeste Bohlen, "Latest Russian Election Returns Favor Kremlin Supporters," *The New York Times* (December 20, 1999) http://nytimes.com/yr/mo/day/late/20russia-nyt.html.

50. "A Grubby Spectacle," *The Economist* (December 18, 1999). http://www.economist.com/editorial/justforyou/19991218/sa8212.html.

51. Associated Press, "Putin's Plan to Increase Central Power Wins Support," *The New York Times* (July 20, 2000) http://www.nytimes.com/library.world/europe/072000russia-politics.html.

52. Runyan, "Action on the Front Lines," 21.

53. Michael Wines, "Russia Voting After Rancorous Campaign," *The New York Times* (December 19, 1999) http://nytimes.com/library/world/europe/121999russia-elect.html.

54. Erich G. Frankland, "Green Revolutions?: the Role of Green Parties in Eastern Europe's Transition, 1989–94," *East European Quarterly* 24:3 (September 1995): 315–45, at 339.

55. Frankland, "Green Revolutions?" 339–41; quote at 340–41.

56. Frankland, "Green Revolutions?" 341.

57. Anna Bramwell. *The Fading of the Greens*, viii.

58. Anna Bramwell. *The Fading of the Greens*, 204.

59. Switzer and Bryner, *Environmental Politics*, 40.

60. For a discussion of this debate in the context of the United States, see Michael X. Delli Carpini and Scott Keeter, *What Americans Know about Politics and Why It Matters* (New Haven, Conn.: Yale University Press, 1996); the classic study of public policy in America that is the source of many theoretical insights is V.O. Key, Jr., *Public Opinion and American Democracy* (New York: Knopf, 1961).

61. Mary Douglas and Aaron Wildavsky, *Risk and Culture* (Berkeley: University of California Press, 1982), and Aaron Wildavsky, *Searching for Safety* (New Brunswick, N.J.: Transaction Publishers, 1988).

62. Robert C. Paehlke, *Environmentalism and the Future of Progressive Politics* (New Haven: Yale University Press, 1989).

63. Ronald Inglehart, *The Silent Revolution: Changing Values and Political Styles Among Western Publics* (Princeton, N.J.: Princeton University Press, 1977).

64. Ronald Inglehart, "Public Support for Environmental Protection: Objective Problems and Subjective Values in 43 Societies," *PS: Political Science and Politics* (March 1995): 57–72, at 57.

65. Inglehart, "Public Support for Environmental Protection," 59.

66. Inglehart, "Public Support for Environmental Protection" 60.

67. Inglehart, "Public Support for Environmental Protection," 65.

68. Inglehart, "Public Support for Environmental Protection," 70–71.

69. See Uday Desai, ed., *Ecological Policy and Politics in Developing Countries* (Albany, NY: State University of New York Press, 1998); Marian A. L. Miller, *The Third World in Global Environmental Politics* (Boulder, Colo.: Lynne Reinner Publishers, 1995).

70. Missy Ryan, "Arrested Development" *National Journal* (June 10, 2000): 1820–25; quote at 1821.

71. Ryan, "Arrested Development," 1822–23.

72. See Kenneth Arrow et al., "Economic Growth, Carrying Capacity, and the Environment" *Ecological Economics* 15 (2): 91–95.

73. Riley E. Dunlap and Angela G. Mertig, "Global Concern for the Environment: Is Affluence a Prerequisite?" 51 *Journal of Social Issues* (1995): 121–37.

74. While Inglehart appears to be correct in arguing that postmaterialists values are associated with strong support for environmental values, other factors are also important here. See S. R. Brechin and W. Kempton, Global Environmentalism: A Challenge to the Postmaterialist Thesis? *Social Science Quarterly* 75 (2) (1994): 245–69.

75. For interesting studies of developing country environmental politics, see Uday Desai, ed., *Ecological Policy and Politics in Developing* Countries (Albany: State University of New York Press, 1998).

76. Riley E. Dunlap, George H. Gallup, Jr., and Alec M. Gallup, *Health of the Planet* (Princeton, N.J.: Gallup International Institute, May 1993): v.

77. Adapted from Robert W. Kates, "Sustaining Life on the Earth," *Scientific American* (October 1994): 114–22, at 120.

78. Donald E. Blake, Neil Guppy, and Peter Urmetzer, "Canadian Public Opinion and Environmental Action: Evidence from British Columbia," *Canadian Journal of Political Science* 30:3 (September 1997): 451–72, at 455–56.

79. Blake, Guppy, and Urmetzer, "Canadian Public Opinion and Environmental Action," 454–55.

80. Blake, Guppy, and Urmetzer, "Canadian Public Opinion and Environmental Action," 461–62.

81. Blake, Guppy, and Urmetzer, "Canadian Public Opinion and Environmental Action," 469.

82. Jureg Altwegg, "Finally, the French May Be Going Green," *Frankfurter Allgemeine Zeitung* (July 10, 2000): 7.

83. "Taxes. Eco-nomics," *The Economist* (June 15, 1996).

84. William M. Lafferty and James Meadowcroft, eds., *Implementing Sustainable Development: Strategies and Initiatives in High Consumption Societies* (London: Oxford University Press, forthcoming).

85. Oluf Langhelle, "Norway: Reluctantly Carrying the Torch," in Lafferty and Meadowcroft, eds., *Implementing Sustainable Development*.

86. Langhelle, "Norway."

87. Katarina Eckerberg, "Sweden: Progression Despite Recession" in Lafferty and Meadowcroft, eds., *Implementing Sustainable Development*.

88. Eckerberg, "Sweden: Progression Despite Recession."

89. Marie-Louise van Muijen, "The Netherlands: Ambitious on Goals, Ambivalent on Action," in Lafferty and Meadowcroft, eds., *Implementing Sustainable Development*.

90. Bramwell. *The Fading of the Greens*, 206.

91. Christiane Beuermann, "Germany: Regulation and the Precautionary Principle," in Lafferty and Meadowcroft, eds., *Implementing Sustainable Development*.

92. Beuermann, "Germany: Regulation and the Precautionary Principle."

93. Elim Papadakis, "Australia: Ecological Sustainable Development in the National Interest," in Lafferty and Meadowcroft, eds., *Implementing Sustainable Development*.

94. Yukiko Fukasaku, "Energy and Environmental Policy Integration," *Energy Policy* 23:12 (1995): 1063–76, at 75; for a broader look at sustainability in Japan, see Miranda Schreurs, "Japan: Law, Technology, and Aid," in Lafferty and Meadowcroft, eds., *Implementing Sustainable Development*.

95. Yumoto Nororu, "Target 2010: The Conservation Challenge," *Look Japan* (April 1998): 4–9.

Chapter 4

1. Edith Brown Weiss, Stephen C. McCaffrey, Daniel Barstow Magraw, Paul C. Szasz, and Robert E. Lutz, *International Environmental Law and Policy* (New York: Aspen Law & Business, 1998): xxiii.

2. For an introduction to these efforts, see Adam Rogers, *The Earth Summit* (Los Angeles: Global View Press, 1993).

3. Robert O. Keohane and Joseph S. Nye Jr., "Globalization: What's New, What's Not? (And So What?)," 118 *Foreign Policy* (Spring 2000): 104–19, at 106–07.

4. Keohane and Nye, "Globalization," 115.

5. Keohane and Nye, "Globalization," 117.

6. Curtis Runyan, "Action on the Front Lines" *World Watch* (November–December 1999): 12–21, at 12.

7. For an overview of NGOs, see World Resources Institute, *World Resources 1992–93* (New York: Oxford University Press, 1992): 219–21.

8. Lee A. Kimball, *Forging International Agreement: Strengthening Inter-governmental Institutions for Environment and Development* (Washington, D.C.: World Resources Institute, 1992): 69.

9. "Greenpeace Means Business: Environmentalism," *The Economist* (August 19, 1995) http://www.economist.com/archive/view.cgi.

10. World Resources Institute, *World Resources 1992–93*, 68–69.

11. World Resources Institute, *World Resources 1994–95*, (1994), 225.

12. The Commission on Global Governance, *Our Global Neighborhood* (New York: Oxford University Press, 1995).

13. Bernard Wysocki, Jr., "The WTO: the Villain in a Drama It Wrote," *The Wall Street Journal* (December 6, 1999): A1.

14. World Business Council for Sustainable Development, http://www.wbcsd.org.

15. Lynton Keith Caldwell, *International Environmental Policy* (Chapel Hill, N.C.: Duke University Press, 1996, 3rd ed.): 282–86.

16. World Resources Institute, *World Resources 1992–93* (1992), 221–22.

17. World Resources Institute, *World Resources 1992–93* (1992), 232.

18. World Resources Institute, *World Resources 1992–93* (1992), 230.

19. Robert O. Keohane, Peter M. Haas, and Marc A. Levy, "Improving the Effectiveness of International Environmental Institutions," in Keohane, Haas, and Levy, *Institutions for the Earth* (Cambridge, Mass.: The MIT Press, 1993): 397–426.

20. David G. Victor and Eugene B. Skolnikoff, "Translating Intent into Action: Implementing Environmental Commitments," *Environment* Vol. 41 (March 1999): 16–20, 39–44, at 18.

21. Victor and Skolnikoff, "Translating Intent into Action," 42–43. See also, David G. Victor, Kai Raustiala, and Eugene B. Skolnikoff, *The Implementation and Effectiveness of International Environmental Commitments: Theory and Practice* (Cambridge, Mass.: MIT Press, 1998).

22. Philip Shabecoff, *A New Name for Peace: International Environmentalism, Sustainability Development, and Democracy* (Hanover, N.H.: University Press of New England, 1996): 73.

23. World Resources Institute, *World Resources 1992–93* (1992): 230.

24. Martin W. Holdgate, "Pathways to Sustainability," 37 *Environment* (November 1995): 16–20, 38–42; the figure on private capital flows is at p. 50.

25. Kumi Naidoo, "The New Civic Globalism," *The Nation* 270 (May 8, 2000): 34–36.

26. This section is adapted from Gary C. Bryner, "Agenda 21: Myth or Reality?" in Norman J. Vig and Regina S. Axelrod, *The Global Environment: Institutions, Law, and Policy* (Washington, D.C.: CQ Press, 2000): 157–89, and Gary C. Bryner, "Implementing Global Environmental Agreements in the Developing World," *Colorado Journal of International Environmental Law and Policy*, 1997 yearbook (1998): 1–25.

27. World Commission on Environment and Development, *Our Common Future* (New York: Oxford University Press, 1987).

28. For a review of the UNCED meeting, see Michael Keating, *Agenda for Change: A Plain Language Version of Agenda 21 and the Other Rio Agreements* (Geneva: Center for Our Common Future, 1994); Michael Grubb, et al., *The Earth Summit Agreements: A Guide and Assessment* (London: Earthscan, 1993); Adam Rogers, *The Earth Summit: A Planetary Reckoning* (Los Angeles: Global View Press, 1993); Daniel Sitarz, *Agenda 21: The Earth Summit Strategy to Save Our Planet* (Boulder, Colo.: Earthpress, 1993).

29. "PrepCom 4 Adopts Draft Declaration of Principles for Rio Summit," *Earth Summit Update* (April 1992): 2.

30. Rio Declaration on Environment and Development, Principle 2.

31. United Nations, Agenda 21: Programme of Action for Sustainable Development; Rio Declaration on Environment and Development; Statement of Forest Principles (1992). United Nations Framework Convention on Climate Change, http://www.unep.ch/iucc/begincon.html; Convention on Biological Diversity, http://www.unep.ch/biodiv.html.

32. "Pressure for Specific Funding Level Expected in Rio," *Earth Summit Update* (May 1992): 2.

33. "PrepCom 4 Forwards Agenda 21 to Rio; Many Ambitious Proposals Are Blocked" *Earth Summit Update* (April 1992): 1, 5; "Agenda 21 Chapter-by-Chapter Summary," *Earth Summit Update* (May 1992): 4–5.

34. "Pressure for Specific Funding Level Expected in Rio," *Earth Summit Update*, 2.

35. Frank Edward Allen and Rose Gutfeld, "Earth Summit Neglects Major Issues of Poverty, Drought, and Population," *Wall Street Journal* (June 11, 1992): 1.

36. See Lester R. Brown, Michael Renner, and Christopher Flavin, *Vital Signs, 1997* (Washington, D.C.: Worldwatch Institute, 1997): 57–61.

37. See E. O. Wilson, ed., *Biodiversity* (Washington, D.C.: National Academy Press, 1988): 3–18.

38. Brown, Renner, and Flavin, *Vital Signs, 1997.*

39. Paula DiPerna, "Five Years After the Rio Talkfest: Where Is the Money?" *The Earth Times*, January 25, 1997, http://www.earthtimes.org.

40. United Nations General Assembly, 19th special session, Agenda item 8, "Overall Review and Appraisal of the Implementation of Agenda 21" (June 27, 1997), II. Assessment of Progress Made Since the United Nations Conference on Environment and Development, paragraphs 7–8, gopher://gopher.un.org:70/00/ga/docs/S-19/plenary/AS19-29.TXT.

41. "Overall Review and Appraisal," paragraphs 17–20.

42. "Overall Review and Appraisal of the Implementation of Agenda 21", paragraphs 9–10.

43. UNGASS, III. Implementation in Areas Requiring Urgent Action, paragraph 22.

44. UNGASS, III. Implementation in Areas Requiring Urgent Action, paragraphs 23–32.

45. UNGASS, III. Implementation in Areas Requiring Urgent Action, paragraphs 76–115.

46. UNGASS, III. Implementation in Areas Requiring Urgent Action, paragraph 137.

47. *Earth Negotiations Bulletin*, vol. 5, no. 88 (June 30, 1997), http://www.iisd.ca/linkages/csd/enb0588e.html#1.

48. *Earth Negotiations Bulletin*, vol. 5, no. 88 (June 30, 1997), http://www.iisd.ca/linkages/csd/enb0588e.html#1.

49. Natural Resources Defense Council and Cape 2000, *Four in '94 Assessing National Actions to Implement Agenda 21: A Country-by-Country Progress Report* (May 1994).

50. Konrad Moltke, "Why UNEP Matters," in Helge Ole Bergesen and Georg Parmann, eds., *Green Globe Yearbook 1996* (Oxford: Oxford University Press, 1996): 55–64, at 61.

51. Moltke, "Why UNEP Matters," 114.

52. Moltke, "Why UNEP Matters," 114.

53. Moltke, "Why UNEP Matters," 61–63.

54. Keohane, Haas, and Levy, "The Effectiveness of International Environmental Institutions," 5.

55. "Overall Review and Appraisal," paragraphs 11–12.

56. "Overall Review and Appraisal," paragraph 13.

57. Congress of the United States, Office of Technology Assessment, *Energy in Developing Countries* (Washington, D.C.: U.S. Government Printing Office, 1991): 3–19.

58. Morris Miller, *Debt and the Environment* (United Nations: United Nations Publications, 1991): 46.

59. Miller, *Debt and the Environment*, 46.

60. Miller, *Debt and the Environment*, 46.

61. The World Bank, *World Development Report* (New York: Oxford University Press, 1988).

62. Jyoti Shankar Singh, "How to Reduce the Debt Burden," *The Earth Times* (October 1–15, 1996): 12.

63. Singh, "How to Reduce the Debt Burden," 12.

64. Singh, "How to Reduce the Debt Burden," 12.

65. Singh, "How to Reduce the Debt Burden," 12.

66. Paul Lewis, "Debt-Relief Cost for the Poorest Nations," *The New York Times* (June 10, 1996): C2; Paul Lewis, "I.M.F. and World Bank Clear Debt Relief," *The New York Times* (September 30, 1996): C2; editorial, "The Third-World Debt Crisis," *The New York Times* (June 26, 1996): A14.

67. See Bruce Rich, *Mortgaging the Earth: The World Bank, Environmental Impoverishment, and the Crisis of Development* (Boston: Beacon Press, 1994); Kevin Danaher, ed., *50 Years Is Enough: The Case Against the World Bank and the International Monetary Fund* (Boston: South End Press, 1994).

68. Pratap Chatterjee and Matthias Finger, *The Earth Brokers: Power, Politics, and World Development* (London: Routledge, 1994); Johan Holmberg, ed., *Making Development Sustainable: Redefining Institutions, Policy, and Economics* (Washington, D.C.: Island Press, 1992).

69. Andrew Steer, "Overview: The Year in Perspective," *Environment Matters*: 4–7.

70. World Bank, *World Bank Environmental Projects: July 1986–June* 1996 (Washington, D.C.: World Bank, 1996): 51–68.

71. World Bank, *World Bank Environmental Projects: July 1986–June 1996.*

72. World Bank, *World Bank Environmental Projects: July 1986–June 1996.*

73. World Bank, *World Bank Environmental Projects: July 1986–June 1996.*

74. Amory Lovins and Hunter Lovins, "The Next Energy Crisis? Efficient Energy Use vs. Producing More Power," *Popular Science*, vol. 249 (September, 1996): 89.

75. Lovins and Lovins, "The Next Energy Crisis?" 89.

76. Laura H. Kosloff and Mark C. Trexler, "Global Warming, Climate-Change Mitigation, and the Birth of a Regulatory Regime," *Environmental Law Reporter* vol. 27 (January 1997): 10012–18.

77. For a more in-depth discussion of these issues, see Gary C. Bryner, *From Promises to Performance: Achieving Global Environmental Goals* (New York: W. W. Norton, 1998).

78. Miller, *Debt and the Environment*, 46.

79. Jane Perlez, "African Dilemma: Food Aid May Prolong War and Famine," *The New York Times* (May, 12, 1991): A1.

80. Global Environment Facility, "The Restructured Global Environment Facility," http://www.worldbank.org/html/gef/intro/revqa.htm.

81. Hilary F. French, "Learning from the Ozone Experience" in Lester R. Brown, et al., *State of the World 1997* (New York: W. W. Norton, 1997): 151–72, at 162–63, 165.

82. French, "Learning from the Ozone Experience," 162–63.

83. French, "Learning from the Ozone Experience," 163.

84. French, "Learning from the Ozone Experience," 163.

85. French, "Learning from the Ozone Experience," 163.

86. Global Environment Facility, "The Restructured Global Environment Facility."

87. Global Environment Facility, "The Restructured Global Environment Facility."

88. Global Environmental Fund, Quarterly Operational Report, July 1996, http://www.worldbank.org/html/gef/Welcome.html.

89. Global Environmental Fund, Quarterly Operational Report, July 1996.

90. "Montreal Protocol Parties Reach Accord on Three-Year, $440 Million Package," *International Environment* (December 8, 1999): 978.

91. French, "Learning from the Ozone Experience."

92. World Resources Institute, *World Resources 1994–95*, 230.

93. David Fairman, "The Global Environmental Facility: Haunted by the Shadow of the Future," in Robert O. Keohane and Marc A. Levy, eds., *Institutions for Environmental Aid* (1996): 55–88.

94. Fairman, "The Global Environmental Facility."

95. Elizabeth DeSombre and Joanne Kauffman, "The Montreal Protocol Multilateral Fund: Partial Success Story," in Robert O. Keohane and Marc A. Levy, eds., *Institutions for Environmental Aid* (1996): 89–126.

96. Jack Freeman, "Downhill: The Road from Rio to Kyoto," *The Earth Times* December 16–31, 1997, 7–8.

97. For a defense of open trade, see Gary Burtless, Robert Z. Lawrence, Robert E. Litan, and Robert J. Shapiro, *Globaphobia: Confronting Fears About Open Trade* (Washington, D.C.: Brookings Institution, 1998).

98. These issues are discussed in David Hunter, James Salzman, and Durwood Zaelke, *International Environmental Law and Policy* (New York: Foundation Press, 1998): 1182–86.

99. Article XX of GATT; see Hunter, Salzman, and Zaelke, *International Environmental Law and Policy*, 1189.

100. See Ralph Nader et al., *The Case Against Free Trade: GATT, NAFTA, and the Globalization of Corporate Power* (San Francisco: Earth Island Press, 1993).

101. Jack L. Goldsmith and John C. Yoo, "Seattle and Sovereignty," *The Wall Street Journal* (December 6, 1999): A35

102. Douglas A. Irwin, "How Clinton Botched the Seattle Summit," *The Wall Street Journal* (December 6, 1999): A34.

103. Margaret Kriz, "The Greening of Free Trade," *National Journal* (November 20, 1999): 3394–96, at 3396.

104. Goldsmith and Yoo, "Seattle and Sovereignty."

105. Wysocki, "The WTO: the Villain in a Drama It Wrote."

106. Kriz, "The Greening of Free Trade," 3394–96.

107. Jeffrey E. Garten, "CEOs: Prepare for More Protests," *The Wall Street Journal* (December 6, 1999): A34.

108. Steven Greenhouse and Joseph Kahn, "U.S. Effort to Add Labor Standards to Agenda Fails," *The New York Times* (December 3, 1999): A1.

109. Lori Nitschke, "U.S., Trading Partners at Crossroads in Seattle," *CQ Weekly* (November 27, 1999): 2826–33, at 2827.

110. Brink Lindsey, Daniel T. Griswold, Mark A. Groombridge, and Aaron Lukas, "Seattle and Beyond: A WTO Agenda for the New Millennium," Cato Institute (November 4, 1999), http://www.freetrade.org/pubs/pas/tpa-008es.html.

111. Nitschke, "U.S., Trading Partners at Crossroads in Seattle," 2831.

112. "World Trade Organization: Organizational Structure," *CQ Weekly* (November 27, 1999): 2831.

113. "The Clinton Administration Agenda for The Seattle WTO," (November 24, 1999), http://www.whitehouse.gov/WH/New/WTO-Conf-1999/factsheets/fs-007.html.

114. Executive Order 13141 (November 14, 1999), http://www.pub.white-house.gov/uri-res/I2R?urn:pdi://oma.eop.gov.us/1999/11/16/5.text.2

115. Kriz, "The Greening of Free Trade," 3396.

116. World Resources Institute, *World Resources 1994–95* (1994): 225.

117. See, generally, Jan Knippers Black, *Development in Theory and Practice* (Boulder, Colo.: Westview Press, 1991); H. Jeffrey Leonard et al., *Environment and the Poor: Development Strategies for a Common Agenda* (Washington, D.C.: Overseas Investment Council, 1989).

118. United Nations Environment Program, *Global Environmental Outlook* (New York: Oxford University Press, 1997): 2.

119. United Nations Environment Program, *Global Environmental Outlook*, 3.

120. Mark MacKinnon, "On the Event's 30th Birthday, Earth Day's a Hit Worldwide," *The Globe and Mail* (April 24, 2000), http://www.globeand mail.com/gam/Environment/20000422/UEARTM.html.

Chapter 5

1. Wayne A. Morrissey and John R. Justis, "Global Climate Change," CRS Issue Brief for Congress, (May 13, 1999) http://www.cnie.org/nle/clim-2.html.

2. G. Tyrel Miller, Jr., *Living in the Environment* (Pacific Grove, Calif.: Brooks Cole, 11th ed., 2000): 500.

3. William K. Stevens, "Moving Slowly Toward Energy Free of Carbon," *The New York Times* (October 31, 1999): 36.

4. "U.S. Greenhouse Gas Emissions Slow, But Continue Steady Increase, DOE says," *Environmental Reporter* (November 12, 1999): 1274.

5. U.S. Global Change Research Program Seminar Series, "What's Driving Climate Change in the Twentieth Century—Changes in Solar Radiation or the Buildup of Greenhouse Gases?" e-mail message from Carla Mitchell, mitchell @usgcrp.gov (November 18, 1999).

6. Among the leading scientific studies: Intergovernmental Panel on *Climate Change, Climate Change: The IPCC Scientific Assessment* (Cambridge, England: Cambridge University Press, 1990); Intergovernmental Panel on Climate Change, *Climate Change 1994* (Cambridge, England: Cambridge University Press, 1995). Strong endorsements of the scientific consensus and the need for policy actions include Ross Gelbspan, *The Heat Is On* (Reading, Mass.: Addison Wesley, 1997) and Thomas R. Casten, *Turning Off the Heat* (Amherst, N.Y.: Prometheus Books, 1998).

7. See, for example, Thomas Gale Moore, *Climate of Fear: Why We Shouldn't Worry about Global Warming* (Washington, D.C.: Cato Institute, 1998); Robert C. Balling, Jr., "Global Warming: Messy Models, Decent Data, and Pointless Policy," in Ronald Bailey, ed., *The True State of the Planet* (New York: The Free Press, 1985): 83–108.

8. See, for example, Wilfred Beckerman, *Through Green-Colored Glasses: Environmentalism Reconsidered* (Washington, D.C.: Cato Institute, 1996).

9. Intergovernmental Panel on Climate Change, *Climate Change: The IPCC Scientific Assessment* (Cambridge: Cambridge University Press, 1990).

10. Intergovernmental Panel on *Climate Change, Climate Change 1995: The Science of Climate Change: Contribution of Working Group 1 to the Second Assessment Report of the Intergovernmental Panel on Climate Change* (Cambridge: Cambridge University Press, 1996).

11. For a helpful overview of the scientific issues surrounding climate change, see John Houghton, *Global Warming: The Complete Briefing* (Cambridge: Cambridge University Press, 2nd ed., 1997).

12. R.A. Kerr, "Hansen vs. The World on the Greenhouse Threat": *Science* 244: 10431–43; letters section, *Science* 245 (1989): 451–52.

13. James A. Baker III, "Remarks by the Honorable James A. Baker III, Secretary of State," before the Response Strategies Working Group, Intergovernmental Panel on Climate Change. (Washington, D.C.: Department of State, January 30, 1989).

14. Gary C. Bryner, *Blue Skies, Green Politics: The Clean Air Act of 1990 and Its Implementation.* (Washington, D.C.: CQ Press, 1995): 114–16.

15. Gary C. Bryner, ed., *Global Warming and the Challenge of International Cooperation.* (Provo, Utah: David M. Kennedy Center/Brigham Young University, 1992): 103–04.

16. Gary C. Bryner. *U.S. Land and Natural Resources Policy.* (Westport, Conn.: Greenwood Press, 1998): 195–96.

17. United States of America. *The Climate Change Action Plan.* (Washington, D.C.: U.S. Department of State, 1993).

18. U.S. Department of Energy. *The Climate Change Action Plan: Technical Supplement* (Springfield, Va.: National Technical Information Service, 1994): 9–10.

19. U.S. Department of Energy, *The Climate Change Action Plan,* 37–70.

20. Christopher Flavin. "Climate Policy: Showdown in Berlin," 8 *World Watch* (July/August 1995): 8–9.

21. Intergovernmental Panel on Climate Change. *Climate Change 1995: The Science of Climate Change* (Cambridge: Cambridge University Press, 1996): 4–5.

22. Associated Press, "Nations Urged to Pass Laws on Emissions," *The New York Times* (July 19, 1996): A5.

23. Environmental Defense Fund. "U.S. Acts on Global Warming at Geneva." *EDF Letter,* (September 1996): 1.

24. Flavin, "Climate Policy: Showdown in Berlin."

25. John H. Cushman, Jr. "U.S. Emits Greenhouse Gases at the Highest Rate in Years." *The New York Times* (October 21, 1997): 14.

26. John H. Cushman, Jr., "Why the U.S. Fell Short of Ambitious Goals for Reducing Greenhouse Gases." *The New York Times* (October 20, 1997): A9.

27. Gary Bryner, "Congressional Decisions About Regulatory Reform: The 104th and 105th Congresses," in Ken Sexton, Alfred A. Marcus, K. William Easter, and Timothy D. Burkhardt, eds., *Better Environmental Decisions: Strategies for Governments, Businesses, and Communities* (Washington, D.C.: Island Press, 1999): 91–112.

28. U.S. Congress, S. Res. 98, 1997.

29. Neil Franz. "Congress Prepares for Debate Over Global Warming Treaty," *Environment and Energy Update* (November 20, 1997).

30. William K. Stevens. "Despite Pact, Gases Will Keep Rising," *New York Times.* (December 1997): A10.

31. John M. Broder. "Clinton Adamant on 3rd World Role in Climate Accord." *The New York Times* (December 12, 1997): A1.

32. John H. Cushman, Jr. "U.S. Signs a Pact to Reduce Gases Tied to Warming," *The New York Times* (13 November, 1998): A1.

33. Verena Schmitt-Roschmann, "Bonn Meeting Leaves Major Decisions on Kyoto Protocol for 2000," *Environment Reporter* (November 12, 1999): 1274–75.

34. John J. Fialka and Jackie Calmes. "Clinton Proposes Global-Warming Plan," *The Wall Street Journal* (October 23, 1997): 2.

35. John H. Cushman Jr. "Clinton Alters His Approach Over Warming." *The New York Times* (October 21, 1997): A1.

36. Charles Pope, "Opposition to Global Warming Treaty Is Cropping Up in Spending Bills," *Congressional Quarterly Weekly Report* (August 1, 1998): 2107–08, at 2108.

37. Pope, "Opposition to Global Warming Treaty."

38. Bonner R. Cohen, Bonner R. "US Environmental Agency Accused of Being Too Hasty on Climate Change" *The Earth Times* (July 20, 1998) http://www.earthtimes.com/jul/washingtonusenvironmentalagencyjul20_98.htm.

39. U.S. Congress, H.R. 4194 (1999).

40. Charles Pope. "Opposition to Global Warming Treaty Is Cropping Up in Spending Bills," 2108.

41. Greenwire, "Climate Change: Talks Enter Key Phase: US to Sign Pact?" (November 11, 1998).

42. Greenwire, "Climate Change II: Signature Sparks Strong Reactions?" (November 13, 1998).

43. 106th Congress, H.R. 2466; Charles Pope, "Senate Clears Interior Bill, Setting Stage for Post-Veto Talks on Policy Riders, Funding Levels," *CQ Weekly* (October 23, 1999): 2527–28.

44. Joby Warwick. "Turning Cool Toward the Kyoto Accords," *The Washington Post National Weekly Edition* (February 23, 1998): 31.

45. Christopher Flavin. "Last Tango in Buenos Aires." *World Watch 11* (November/December, 1998): 10–18.

46. Neil Franz, "Congress Prepares for Debate Over Global Warming Treaty."

47. John Houghton. *Global Warming: The Complete Briefing* (Cambridge: Cambridge University Press, 1987).

48. Ross Gelbspan, *The Heat Is On.*

49. U.S. Congress, Office of Technology Assessment. *Building Energy Efficiency* (Washington, D.C.: U.S. Government Printing Office, 1992).

50. Amory Lovins, *Soft Energy Paths* (New York: Harper Colophon, 1979); Amory Lovins, *World Energy Strategies* (New York: Harper Colophon, 1980).

51. Walter A. Rosenbaum, *Environmental Policy and Politics* (Washington, D.C.: CQ Press, 1998: 261–96

52. Gelbspan, *The Heat Is On.*

53. James L. Sundquist, *Congressional Reform and Effective Government.* (Washington, D.C.: Brookings Institution, revised edition, 1992); James A. Thurber, *Divided Democracy: Cooperation and Conflict Between the President and Congress.* (Washington, D.C.: CQ Press, 1991).

54. Robert D. Putnam, "Diplomacy and Domestic Politics: The Logic of Two-Level Games," *International Organization.* Vol. 48, no. 2 (1988): 427–60.

55. National Academy of Public Administration. *Setting Priorities, Getting Results: A New Direction for EPA* (Washington, D.C.: NAPA, 1995).

56. Christopher Flavin and Seth Dunn, "Climate of Opportunity: Renewable Energy After Kyoto," *Renewable Energy Policy Project Issue Brief* No. 11 (July 1998).

57. J. Clarence Davies and Jan Mazurek, *Pollution Control in the United States: Evaluating the System* (Washington, D.C.: Resources for the Future, 1998).

58. Michael E. Kraft, "Environmental Policy in Congress: From Consensus to Gridlock," in Norman J. Vig and Michael E. Kraft, eds., *Environmental Policy in the 1990s* (Washington, D.C.: CQ Press, fourth edition, 2000): 121–44.

59. Ed Gillespie and Rob Schellhas, eds. *Contract with America* (New York: Times Books, 1994): 125–41.

60. Cited in World Resources Institute, *World Resources 1998–99* (New York: Oxford University Press, 1998): 176.

61. State and Territorial Air Pollution Program Administrators and the Association of Local Air Pollution Control Officials, *Reducing Greenhouse Gases and Air Pollution: A Menu of Harmonized Options* (Washington, D.C.: STAPPA/ALAPCO, 1998): xx.

62. The information on state innovations comes from Josh Wilson, "Power Plays" *MotherJones Interactive* http://bsd.mojones.com/news_wire/wilson.html.

63. Clinton and Gore, "The Climate Change Action Plan."

64. Clinton and Gore, "The Climate Change Action Plan," 33–70.

65. E-mail from Ken Bossong, SUN DAY campaign, kbossong@cais.com (October 14, 1999).

66. See Eric R. A. N. Smith, *Energy, the Environment, and Public Opinion* (Lanham. Md.: Rowman and Littlefield, forthcoming).

67. Flavin and Dunn, "Climate of Opportunity."

68. Curtis Moore and Alan Miller, *Green Gold: Japan, Germany, and the United States, and the Race for Environmental Technology.* (Boston: Beacon Press, 1994).

69. R. A. Kerr, "The Next Oil Crisis Looms Large—And Perhaps Close," *Science* 281 (1998): 1128–31.

70. Laura B. Campbell, "COP-5: Toward Implementation of the Climate Change Treaty and Kyoto Protocol," *International Environmental Reporter* (December 8, 1999): 1014–17, at 1014.

71. Schmitt-Roschmann, "Bonn Meeting Leaves Major Decisions On Kyoto Protocol for 2000," 1274–75.

72. Campbell, "COP-5," 1017.

73. Dan Lashof, "Ye of little faith, Kyoto is not dead," *Grist Magazine* (January 25, 2000) http://www.gristmagazine.com/grist/heatbeat/debates, accessed January 25, 2000.

74. Campbell, "COP-5," 1015.

75. Sonni Efron, "Japan Reports Reduction in Greenhouse Gas Emissions," *Los Angeles Times* (January 29, 2000), http://latimes.com/news/science/environ/2000.

76. Michael Grubb, with Christian Vrolijk and Duncan Brack, *The Kyoto Protocol: A Guide and Assessment* (London: Royal Institute of International Affairs, 1999).

77. Grubb, *The Kyoto Protocol*, 29–30.

78. Grubb, *The Kyoto Protocol*, 32–34.

79. Grubb, *The Kyoto Protocol*, 34–35.

80. Grubb, *The Kyoto Protocol*, 82.

81. Grubb, *The Kyoto Protocol*, 35–36, 49.

82. Pew Center on Global Climate Change, "Developing Countries & Global Climate Change: Electric Power Options in China" (May 2000). http://www.pewclimate.org/projects/pol_china.html.

83. Pew Center on Global Climate Change, "Developing Countries & Global Climate Change: Electric Power Options in Brazil" (May 2000). http://www.pewclimate.org/projects/pol_brazil.html.

84. Pew Center on Global Climate Change, "Developing Countries & Global Climate Change: Electric Power Options in Argentina" (May 2000). http://www.pewclimate.org/projects/pol_argentina.html.

85. "Progress on Ozone Protection Only the Beginning," Environment News Service (July 12, 2000) http://ens.lycos.com/ens/jul2000/2000L-07-12-11.html

86. Grubb, *The Kyoto Protocol*, 107.

87. Grubb, *The Kyoto Protocol*, 50–51.

88. Grubb, *The Kyoto Protocol*, 258.

89. Grubb, *The Kyoto Protocol*, 51–52.

90. Grubb, *The Kyoto Protocol*, 112.

91. Grubb, *The Kyoto Protocol*, 54–55.

92. Grubb, *The Kyoto Protocol*, 59.

93. Grubb, *The Kyoto Protocol*, 112.

94. Grubb, *The Kyoto Protocol*, 255, 276.

95. Bureau of National Affairs, "Outlook 2000," *International Environmental Reporter* (February 2, 2000): 116–24.

96. Bernd Kasemir, Daniela Schibli, Susanne Stoll, and Carlo C. Jaeger, "Involving the Public in Climate and Energy Decisions," *Environment* vol. 42 (April 2000): 32–42.

97. David Victor, "Kyoto Is Dead," *Grist Magazine* (January 25, 2000) http://www.gristmagazine.com/grist/heatbeat/debates, accessed January 25, 2000.

98. Center for Sustainable Development in the Americas, "An Annotated Glossary of Commonly Used Climate Change Terms," http://www.csdanet.org/glossary.html.

99. Laura H. Kosloff and Mark C. Trexler, "Global Warming, Climate-Change Mitigation, and the Birth of a Regulatory Regime," *Environmental Law Report* 27 (January 1997), at 10012-18.

100. Clinton and Gore, "The Climate Change Action Plan," p. 8.

101. These projects are discussed in Kosloff and Trexler, "Global Warming."

102. Annie Petsonk, Daniel J. Dudek, and Joseph Goffman, "Market Mechanisms and Global Climate Change: An Analysis of Policy Instruments" (Arlington, Va.: Pew Center on Global Climate Change, 1999).

103. Petsonk, Dudek, and Goffman, "Market Mechanisms," 7–8.

104. Flavin, "Last Tango in Buenos Aires," *World Watch*, 14–15.

105. World Resources Institute, *World Resources* 1998–99, 176.

106. See Daniel Sarewitz and Roger Pielke Jr. "Breaking the Global-Warming Gridlock," *The Atlantic Monthly* (July 2000) www.theatlanticmonthly-bin/o/issues/2000/07/sarewitz.htm.

107. Sebastian Oberthuer and Hermann E. Ott, *The Kyoto Protocol: International Climate Policy for the 21st Century* (Berlin: Springer, 1999): 235.

108. Oberthuer and Ott, *The Kyoto Protocol*, 235.

109. For more on the challenges in making flexible mechanisms work, see Robert Repetto, "The Clean Development Mechanism: Institutional Breakthrough or Institutional Nightmare?" Wirth Chair in Environmental and Community Development Policy, Institute for Policy Implementation, University of Colorado at Denver (April 3, 2000).

110. Sarewitz and Pielke, "Breaking the Global-Warming Gridlock."

111. Ambuj D. Sagar, "A 'Polluters Get Paid' Principle?" *Environment* (November 1999): 4–5.

112. John Lanchbery, "Expectations for the Climate Talks in Buenos Aires," *Environment* 40: (October 1998): 16–20, 42–45.

113. Jon Naimon and Debra S. Knopman, "Reframing the Climate Change Debate," Democratic Leadership Council and the Progressive Policy Institute (November 1999) www.dlcppi.org/texts/commerce/climate/htm.

114. See Paul Hawken, Amory Lovins, and L. Hunter Lovins, *Natural Capitalism: Creating the Next Industrial Revolution* (Boston: Little, Brown, 1999); Joseph J. Romm, *Cool Companies: How the Best Businesses Boost Profits and Productivity by Cutting Greenhouse Gas Emissions* (Washington, D.C.: Island Press, 1999); Curtis Moore and Alan Miller, *Green Gold: Japan, Germany, the United States, and the Race for Environmental Technology* (Boston: Beacon Press, 1994).

115. See Repetto, "The Clean Development Mechanism," 27–32.

116. Sarewitz and Pielke, "Breaking the Global-Warming Gridlock."

117. Sarewitz and Pielke, "Breaking the Global-Warming Gridlock."

118. Sarewitz and Pielke, "Breaking the Global-Warming Gridlock."

119. Mark MacKinnon, "On the Event's 30th Birthday, Earth Day's a Hit Worldwide." *The Globe and Mail* (April 24, 2000) http://www.globeandmail.com /gam/Environment/20000422/UEARTM.html.

Chapter 6

1. Susan Griffin, *A Chorus of Stones* (New York: Anchor Books, 1992): 178.

2. See Lester R. Brown, et al., *The State of the World 2000* (New York: W. W. Norton and Company, 2000), especially chapter 1.

3. Lamont C. Hempel, "Conceptual and Analytic Challenges in Building Sustainable Communities," in Daniel A. Mazmanian and Michael E. Kraft, eds., *Toward Sustainable Communities: Transition and Transformations in Environmental Policy* (Cambridge, Mass.: MIT Press, 1999): 43–74, at 44.

4. See Barry Commoner, *Making Peace with the Planet* (New York: Pantheon, 1990).

5. Aldo Leopold, *A Sand County Almanac* (New York: Ballantyne Books, 1966): 238–39.

6. Dale Jamieson, "Sustainability and Beyond," NRLC Public Land Policy Discussion Paper Series (PL02) (Boulder, Colo.: Natural Resources Law Center, 1996): 12.

7. See Joanna Burger and Michael Gochfeld, "The Tragedy of the Commons: 30 Years Later," *Environment* vol. 40 (December 1998), and letters it prompted by

Lawrence Lundgren and Paul Burnet, and a response by Hardin, in "The Tragedy of the Commons Revisited," *Environment* vol. 41 (March 1999): 4–5, 45.

8. For a helpful overview and assessment of the functioning of consensus-based groups, see Douglas S. Kenney, "Arguing About Consensus: Examining the Case Against Western Watershed Initiatives and Other Collaborative Groups Active in Natural Resource Management" (Boulder, Colo.: Natural Resources Law Center, University of Colorado School of Law, 2000).

9. Robin Gregory, "Using Stakeholder Values to Make Smarter Environmental Decisions," *Environment* vol. 42 (June 2000): 34–44, at 35.

10. Douglas S. Kenney, "Innovations in Forestry: The Controversy Over Collaborative Planning and Management" (Boulder, Colo.: Natural Resources Law Center, University of Colorado School of Law, 2000).

11. Kenney, "Innovations in Forestry."

12. Lester Brown, et al., eds., *State of the World 2000*, especially chapter 2.

13. Neil E. Harrison, *Constructing Sustainable Development* (Albany, N.Y.: State University of New York Press, 2000).

14. Daniel A. Mazmanian and Michael E. Kraft, "The Three Epochs of the Environmental Movement" in Mazmanian and Kraft, eds., *Toward Sustainable Communities: Transitions and Transformations in Environmental Policy* (Cambridge, Mass.: MIT Press, 1999): 3–42.

15. Ranji Kothari, quoted in Dale Jamieson, "Sustainability and Beyond," NRLC Public Land Policy Discussion Paper Series (PL02) (Boulder, Colo.: Natural Resources Law Center, 1996): 16.

16. Dale Jamieson, "Sustainability and Beyond," 12.

17. Michael Sandel, *Democracy's Discontent* (Cambridge, Mass.: Harvard University Press, 1996): 46.

18. Sandel, *Democracy's Discontent*, 350.

19. John Rawls, *A Theory of Justice* (Cambridge: Harvard University Press, revised edition, 1999): 13.

20. Rawls, *A Theory of Justice*, 13.

21. Rawls, *A Theory of Justice*. Also, for a thoughtful critique of Rawls, see Thomas Nagel, "Justice, Justice, Shalt Thou Pursue," *The New Republic* (October 25, 1999): 36–41.

22. John Rawls, *The Law of Peoples, with "The Idea of Public Reason Revisited."* (Cambridge: Harvard University Press, 1999).

23. The story and Singer's interpretation are discussed in Peter Berkowitz, "Other People's Mothers: The Utilitarian Horrors of Peter Singer," *The New Republic* (January 10, 2000): 27–37, at 28.

24. Orlando Patterson, "The Liberal Millennium," *The New Republic* (November 11, 1999): 54–63.

25. "America's World," *The Economist* (October 23, 1999): 15–16.

26. The speech was reported in Barbara Crossette, "Helms, in Visit to UN, Warns of U.S. Pullout," *The New York Times* (January 21, 2000): A1.

27. Alan Wolfe, "A Necessary Good" (review of Garry Wills, A Necessary Evil: A History of American Distrust of Government), *The New Republic* (November 1, 1999): 37–40.

28. Garry Wills, *A Necessary Evil: A History of American Distrust of Government* (New York: Simon and Schuster, 1999).

29. See, for example, the World Federalist Association, "Common Responsibility in the 1990s: The Stockholm Initiative on Global Security and Governance" (Stockholm: Office of the Prime Minister, 1991).

30. For a discussion of institutional innovations for the environment, see The Commission on Global Governance, *Our Global Neighbourhood* (Oxford: Oxford University Press, 1995); Daniel C. Esty, *Greening the Gatt: Trade, Environment, and the Future* (Washington, D.C.: Institute for International Economics, 1994).

31. Karen T. Litfin, ed., *The Greening of Sovereignty in World Politics* (Cambridge, Mass.: The MIT Press, 1998): 3.

32. Paul Wapner, *Environmental Activism and World Civic Politics* (Albany: SUNY Press, 1996): 9–10.

33. Wapner, *Environmental Activism and World Civic Politics*, 15.

34. For more on this debate, see Peter M. Haas, Robert O. Keohane, and Marc A. Levy, *Institutions for the Earth: Sources of Effective International Environmental Protection* (Cambridge, Mass.: MIT Press, 1993); and Oran R. Young, ed., *Global Governance: Drawing Insights from the Environmental Experience* (Cambridge, Mass.: MIT Press, 1997).

35. Kai Bird, "A Foreign Policy for the Common Citizen," *The Nation* 270 (May 8, 2000): 11–12.

36. Robert Wright, "Continental Drift," *The New Republic* (January 17, 2000): 18–23, at 20.

37. Wright, "Continental Drift," 23.

38. Bruce Cumings, "The American Ascendancy: Imposing a New World Order," *The Nation* 270 (May 8, 2000): 13–20.

39. For more on this argument, see William Greider, "Ambassador Babbitt," *The Nation* 270 (May 8, 2000): 27–30.

40. Mark Hertsgaard, "A Global Green Deal," *Time: Special Edition, Earth Day 2000* (Spring 2000): 84–85.

SUGGESTIONS FOR FURTHER READING

Environmental Problems

Beckerman, Wilfred, *Through Green-Colored Glasses: Environmentalism Reconsidered* (Washington, D.C.: Cato Institute, 1996).

Brown, Lester R., et al., *State of the World 2000* (New York: W. W. Norton, 2000).

Commoner, Barry, *Making Peace with the Planet* (New York: Pantheon, 1990).

The Commission on Global Governance, *Our Global Neighborhood* (New York: Oxford University Press, 1995).

Caldwell, Lynton Keith, *International Environmental Policy* (Chapel Hill, N.C.: Duke University Press, 1996, 3rd ed.).

Davies, J. Clarence, and Jan Mazurek, *Pollution Control in the United States: Evaluating the* System (Washington, D.C.: Resources for the Future, 1998).

Douglas, Mary, and Aaron Wildavsky, *Risk and Culture* (Berkeley: University of California Press, 1982).

Easterbrook, Gregg, A *Moment on the Earth: The Coming Age of Environmental Optimism* (New York: Viking, 1995).

Feshback, Murray, and Alfred Friendly Jr., *Ecocide in the USSR* (New York: Basic Books, 1992).

Heilbroner, Robert L., *An Inquiry into the Human Prospect* (New York: Norton, 1991).

Jancar-Webster, Barbara, ed., *Environmental Action in Eastern Europe: Responses to Crisis* (Armonk, New York: M. E. Sharpe, 1993).

Leopold, Aldo, *A Sand County Almanac* (New York: Ballantyne Books, 1966).

Miller, G. Tyrel, Jr., *Living in the Environment* (Pacific Grove, Calif.: Brooks Cole, 11th ed., 2000).

Morone, Joseph G., and Edward J. Woodhouse, *Averting Catastrophe: Strategies for Regulating Risky Technologies* (Berkeley: University of California Press, 1986).

Ophuls, William, and A. Stephan Boyan Jr., *Ecology and the Politics of Scarcity Revisited* (New York: W. W. Freeman, 1992).

Sandler, Todd, *Global Challenges* (Cambridge: Cambridge University Press, 1997).

Simon, Julian, *The Ultimate Resource 2* (Princeton, N.J.: Princeton University Press, 1996).

Simon, Julian and Herman Kahn, *The Resourceful Earth: A Response to Global 2000* (New York: Basil Blackwell, 1984).

United Nations Development Program, *Human Development Report 1997* (New York: Oxford University Press, 1997).

United Nations Environment Program, *Global Environmental Outlook* (New York: Oxford University Press, 1997).

The World Bank, *Advancing Sustainable Development* (Washington, D.C.: The World Bank, 1997).

World Commission on Environment and Development, *Our Common Future* (New York: Oxford University Press, 1997).

World Resources Institute, *World Resources: A Guide to the Global Environment 1998–99* (New York: Oxford University Press, 1998).

Climate Change

Bryner, Gary C., ed., *Global Warming and the Challenge of International Cooperation* (Provo, Utah: David M. Kennedy Center/Brigham Young University, 1992).

Casten, Thomas R., *Turning Off the Heat* (Amherst, N.Y.: Prometheus Books, 1998).

Grubb, Michael, with Christian Vrolijk and Duncan Brack, *The Kyoto Protocol: A Guide and Assessment* (London: Royal Institute of International Affairs, 1999).

Gelbspan, Ross, *The Heat Is On* (Reading, Mass.: Addison Wesley, 1997).

Houghton, John, *Global Warming: The Complete Briefing* (Cambridge: Cambridge University Press, 2nd ed., 1997).

Moore, Thomas Gale, *Climate of Fear: Why We Shouldn't Worry about Global Warming* (Washington, D.C.: Cato Institute, 1998).

Intergovernmental Panel on Climate Change, *Climate Change: The IPCC Scientific Assessment* (Cambridge: Cambridge University Press, 1990).

Intergovernmental Panel on Climate Change, *Climate Change 1995: The Science of Climate Change: Contribution of Working Group 1 to the Second Assessment Report of the Intergovernmental Panel on Climate Change* (Cambridge: Cambridge University Press, 1996).

Intergovernmental Panel on Climate Change, *Climate Change: The IPCC Scientific Assessment* (Cambridge: Cambridge University Press, 1990).

Intergovernmental Panel on Climate Change, *Climate Change 1994* (Cambridge: Cambridge University Press, 1995).

Intergovernmental Panel on Climate Change,. *Climate Change 1995: The Science of Climate Change* (Cambridge: Cambridge University Press, 1996).

Romm, Joseph J., *Cool Companies: How the Best Businesses Boost Profits and Productivity by Cutting Greenhouse Gas Emissions* (Washington, D.C.: Island Press, 1999).

United States of America. *The Climate Change Action Plan.* (Washington, D.C.: U.S. Department of State, 1993).

Environmental Politics and Social Movements

Berry, Jeffrey M., *The New Liberalism: The Rising Power of Citizen Groups* (Washington, D.C.: Brookings Institution, 1999).

Bramwell, Anna, *The Fading of the Greens: The Decline of Environmental Politics in the West* (New Haven: Yale University Press, 1994).

Bryner, Gary C., *From Promises to Performance: Achieving Global Environmental Goals* (New York: W. W. Norton, 1998).

Bullard, Robert D., ed., *Confronting Environmental Racism: Voices from the Grassroots* (Boston: South End Press, 1993).

Bunyan Bryant, ed., *Environmental Justice: Issues, Policies, and Solutions* (Washington, D.C.: Island Press, 1995).

Dowie, Mark, *Losing Ground: American Environmentalism at the Close of the Twentieth Century* (Cambridge, Mass.: MIT Press, 1995).

Freeman, Jo and Victoria Johnson, *Waves of Protest: Social Movements Since the Sixties* (Lanham, Md.: Rowman & Littlefield, 1999).

Haas, Peter M., Robert O. Keohane, and Marc A. Levy, *Institutions for the Earth: Sources of Effective International Environmental Protection* (Cambridge, Mass.: MIT Press, 1993).

Hays, Samuel P., *Beauty, Health, and Permanence: Environmental Politics in the United States 1955–1985* (Cambridge: Cambridge University Press, 1987).

Inglehart, Ronald, *The Silent Revolution: Changing Values and Political Styles Among Western Publics* (Princeton, N.J.: Princeton University Press, 1977).

John, DeWitt, *Civic Environmentalism* (Washington, D.C.: CQ Press, 1994).

Kamieniecki, Sheldon, ed., *Environmental Politics in the International Arena: Movements, Parties, Organizations, and Policy* (Albany: SUNY Press, 1993).

Ladd, Everett Carll, and Karlyn H. Bowman, *Attitudes Toward the Environment: Twenty-Five Years After Earth Day* (Washington, D.C.: American Enterprise Institute for Public Policy Research, 1995).

Lewis, Martin W. *Green Delusions* (Durham, N.C.: Duke University Press, 1992).

Litfin, Karen T., ed., *The Greening of Sovereignty in World Politics* (Cambridge, Mass.: The MIT Press, 1998).

Manes, Christopher, *Green Rage* (Boston: Little, Brown, 1990).

Merchant, Carolyn, *Radical Ecology* (New York: Routledge, 1992).

Merchant, Carolyn, ed., *Ecology* (Atlantic Highlands, N.J.: Humanities Press, 1994).

Meyer, David S., and Sidney Tarrow, eds. *The Social Movement Society* (Lanham, Md.: Rowman & Littlefield, 1998).

Paehlke, Robert C., *Environmentalism and the Future of Progressive Politics* (New Haven, Conn.: Yale University Press, 1989).

Parkin, Sara, *Green Parties: An International Guide* (London: Heretic Books, 1989).

Richardson, Dick, and Chris Rootes, eds. *The Green Challenge: The Development of Green Parties in Europe* (London: Routledge, 1995).

Rose-Ackerman, Susan, *Controlling Environmental Policy: The Limits of Public Law in Germany and the United States* (New Haven, Conn.: Yale University Press, 1995).

Rosenbaum, Walter, *Environmental Politics and Policy* (Washington, D.C.: CQ Press, 4th ed., 1998).

Shabecoff, Philip, *Earth Rising: American Environmentalism in the 21st Century* (Washington, D.C.: Island Press, 2000).

Shabecoff, Philip, *A New Name for Peace: International Environmentalism, Sustainability Development, and Democracy* (Hanover, N.H.: University Press of New England, 1996).

Switzer, Jacqueline Vaughn, with Gary Bryner, *Environmental Politics: Domestic and Global Dimensions* (New York: St. Martin's Press, 1998).

Victor, David G., Kai Raustiala, and Eugene B. Skolnikoff, *The Implementation and Effectiveness of International Environmental Commitments: Theory and Practice* (Cambridge, Mass.: MIT Press, 1998).

Vig, Norman J., and Regina S. Axelrod, *The Global Environment: Institutions, Law, and Policy* (Washington, D.C.: CQ Press, 2000).

Vig, Norman J., and Michael E. Kraft, eds., *Environmental Policy* (Washington, D. C.: CQ Press, 2000).

Vogel, David, *National Styles of Regulation: Environmental Policy in Great Britain and the United States* (Ithaca, N.Y.: Cornell University Press, 1986).

Wapner, Paul *Environmental Activism and World Civic Politics* (Albany: State University of New York Press, 1995).

Young, Oran Y., ed., *Global Governance: Drawing Insights from the Environmental Experience* (Cambridge, Mass.: MIT Press, 1997).

Sustainability

Grubb, Michael, et al., *The Earth Summit Agreements: A Guide and Assessment* (London: Earthscan, 1993).

Hawken, Paul, *The Ecology of Commerce* (New York: Harper Business, 1993).

Hawken, Paul, Amory Lovins, and L. Hunter Lovins, *Natural Capital: Creating the Next Industrial Revolution* (Boston: Little, Brown, 1999).

Harrison, Neil E., *Constructing Sustainable Development* (Albany, N.Y.: SUNY Press, 2000).

Harrison, Paul, *The Third Revolution: Population, Environment, and a Sustainable World* (London: Penguin Books, 1993).

Holmberg, Johan, ed., *Making Development Sustainable: Redefining Institutions, Policy, and Economics* (Washington D.C.: Island Press, 1992).

Lee, Kai N., *Compass and Gyroscope: Integrating Science and Politics for the Environment* (Washington, D.C.: Island Press, 1993).

Lafferty, William, and James Meadowcroft, eds., *Implementing Sustainable Development: Strategies and Initiatives in High Consumption Societies* (London: Oxford University Press, forthcoming).

Mazmanian, Daniel A., and Michael E. Kraft, eds., *Toward Sustainable Communities: Transition and Transformations in Environmental Policy* (Cambridge, Mass.: MIT Press, 1999).

Milbraith, Lester, *Envisioning a Sustainable Society* (Albany: State University of New York Press, 1991).

Moore, Curtis, and Alan Miller, *Green Gold: Japan, Germany, and the United States and the Race for Environmental Technology* (Boston: Beacon Press, 1994).

Orr, David, *Ecological Literacy: Education and the Transition to a Postmodern World* (Albany, N.Y.: State University of New York Press, 1992)

Pirages, Dennis C., *Building Sustainable Societies: A Blueprint for a Post-Industrial World* (Armonk, N.Y.: M. E. Sharpe, 1996).

The President's Council on Sustainable Development, *Sustainable Development: A New Consensus* (Washington, D.C.: U.S. Government Printing Office, 1996).

Rogers, Adam Rogers, *The Earth Summit: A Planetary Reckoning* (Los Angeles: Global View Press, 1993).

Sitarz, Daniel, ed., *Agenda 21: The Earth Summit Strategy to Save Our Planet* (Boulder, Colo.: EarthPress, 1993).

World Commission on Environment and Development, *Our Common Future* (New York: Oxford University Press, 1987).

SELECTED WEB SITES FOR ENVIRONMENTAL ISSUES

U.S. Government Agencies and Congress

Environmental Protection Agency: www.epa.gov

Department of Energy: www.doe.gov

Department of the Interior: www.doi.gov

Congressional Record: www.access.gpo.gov/su_docs/aces/aces150.html

Federal Register: www.access.gpo.gov/su_docs/aces/aces140.html

Code of Federal Regulations: www.access.gpo.gov/nara/cfr/index.html

President's Council on Sustainable Development:
www.whitehouse.gov/PCSD

United Nations Agencies

UN Development Programme: www.undp.org/

UN Environment Programme: www.unep.org/

UN Commission on Sustainable Development: www.un.org/esa/sustdev

UN Population Fund: www.unfpa.org/

World Health Organization: www.who.org/

World Meterological Organization: www.wmo.ch/

Intergovernmental Panel on Climate Change: www.ipcc.ch/

UN Framework Convention on Climate Change: www.unfccc.de

Other International Agencies

Organization for Economic Cooperation and Development,
Environment Directorate: www.oecd.org/env

World Trade Organization, Environment and Trade Operation:
www.wto.org/wto/environ/environ.html

North American Free Trade Agreement,
Commission on Environmental Cooperation: www.cec.org/

World Bank: www.worldbank.org/

International Monetary Fund: www.imf.org/

Global Environment Facility: www.gefweb.com/geftext.htm

International Court of Justice: www.icj-cij.org

Environmental Groups

Center for International Environmental Law: www.igc.apc.org

Clean Air Network: www.cleanair.net/

EcoJustice Network: www.igc.org/envjustic

Environmental Defense: www.edf.org

Environmental Law Institute: www.eli.org

Friends of the Earth: www.foe.org

Greenpeace: www.greenpeace.org

National Audubon Society: www.audubon.org

National Wildlife Federation: www.nwf.org

Natural Resources Defense Council: www.nrdc.org

The Nature Conservancy, www.tnc.org/

Sierra Club: www.sierraclub.org

World Wide Fund for Nature: www.wwf.org

Industry Groups and Trade Associations

World Business Council for Sustainable Development: www.wbcsd.ch/

Dow Chemical Company: www.dow.com/homepage/index.html

Environmental News Services and Information

Bureau of National Affairs, Environment Reporter:
www.bna.com/resources/ENR

Bureau of National Affairs, Daily Environment Reporter:
www.bna.com/resources/DER

Bureau of National Affairs, International Environment Reporter:
www.bna.com/resources/IER

Daily Reuters Wire Service—environmental news: www.planetark.org

E&E Newsline: www.eenews.net.

European Daily Environmental New Service: www.ends.co.uk/envdaily

Grist Magazine: www.gristmagazine.com/grist/daily/

Lycos Environmental News Service: www.ens.lycos.com

Which World? Scenarios for the 21st Century, Social and Political Trends,"
mars3.gps.caltech.edu/whichworld/explore/trends/trendssoc.html

World Resources Institute: www.wri.org

WorldWatch Institute: www.worldwatch.org

Index

About the Author

Gary C. Bryner is director of the Natural Resources Law Center and research professor of law at the University of Colorado School of Law. He has also been a professor of political science at Brigham Young University, where he directed the Public Policy Program. His other books on environmental policy and politics include *Blue Skies, Green Politics: The Clean Air Act of 1990 and Its Implementation; From Promises to Performance: Achieving Global Environmental Goals; U.S. Land and Natural Resources Policy;* and, with Jacqueline Vaughn Switzer, *Environmental Politics: Domestic & Global Dimensions.* His research focuses on federalism, intergovernmental relations, the interaction of domestic and global policies, and other issues of governance in the context of environmental and other public policies, and he has also written about affirmative action, welfare reform, and constitutional law. He has been a guest scholar at the Brookings Institution, the National Academy of Public Administration, and the Natural Resources Defense Council.